"A first-rate true crime book necessarily requires two elements—a powerful and intriguing story, and a writer who can capture its soul. *Homicide Miami* has both. I highly recommend this story of murder and greed at their worst."

—Vincent Bugliosi, #1 *New York Times* bestselling author
of *Helter Skelter* and *Divinity of Doubt*

"Torture murder for sex has, unfortunately, become yesterday's news. It is what serial killers are all about. Torture murder for money is rare. This is what gives Peter Davidson's new book its punch. The two main characters in this sordid drama of predatory psychopaths are the embodiment of what we mean by 'evil.' Lugo and especially Dorbal are poster children for the death penalty. But they are as fantastical for stupidity as they are for depravity. First a bungled murder, then a bungled theft and a bungled dismemberment, foiled when a woman's hair jams the killers' electric saw . . . Davidson said his book is not for the squeamish. True. But once you start it you can't put it down."

—Dr. Michael H. Stone, professor of clinical psychiatry,
Columbia College of Physicians and Surgeons,
and host of *Most Evil* on Investigation Discovery

Berkley titles by Peter Davidson

DEATH BY CANNIBAL
MURDER AT HOLY CROSS
HOMICIDE MIAMI
BONES ON THE BEACH

HOMICIDE MIAMI

THE MILLIONAIRE KILLERS

PETER DAVIDSON

BERKLEY BOOKS, NEW YORK

THE BERKLEY PUBLISHING GROUP
Published by the Penguin Group
Penguin Group (USA) Inc.
375 Hudson Street, New York, New York 10014, USA

USA / Canada / UK / Ireland / Australia / New Zealand / India / South Africa / China

Penguin Books Ltd., Registered Offices: 80 Strand, London WC2R 0RL, England
For more information about the Penguin Group, visit penguin.com.

HOMICIDE MIAMI

A Berkley Book / published by arrangement with the author

Berkley Books are published by The Berkley Publishing Group,
BERKLEY® is a registered trademark of Penguin Group (USA) Inc.
The "B" design is a trademark of Penguin Group (USA) Inc.

For information, address: The Berkley Publishing Group,
a division of Penguin Group (USA) Inc.,
375 Hudson Street, New York, New York 10014.

ISBN: 978-0-425-22901-9

PUBLISHING HISTORY
First Berkley mass-market edition / August 2009

PRINTED IN THE UNITED STATES OF AMERICA

10 9 8 7 6 5 4 3

Cover photos: *Amber Ink* © Jupiterimages; *Street* by Photos.com/Jupiterimages; *Crime Scene*
by Miami-Dade Police Department.
Cover design by Erika Fusari.
Interior text design by Kristin del Rosario.

ALWAYS LEARNING   **PEARSON**

For Frank Griga and Krisztina Furton,
and for Marc Schiller

WHO'S WHO

The Victims

Krisztina Furton
Frank Griga
Marcelo Schiller

The Musclemen

Jorge Delgado
Noel Adrian Doorbal
Mario Gray
Danny Lugo
John Carl Mese
Stevenson Pierre
John Raimondo
Mario Sanchez
Carlton Weekes

The Lawmen

Sergeant Luis Alvarex
Detective Gus Baez

Detective Iris Deegan
Detective Nicholas Fabregas
Detective Bobby Fernandez
Sergeant Donna Ganz
Detective Sal Garafalo
Detective Al Harper
Detective Richard Hellman
Sergeant Felix Jimenez
Detective John King
Detective Gary Porterfield

The Private Detective

Ed Du Bois

The Lead Prosecutor

Gail Levine

The Defense Lawyers

Penny Burke
Bruce Fleischer
Ron Guralnick
Anthony Natale

The Judge

Alex Ferrer

Significant Others

Cynthia Eldridge
Sabina Petrescu
Lillian Torres

The Medical Examiner

Dr. Roger Mittleman

HOMICIDE
MIAMI

INTRODUCTION

June 3, 1995
6:30 A.M.

Only three days into the official start of hurricane season and the citizens of South Florida were already keeping a watchful eye on the western Caribbean. The season's first named tropical storm, Allison, was churning its way toward the Florida peninsula.

Ever since 1992, when a category five hurricane named Andrew devastated much of Miami, residents who could afford it spent small fortunes fortifying their homes against the destructive forces of Mother Nature. They also spent small fortunes shielding themselves from the wave of violent crime that had washed over the region, buying homes in gated communities where they were protected by hi-tech security systems and rent-a-cops.

But it wasn't a team of rent-a-cops that assembled just before dawn in the public park near the district police station in suburban Miami Lakes. Instead, it was an army of real cops, members of the Metro-Dade Police Department, the MDPD, the agency responsible for enforcing law and

maintaining order in the unincorporated areas of what then
was known as Dade County.[1]

This morning the quiet park served as the staging area
for squads of homicide detectives, hostage negotiators,
crime scene investigators, and heavily armed SWAT members. Most of the lawmen wore bulletproof vests and raid
jackets with the word *police* emblazoned on the front and
back. Promptly at seven, the cops were briefed by their
commanders who informed them that they were investigating the disappearance of a wealthy young couple.

With warrants in hand, at half past seven the lawmen
fanned out across the county in a coordinated hunt for the
couple, who had disappeared two weeks earlier. Investigators were certain they had been abducted by a ruth-
less band of musclemen who plotted murders while they
pumped iron, targeting wealthy Floridians for extortion
and death. Their diabolical plan: Kidnap and torture their
victims. Force them to sign over their assets. Plunder their
possessions. Then kill them.

Within an hour all the warrants had been served and
two members of the gang were in police custody, but the
lawmen were unable to locate the missing couple. In all,
investigators would eventually file charges against ten men
and two women. Among them were a county corrections
officer, a Cuban-born businessman, two personal trainers,
an accountant, a former Special Forces soldier, a buxom
stripper, and a lovelorn nurse. They were charged with
crimes ranging from accessory after the fact to money laundering, racketeering, extortion, kidnapping, and murder.

Seven of the men and both women would strike deals
with prosecutors, agreeing to tell all in exchange for
immunity, reduced charges, or lenient sentences. They
also agreed to testify against the three muscle-bound men

---

[1]In a 1997 referendum, Dade County voters approved renaming
Florida's most populous county Miami-Dade County. The Metro-Dade
Police Department became the Miami-Dade Police Department.

investigators said were the gang's ringleaders. Their trial spanned ten weeks. Ninety-eight witnesses testified against the trio, and prosecutors introduced more than twelve hundred pieces of evidence.

This is the shocking true story of the criminal enterprise known as the Sun Gym gang. It's also a story about insatiable greed, unsuspecting victims, and a trial, the longest and costliest in county history. This book is not for the squeamish. It reveals all the gruesome details of the gang's crimes, which were so heinous, so evil, lawmen at first didn't believe they ever happened. They changed their minds, however, when they learned that they happened again.

CHAPTER ONE

ON GOLDEN BEACH

May 24, 1995, should have been yet another wonderful day for self-made millionaire Frank Griga. In the morning the handsome telecommunications entrepreneur drove his canary yellow Lamborghini Diablo fifteen miles to a marine supply store in Fort Lauderdale where he purchased Jet Ski accessories—two helmets, a pair of life vests, and a case of marine oil. Later, his friend Lloyd Alvarez drove him to a boat ramp near Hollywood Beach where the thirty-three-year-old businessman took delivery of a brand new, six thousand dollar Sea-Doo XP 800, a top-of-the-line personal watercraft. Frank could hardly wait to take it out. Although pressed for time—he had agreed to a dinner meeting to discuss investing in a South Asian telecommunications venture—nothing could keep the wealthy telecom executive from test-driving his new water toy.

It was 6:30 P.M. when Frank donned a life vest. A light breeze blew in from the ocean as he climbed aboard the Sea-Doo and steered it into the middle of the Intracoastal, the inland waterway that separates mainland Florida from the chain of barrier islands that lie offshore. Frank revved the engine, made three wide circles, and gave Lloyd a thumbs-up. Then he turned the Sea-Doo south toward his waterfront villa eight miles away in Golden Beach, a tiny barrier island town wedged between the Intracoastal Waterway on the west and the Atlantic Ocean on the east. When Frank arrived, Lloyd was waiting for him on the villa's backyard dock. He helped Frank hoist the Sea-Doo out of the water after the test-drive.

The town of Golden Beach is less than two miles long and about a half-mile wide. It's located fifteen miles north of downtown Miami and just minutes from South Beach, the world famous neon-lit Art Deco district at the southern end of Miami Beach. State Road A1A, which in Golden Beach is also known as Ocean Boulevard, separates the beach-front homes on the Atlantic from those on the Intracoastal. It's the only road through the exclusive seaside community. Pedestrians are not wanted on Golden Beach's stretch of A1A—there is no sidewalk on either side of the palm-tree-lined roadway.

The seaside community was developed by brothers R. W. and Henry Ralston during the Florida land boom of the 1920s. It was to be a tropical paradise for wealthy retirees and snowbirds, but only if they were white, Anglo-Saxon, and Protestant. The Ralstons purchased large tracts of mostly mangrove swamps and muck on the northern-most end of the narrow island, selling oceanfront plots for the then-princely sum of seventy-five hundred dollars each, while those on the Intracoastal went for two thousand dollars. By 1929 there were enough registered voters in Golden Beach to incorporate the tiny town.

The civil rights movement of the 1960s put an end to ownership restrictions, and the town saw an influx of young professionals and movers and shakers of all faiths and skin tones. Wealthy immigrants, Jews, even a Saudi sheik and his family, settled there. By the 1970s, the once-sleepy

winter retreat for white Anglo-Saxon Protestants had transformed into a year-round community. Latin singing star
Ricky Martin is "Livin' La Vida Loca" in a magnificent
beachfront home there. Rocker Eric Clapton's 1974 album
461 Ocean Boulevard—one of the most famous rock-and-
roll albums ever—took its title from the beachfront house
he stayed in while recording it at a Miami studio. Two years
later, the Eagles recorded their 1976 album *Hotel California* in Florida while living in Golden Beach. In the 1980s,
191 Ocean Boulevard achieved fame as "the *Miami Vice*
house," where many scenes from the popular TV series
were filmed. Even the Material Girl, Madonna, left her
mark on the tiny town when she bared her body on its sandy
beach for a photo that appeared in her 1992 book *Sex.*

There are no high-rises on Golden Beach. Through the
years it has remained an oasis of low-rise mansions and
villas wedged between miles of oceanfront glass and steel
towers in Sunny Isles to the south and Hallandale to the
north. There are no stores, offices, nightclubs, or restaurants in Golden Beach, not even a post office. The town
contracts with neighboring communities to fight its fires
and supply its water, but the seaside community does have
its very own police department. In 1995, Chief Stanley
Kramer and the twelve sworn officers under his command
kept a watchful eye on the enclave's nine hundred residents
and the three hundred and twenty-five single-family villas
they lived in.

It's not the most exciting police job in South Florida.
Golden Beach recorded no violent crimes and just three
burglaries in 1994. For the most part, the town's lawmen
spend their shifts issuing speeding tickets to motorists on
Ocean Boulevard and conducting routine patrols on the
beach and along the town's seven residential streets.

But life in the exclusive enclave wasn't always so serene.
There had been drug busts and home invasions in the
1970s. In 1979, Carroll Rosenbloom, the seventy-two-year-
old owner of the NFL's Rams, had just arrived at his oceanfront vacation home when he decided to take a dip in the

Atlantic. He drowned. Rumors swirled that the controversial football team owner had been murdered by angry gamblers, but an investigation found no evidence of foul play and Rosenbloom's death was ruled an accident. Later that year an airline pilot was shot dead during a home invasion robbery. The next year there were forty-four burglaries.

Golden Beachers were frightened, and with good reason. Miami-Dade, Florida's most populous county, home to more than two million men, women, and children in 1990, had become a very scary place. It was the undisputed cocaine-smuggling capital of the world. Billions of dollars in drug money poured into the city. The money found its way into luxury car dealerships and dozens of new oceanfront hotels and condominium developments. With the area awash in drug money, there was an explosion in violent crime, especially murders and home invasion robberies.

Just ten years earlier, the county was forced to absorb thousands of refugees during the massive Mariel Boat Lift, when Cuban dictator Fidel Castro announced that anyone who wanted to leave Cuba could do so. Among the new refugees were criminals who were freed from the island nation's prisons and mentally ill men and women who were released from its mental hospitals. By the mid-eighties the county was well on its way to recording the highest crime rate in the nation. Its criminal justice system was overwhelmed, its courts disposing of cases with plea deals 98 percent of the time.

Golden Beach residents demanded better protection, so the town council took drastic action—it closed off six of the seven streets leading into the western part of the community and funneled all cars through one road, the Strand, where motorists are forced to come to a full stop at a police-manned gatehouse. Visitors could be questioned briefly by a Golden Beach cop. Burglaries nose-dived immediately, from forty-four in 1980 to nineteen the following year. There was only one burglary in 1995.

Unquestionably, Golden Beachers were safer and more secure, so the cops on duty had no reason to be suspicious of the two young men who drove up to the gatehouse shortly before 8 P.M. in a top-of-the-line gold-colored Mercedes. Thirty-two-year-old Danny Lugo was behind the wheel. Noel Adrian Doorbal, twenty-four, sat next to him. This was their third trip to Golden Beach in four days. They were on their way to 308 South Parkway, Frank Griga's home, ostensibly to take him and his girlfriend, Krisztina, to a restaurant where they would discuss a multimillion dollar investment in a telecommunications company that was expanding into South Asia.

Frank, an émigré from Hungary, met the two body-builders the previous Saturday. Attila Weiland, the ex-husband of one of Frank's former lovers, a Hungarian-born exotic dancer named Beatriz Weiland, arranged the meeting. Attila and Beatriz had been among the dozen guests, mostly Hungarians, at Frank's Golden Beach house Friday night for the surprise birthday party Krisztina threw for him. Attila took Frank aside and told him all about Lugo and Doorbal and the deal they wanted to pitch. Frank said he'd be more than happy to listen to what they had to say, so the very next day Lugo and Doorbal, and Attila, too, were at Frank's house.

Doorbal hardly uttered a word while Danny Lugo did all the talking. At six foot one, the swarthy muscleman was an imposing figure and a smooth talker despite a distinctive and annoying lisp, a slight stutter, and a heavy New York accent. To someone less savvy than Frank, Lugo seemed to have an excellent grasp of the opportunity. Lugo told Frank he would need to put up at least five hundred thousand dollars to get in. He mentioned that he had invested five million dollars of his own money.

Frank, however, was not impressed, even though both men were smartly dressed in tailored suits and ties, unusual garb for the two weight lifters who preferred jeans and tightly fitting T-shirts that accented their massive muscles. There was something not quite right about the musclemen who were pitching him, and Frank sensed it. Maybe Frank was put off by Adrian Doorbal's long ponytail or by the

massive muscles that bulged through Danny Lugo's suit
jacket. Whatever it was, he told Attila in Hungarian that he
was not interested in investing his money with Lugo, but
the muscleman was persistent and Frank wasn't ready to
close the door, so he told Lugo and Doorbal that he might
be willing to put up as much as one million dollars if the
company's expansion plans included cell phones. Lugo
promised to find out.

When the meeting ended, Krisztina took the two weight
lifters on a tour of the waterfront mansion, and before the
brawny pair drove off, Frank let Doorbal sit inside his
canary yellow Lamborghini. Like a little boy behind the
wheel of the family car, the muscleman pretended that
he was actually driving the awesome machine, which
was named for a famous Spanish fighting bull renowned
for its strength and fierceness. He imagined what it would
be like to let its powerful V-12 engine roar and take it to
its top speed, 200 mph. Doorbal was certain he would not
have to wait much longer to find out. As far as he was concerned, Frank Griga's yellow Lamborghini would soon
be his.

Over the following days Frank looked over the corporate
information package Lugo had left behind. It was complete
with authentic color brochures, pie charts, graphs, and other
data for Interling International, a legitimate telephone company with plans to expand into India, but he had no intention of investing his money with the smooth-talking New
Yorker. Frank was just stringing him along, picking his
brain.

"He liked to talk to people about businesses," said
Amado Garcia, Frank's accountant. "I don't recall him
actually getting into other businesses. He compared all
others to his, and his was always better, more profitable."

While Frank may have been picking Lugo's brain, he
had no way of knowing that Lugo and Doorbal were gun-
toting wolves in sheep's clothing, and while Interling was
a real company, their investment scheme was completely
bogus. Underneath his Armani suit Danny Lugo was a

mass of muscle—an incredibly strong two-hundred pound bodybuilding ex-con, a pathological liar, and the mastermind behind the Sun Gym gang.

With dark skin and a Dutch surname, diminutive but muscular Adrian Doorbal, a once-scrawny runt from the Caribbean who transformed into a hunky strongman by endlessly pumping iron and taking steroids, was Lugo's cousin through marriage, his disciple and devoted lieutenant. The steroids made him prone to sudden rages and tantrums. Among others lurking behind the scenes was John Carl Mese, the gang's financial guru, a prominent Miami businessman with an impressive resume: certified public accountant, financial consultant, and accounting instructor at two local universities.

While Frank showered and dressed, Lugo and Doorbal waited for him downstairs. Happy Birthday banners from Friday's party still hung from the ceiling. A television set tuned to CNN brought news of the O. J. Simpson murder trial in Los Angeles, then in its fourth month. As California prosecutors explained how DNA analysis linked the former NFL running back to the 1994 murders of his ex-wife Nicole and her friend Ron Goldman, Lugo and Doorbal sipped drinks and made small talk with Lloyd Alvarez, who arrived at the waterfront mansion after helping Frank launch the Sea-Doo.

The musclemen were there when Krisztina and Eszter Toth, the Hungarian housekeeper, returned at 8:30 P.M. Eszter was not Frank and Krisztina's maid. She was a once-a-week housecleaner. Toth and her four-year-old daughter Bianca had been living in Frank's house temporarily while she was going through a divorce. Earlier, Krisztina drove Eszter in the blue Dodge Stealth Frank bought her to pick up Bianca in Boca Raton, where the little girl had been visiting with her father. The musclemen said hello to Krisztina and introduced themselves to Eszter and Bianca, who immediately disappeared into their first floor bedroom. Krisztina joined Frank in their bedroom to get ready for dinner, too.

* * *

Frank and Krisztina were all smiles when they came downstairs after ten o'clock. She was gorgeous in an outfit she'd bought on a recent trip to Las Vegas with Frank—red leather miniskirt, red heels, and a matching red leather handbag. An embossed gold eagle decorated the back of her red leather jacket. A stunning sapphire ring Frank bought her adorned one of her fingers, while a sparkling emerald adorned another. As for Frank, he wore a silk shirt, jeans, and crocodile boots. Just as they were about to leave, the phone rang. James Reimer, Frank's friend and stockbroker at Prudential Securities, was on the other end. Frank had hoped he would attend the meeting, too, but the broker said he was too busy and couldn't make it. The two men made plans to discuss the Interling investment the next day instead.

After Frank hung up the phone, he, Krisztina, and the two bodybuilders made their way to the front door. Before they left, the couple took turns patting their dog Chopin good-bye. Once outside they ran into Judi Bartusz, their best friend and neighbor, and the wife of Frank's longtime friend and sometime business partner Gabor Bartusz. Judi had been walking her little dog Lucky when she spotted the gold Mercedes in Frank's driveway. Curious, Judi walked up to the front door.

When Frank opened it, he invited Judi inside. She learned that Frank and Krisztina and the two musclemen were on their way to a late-night supper at Shula's Steak House, the popular Miami Lakes restaurant named for Miami Dolphins coach Don Shula, the winningest coach in National Football League history. It was late, but they decided to go anyway. Judi walked with them to the driveway.

"I was the first one to walk out of the house," Judi remembered. "I was walking with the dog and [Doorbal] was walking down to his car, and he made a little small talk, 'hi,' and 'hi.' And I said, 'I live down the street.' And he said his name was Adrian, and I shook his hand."

As Judi looked on, Frank took his seat behind the wheel of the Lamborghini, while Krisztina sat beside him. Judi waved as the couple drove off, with the Lamborghini following behind the Mercedes. Once past the Golden Beach gatehouse, the two-car caravan traveled south along Route A1A to Sunny Isles Boulevard where they turned right and headed west. With no traffic it's no more than a twenty minute drive from the seaside community to Shula's. Frank and Krisztina expected to be back home by midnight, time enough to pack for an afternoon flight to the Bahamas, where they planned to spend the Memorial Day weekend at Frank's Freeport condominium.

Meanwhile as Judi walked home, she thought about the two men she had met at Frank's house. They were "gangster-looking," she told her husband when she arrived home, and she remarked that the usually laid-back Frank seemed nervous. Even Chopin, Frank and Krisztina's dog, acted strangely. He bolted from the house, something the usually well-behaved canine had never done before. Frank had to chase after him, and it seemed to Judi that Chopin sensed that the musclemen were up to no good.

Judi told Gabor that she feared that Frank and Krisztina were in danger. Sadly, she was right, and before another sun would rise over Golden Beach one of them would be dead, while the other would barely be alive.

CHAPTER TWO

FRANK GRIGA:
THE BOY FROM BUDAPEST

To the Sun Gym gang's leaders it seemed that there would be an infinite supply of rich victims to choose from. Miami, after all, attracts people who have lots of money, and they're not shy about flaunting it. It's "a city fueled by flagrant materialism [and] conspicuous consumption," the alternative weekly *Miami New Times* once observed. Frank Griga wasn't one to hide his success. He was nouveau riche and proud of it, and he reveled in showing it.

Frank Griga grew up in Budapest, Hungary, but he was born in East Berlin on May 19, 1961. His father, a diplomat, was posted there. A preemie, Frank spent the first two months of his life in an incubator. The divided city, the capital of East Germany (the German Democratic Republic), was ground zero in the Cold War, the long and bitter ideological struggle that pitted the free world, led by the United States, against the Communist bloc, led by the Soviet Union. The division of Germany into East and West came about at the end of World War II in 1945, after Russia's Red Army liberated the nations of Eastern and Central

Europe from their Nazi conquerors and occupied eastern Germany. The Soviets ruled with an iron hand, and they set up puppet regimes throughout the region. In 1948, Soviet troops helped Hungary's Communist Party seize political control of the country. As they did in East Germany, Poland, Romania, and Czechoslovakia, the Communists declared Hungary a "People's Republic" and a one-party state. They nationalized industry, turned farms into collectives, and unleashed a brutal secret police force, the AVH, that terrorized the population.

The oppressive Communist regime squashed opposition, suppressed religious worship, and restricted travel— Hungarians were unable leave the country without government permission. The harsh rule sparked a revolution that began on October 23, 1956, in Budapest, Hungary's capital, and spread to the rest of the country. It started as a student-led protest march on the parliament. It ended when Soviet tanks and troops crushed the revolt, killing more than twenty-five hundred Hungarians in bloody fighting.

World tensions were high in the spring of 1961. Frank was just sixteen days old when, on June 4, U.S. President John F. Kennedy left the United States to meet with Soviet ruler Nikita Khrushchev in Vienna, Austria. Instead of easing tensions, the contentious meeting between the American president and the Russian dictator intensified them. When it ended, talk of thermonuclear war was in the air. It was "the most potentially dangerous confrontation since the early 1950s," historian Michael Beschloss noted.

Kennedy called up military reservists and placed America's armed forces on high alert. For his part, Khrushchev scuttled plans to pare down the 1.2 million-man Red Army. Military commanders in both countries drew up plans of attack that would annihilate tens of millions of people in Central and Eastern Europe alone. Four months later the Cuban Missile Crisis brought the superpowers to the brink of nuclear war. This time Miami and most of the eastern United States were in the atomic crosshairs, too. Pentagon war planners estimated that seventy million Americans would perish in a nuclear war with the Soviet Union. President Kennedy asked Congress for $270 million for civil defense.

After taking the world to the brink, tensions between the superpowers eased in the years ahead. As the Cold War thawed, life improved somewhat in Hungary, too. Frank was age five and his sister, Zsuzsanna, was nine when their parents divorced. In the aftermath of the breakup, they moved with their mother to Budapest. Frank relied on his older sister, and their bond became stronger after their mother, Ferencne, suffered a nervous breakdown.

Frank was among the brightest boys in his primary school but he was shy, a trait his sister attributed to his premature birth and the two months he spent in an incubator. By the time he turned twenty, however, Frank was a handsome, five foot ten inch young man with a round face, bright smile, and deep brown eyes who was burning with ambition, but opportunities in Hungary were restricted. He decided to leave his homeland and settle in America.

"Every normal person wanted to leave," said Zsuzsanna, a high school English teacher in Hungary. "There came a time when [Frank] realized there is no future for him and he decided to leave." Fortunately for Frank his coming of age coincided with the beginning of the end of the Communist tyranny.

In the early 1980s, the Hungarian Communist Party reined in the secret police, and even eased travel restrictions. Hungary was arguably the most liberal of the Soviet-bloc nations, its citizens even allowed to view reruns of American television shows. Among Frank's favorites was *Miami Vice*, the groundbreaking cop show that defined Miami. It starred Don Johnson as Sonny Crockett, a former University of Florida football star who served two combat tours in Vietnam before becoming a cop in Miami where he lived on a sailboat with Elvis, his pet alligator.

Crockett and his partner, Rico Tubbs (played by Philip

Michael Thomas), portrayed a pair of undercover Metro-Dade detectives assigned to the vice unit. The crime-fighting duo battled the forces of evil—drug traffickers, foreign agents, and corrupt officials. They raced around town in Ferraris and piloted speedboats on Biscayne Bay. The popular television show captured more than the violence of Miami; it also captured the glamour of the South Florida lifestyle, the sultry sexiness of its women, as well as the colors of the city—the deep pastels of its art deco buildings and the shimmering blues and greens of its waterways. And it launched new styles in men's fashions. Thanks to *Miami Vice*, three-day old facial stubble became fashionable for Miami's men, as did loafers without socks, Ray-Ban sunglasses, and suits worn over T-shirts.

Frank yearned to go to Miami. Despite the Communists' attempts to stamp out capitalism in Hungary, he was a natural born businessman, "a risk taker," said a Hungarian friend who knew him in Budapest and later in Miami. Early on Frank vowed that he would make his fortune there, but his first stop in America was in New York City.

He arrived in the Big Apple in 1985 and went to work washing cars at a foreign car dealership in Manhattan. It wasn't long before he was repairing them. Two years later Frank was living in Miami where he landed a job as a salesman at Prestige Motors, a luxury car dealership that sold Lotuses, Mercedes, Ferraris, Bentleys, and Lamborghinis. Likeable and diligent, he earned a six-figure income as a salesman, but the boy from Budapest wasn't content to sell the high-priced vehicles—he wanted to own them.

The Miami that Frank moved to was a boomtown, a multicultural, multiethnic melting pot vastly different from what it had been just a generation before. According to a demographic study by the Miami-Dade County Department of Planning and Zoning, in 1960 the population of 935,000 consisted mainly of American-born whites and African-

Americans. A mere 5 percent of Miamians were Hispanic. By 1990, the face and pulse of Miami-Dade County had changed dramatically.

Of the two million residents, more than 50 percent were Hispanic, the result mainly of immigration from Cuba, Central America, and South America. Haitian immigrants accounted for 10 percent of the county's population, while immigrants from Europe made up just 2 percent. Within Miami's European population, only about one thousand were Hungarian-born.

He quickly became a hero in Miami's tiny Hungarian community. He invested in the burgeoning 900 phone line business, beginning with 976-CARS, which charged callers for information about used cars. He added other 900 lines such as weather information for boaters and surfers, but he struck it rich when he got into the two billion dollar a year phone sex industry with his own teleporn lines, charging callers as much as five dollars per minute to engage in steamy conversations with telephone actors and actresses. In the beginning the business was taking in three thousand dollars a month. Then he began advertising on television and his income soared. By 1994, Frank had more than forty phone sex lines, among them 9-ROMANCE and 976-TITS. That year Frank netted a whopping $1.9 million after taxes.

"Frank must have been twenty-five or twenty-six when he started to make money," his sister, Zsuzsanna, said. "He was like a kid in a candy store." Zsuzsanna remembers when her brother bought the Lamborghini. "When he picked it up, he was so happy. That was the happiest day in his life, when he picked that car up. If there was anyone making the American dream happen it was Frank. He really wanted to have a slice of it, and he did."

Frank was smart, and he was lucky, too. The phone sex industry emerged in the mid 1980s, just about when he arrived in Miami. By the end of the decade nearly all of the major telephone companies were involved in the business, providing billing services and remitting as much as 50 percent of the money they collected to the sex line operators. Callers could indulge their wildest fantasies with paid actors and actresses whose goal was to keep the caller on the line for as long as possible.

"It's the safest sex there is," Frank would explain to friends. His ads appeared in men's magazines like *Penthouse* and *Hustler*:

LONELY?
Call the Date Line
$1.99 per minute
SATISFACTION GUARANTEED

FANTASIES
CAN COME TRUE
Call Now
Just $2.99 per minute

He featured his cars and his girlfriends in the racy ads, which was how Frank came to meet Krisztina—her stage name was Krista—while scouting South Florida's men's clubs for bodacious young babes to appear in his advertisements.

Krisztina Furton was born in Hungary on March 5, 1972, the younger of Estevan and Elizabeth Furton's two daughters. Her father, a career soldier in the Hungarian army, instilled in her a love of sports, and from an early age Krisztina dreamed of becoming an Olympic swimmer. She began training at age three. As an elementary school student she would rise early every morning and head for the pool before school. She'd go back there again after school. As a young teen, Krisztina concentrated on high-diving, but she tore a ligament in her ankle at age fourteen, forcing her to give up her Olympic dream.

Krisztina arrived in Miami from Hungary in 1992. She was twenty-one years old, she had no money, she spoke no English, and she lacked a green card. But the limber brunette was a five foot, seven inch beauty, and in no time she was dancing at a strip club in Pompano Beach. There she could perform for cash tips, no green card or Social Security number needed.

In less than a year Krisztina had saved enough money for breast implants and a nose job, and she met the love of her life, Frank Griga. They were introduced by Beatriz Weiland, Frank's former lover. Their three-month relationship had ended amicably and they remained friends, so Beatriz had no qualms about introducing Frank to Krisztina. By all accounts it was love at first sight. A few months after they met, Krisztina was living with Frank in Golden Beach.

Even before he met her, the boy from Budapest was living a lavish lifestyle in Miami. He bought his Golden Beach home in 1988, plunking down $650,000 for the waterfront villa with a swimming pool and a boat dock. He dressed in made-to-order Italian suits, ate at posh restaurants, and frequented high-end strip clubs where he would tip the dancers liberally and generously buy rounds of drinks for other club-goers.

"Frank was a flashy guy," recalled next door neighbor Yosef Yoifore. Rumors about Frank were rampant in the tiny seaside community. Neighbors speculated that he was a pimp or a drug dealer; some thought that he was running a call girl service, while others wondered if he was involved in the sex-slave trade.

Frank was also friendly, easygoing, and accessible, a down-to-earth millionaire who would invite tradesman who had come to work on his house to join him for a beer or for a ride on his boat. Despite his wealth, he never forgot where he came from. He stayed close to his roots—godfather to his sister's two children and close to his mother and sister in Budapest, phoning them daily and sending them money.

Like Frank, Krisztina also kept in close contact with her family in Hungary, phoning home every Friday morning to speak with her parents and her married sister, Katia. The couple invited Krisztina's parents to visit them in Miami, paying their airfare and all their expenses. They arrived in late winter, a glorious time of year in South Florida, when the days are sunny, warm, and dry, and the nights are comfortably cool and crisp. They went back to Hungary just before South Florida's weather turned steamy and rainy, reassured that their youngest daughter was safe, happy, and well cared for.

Their concern about their youngest's safety was well-founded. Tourist killings in Florida were well-publicized in Europe and around the world. On September 8, 1993, German tourist Uwe-Wilhelm Rakebrand and his wife, Kathrin, were in Miami less than an hour when their rental car was bumped from behind as they drove from the airport into the city. They heeded the advice given to Miami tourists: Don't stop. When he didn't stop, one of the thugs, a twenty-two year old female, shot him as he drove on the expressway. One week later, a British couple stopped their car at a rest stop on I-10 where three young thugs tried to rob them. Gary Colley and Margaret Jagger were shot. He died, she survived. The attacks gave Florida a black eye. Tourism, Miami's number one industry, fell markedly in 1994. European tourism fell by twenty percent.

Despite the violence around him, life couldn't have been better for the boy from Budapest. He'd found the love of his life and had struck it rich in America. By 1995, in addition to the Lamborghini Diablo, Frank also owned a red Dodge Viper, a blue Dodge Stealth, and a $300,000 yacht, which he named *Foreplay*. He was looking at purchasing an experimental sports car called a Vector for $200,000. His Golden Beach home was worth $700,000. His condominium in the Bahamas was valued at $275,000, while land he owned in Hawaii was worth $200,000. Along with his bank and brokerage accounts and life insurance policies, Frank Griga's net worth as he followed the two musclemen in the Mercedes was more than ten million dollars. But on this night the forces of evil were just one car ahead, and they had been plotting for weeks to take everything away from Frank and Krisztina.

CHAPTER THREE

DANNY LUGO:
THE LEADER OF THE PACK

The Sun Gym gang's death for dollars plot was the brain-child of Danny Lugo, a street-smart native New Yorker and, like Frank Griga, a fan of *Miami Vice*. Lugo was born on April 6, 1963. By all accounts he was smart and precocious, and loved by his parents; Carmen, a house cleaner, and Guillermo, a building superintendent.

Of Puerto Rican heritage, Danny Lugo grew up in a religious Catholic home, one of four children: He had a younger sister and two older half brothers. Fluent in Spanish and English, young Danny attended church regularly and even served as an altar boy. After graduating from Xavier High School where he was an honor student and a star player on the school's football team, Lugo was awarded a scholarship to attend Fordham University in the borough of the Bronx.

"He was an outstanding youngster," says O'Neal Tutein, his coach at Fordham. "Very quiet. A very hard worker. Lived in the weight room. Took good care of himself and the kids liked him." Coach Tutein added that Lugo "was a person of character." But from an early age, Danny Lugo was an accomplished liar. He once told a psychologist that "lying was something he had done almost all his life," adding that he was very good at it, and routinely lied "to get other people to do things for him." What's more, he could lie in two languages—English and Spanish.

Danny Lugo was only six credits shy of earning a degree in computer science when he dropped out of Fordham because, he would later explain, he had not taken some required courses. Lugo felt that he should not have to take them, but he couldn't convince the dean at Fordham, a Jesuit university, to give him a pass, so he swapped textbooks for barbells at a Manhattan health club where he met coworker Lillian Torres. They married in October 1987. It was Lugo's second trip to the altar; a previous marriage ended in divorce just sixth months after it began.

Lillian and Danny moved from New York City to Miami in 1988, along with Lillian's young niece Jessica, the daughter of her deceased brother. At first they lived with a relative in suburban Kendall. After a couple of months the young family settled north and west of downtown Miami, in the city of Hialeah. Three more children, the offspring of Lillian's sister who had died from AIDS, would join them in Miami, too.

Handsome, buff, and blessed with a dazzling smile and charisma, twenty-five-year-old Danny Lugo landed a job selling memberships and working as a personal trainer at the Scandinavian Health and Racquet Club in Kendall, but the young husband was unable to earn enough to support his family. That's because gyms and health clubs are everywhere in South Florida, where looking good and showing off a well-chiseled body is as much a part of the lifestyle as sunshine, sand, and palm trees. Competition for members is fierce, and Danny Lugo had four children to support and expensive tastes—luxury cars, Armani suits, pricey men's clubs, hot-bodied dancers, and gambling jaunts to the Bahamas—and a sense of entitlement. His six-hundred-dollar-a-week salary plus commissions didn't go far enough, so to make ends meet Lugo came up with his first fast-buck scam.

He began using an alias, morphing into David Lowenstein, a lawyer and the U.S. representative of a wealthy Chinese family from Hong Kong with millions of dollars to lend small businesses seeking venture capital. As Lowenstein, he contacted them through classified ads in newspapers, easily winning their confidence and collecting 10 percent of the loan amount in upfront fees along with applications.

Lugo's victims weren't naïve patsies. On the contrary, they were mostly sophisticated businesspeople who believed that the upfront fee was payment for an insurance policy with Lloyd's of London to guarantee repayment of the loan. The victims even flew to Miami where they met with David Lowenstein in hotel rooms or restaurants and personally gave him cashier's checks to cover the advance fees. The checks were made out to Daniel Lugo who, as Lowenstein, simply explained that Lugo was a financial officer with the Chinese family.

In all, the fast-talking con man managed to rake in nearly $300,000 from his unwitting victims, none of whom ever received a loan. Advance fees ranged from $5,200 to $42,000.

Despite the alias, it didn't take long for the FBI to track Lugo down. Agents took him into custody at the Scandinavian Health and Racquet Club in May 1990, marching him out of the gym in handcuffs. At first he denied he was Lowenstein, and he denied that he was a swindler, but in January 1991, Lugo pleaded guilty to fraud. In his statement to the court, he acknowledged his guilt and promised the judge, "It will never happen again for I have learned not to use intelligence for wrong actions."

In a written statement, Lugo explained:

> I thought I wanted to be an entrepreneur. I assumed the victims had a lot of money. I called up people that requested money. They placed ads like "Looking for

$4,000,000 for a project." I also placed these types of advertisements. I saw the ads in entrepreneur magazines like Inc. and Entrepreneur. I called the victims saying I can help them, that for a nominal fee I would get them financing. I tried to bolster my image by saying I was a counsel to trusts and was close to people who had the money to lend. I identified myself as David Lowenstein.

I asked for 10 percent of the loan to cover premiums for guaranteed loans and expenses. I always received payment by check, twice by wire.

The majority of the time I met the people personally at hotel rooms or restaurants and they would give me the check. They already knew to make it out to Daniel Lugo. Some people even would ask me why to Lugo and I would say that's what the trust expected.

And he expressed remorse:

I felt bad for what I have done and for the past year I have felt a prisoner of my own guilt and as a family man I made them suffer, too. The humiliation and embarrassment I will carry for the rest of my life.

Despite what sounded like a heartfelt plea, Lugo was sentenced to four years in federal prison, which he served at a minimum-security facility in the Florida panhandle where he spent his days pumping up and mingling freely with other white-collar criminals.

On October 22, 1992, fifteen months after he was sent to prison, Danny Lugo was released on parole, but the muscular swindler did not keep his promise to the judge. Investigators believe it was while he was behind bars that the hustler from New York learned the ins and outs of Medicare fraud. Not long after he was released, he and a partner allegedly launched several bogus medical supply companies. They rented mailboxes at a Miami postal center, purchased the names, birth dates, and Social Security numbers of actual Medicare recipients, then billed the United States government for medical services never delivered. The scam would set Lugo on the path that would lead him to Frank Griga's front door.

By this time, however, Lugo's marriage to Lillian was on the rocks. Even before he was incarcerated, Lugo, an incorrigible womanizer and adulterer, had taken up with another woman. They met before he went to prison, and they stayed in touch while he served his sentence. On January 3, 1993, just two months after his release, thirty-year-old Danny Lugo and twenty-four-year-old Lucretia Goodridge were married in Miami in a Buddhist ceremony.

He had been a model prisoner; nevertheless Lugo's parole came with strict conditions: He would be on probation for three years, and he was required to return thousands of dollars in restitution to those he had bilked. The length of his probation would be curtailed if and when he made restitution to his victims. While on probation Lugo was prohibited from borrowing money or establishing lines of credit without the permission of his probation officer. He also needed a legitimate job, and within days of his release, Danny Lugo turned up at the testosterone emporium known as Sun Gym looking for work. He met with the gym's owner, Miami accountant and bodybuilding impresario John Carl Mese.

Lugo told Mese about his incarceration, explaining that he'd gotten into trouble because he wanted money to help Lillian and her family. "I saw the kids were lacking," Lugo would say. "Mildred, Lillian's sister, called collect to ask if we can send money to get food. I saw all this and I had to do something," so he used some of the money to bring Mildred and her family from the South Bronx "where they were barely eating."

Mese was impressed, and he bought into Lugo's vision for Sun Gym. If Mese would just give him a chance he would turn Sun Gym into a nationally renowned fitness powerhouse. They'd sell Sun Gym franchises. There would also be Sun Gym Vitamins, Sun Gym Snacks, and a Sun

Gym Wear, a clothing line. They would sell their products through thousands of multilevel marketers with Danny Lugo and John Mese at the top of the pyramid.

And that wasn't all. A team of Sun Gym weight lifters—women as well as men—would tour South Florida, putting on exhibitions at malls and arenas. Lugo even promised to organize a Sun Gym karate team. In no time, he promised, gym membership would quadruple. And Lugo, who fancied himself a computer whiz, claimed that he had developed a program that would revolutionize gym management by making it easier to monitor members' payments and accounts receivable. "We'll make a fortune selling it to other gyms," Lugo vowed. It was all bullshit, but Mese fell for it hook, line, and sinker.

It was, in fact, music to the middle-aged accountant's ears.

For one thing, Mese had invested heavily in a computer software company, so the accountant saw a golden opportunity to bring Lugo's gym management computer program under its umbrella. For another, Sun Gym had been a losing proposition almost from day one, a constant drain on Mese's time and his financial resources. He was constantly behind on the half million dollar mortgage he'd taken out to finance the gym, whose membership was an eclectic mix of serious bodybuilders and narcissistic muscleheads. By 1992, Sun Gym had been steadily losing members to nationally known chains that were springing up throughout South Florida. Gold's Gym had opened in Miami Lakes at a better and more spacious location with more modern equipment and a more upscale clientele. Bally Total Fitness had opened nearby, too, and the two facilities were pulling members away from Sun Gym, especially those members who weren't hell-bent on building muscle mass or achieving the perfect bodybuilder's physique.

What's more, the gym was taking up too much of the accountant's time; his bread and butter, his accounting practice, suffered as a result, so Mese was looking to sell Sun Gym—until he met with Danny Lugo. With someone he could trust, a dynamic and charismatic general manager like Danny Lugo at the helm, Mese reasoned, his dream would at long last come true: Sun Gym would become the Mecca for serious bodybuilders after all, while he devoted his attention to his accounting practice, Mese and Associates.

CHAPTER FOUR

THE MIDAS TOUCH

John Carl Mese, Texas-born but Miami-raised, was a fifty-six-year-old father of two. He was a pillar of the community, a member of the prestigious Miami Shores Country Club and the Kiwanis club, and the founder and owner of Sun Gym, which he opened in 1987. Located at 6135 NW 167th Street, it offered everything for men and women who were deadly serious about building muscle mass and definition: free weights; Hammer, Nautilus, and Cam machines; a juice bar; even babysitting for parents who worked out. And there were mirrors all over, so that every Arnold Schwarzenegger wannabe could watch his muscles grow with every curl and bench press and from every angle. For those who wanted an extra boost, illegal steroids were available, too, but the illicit trade was an under-the-table amenity at Sun Gym.

Mese himself was an avid bodybuilder. A graduate of Miami Edison High School, he took up weight lifting as a college student at Texas A&M, where he majored in accounting. By the time he graduated, he had a sixty-inch

chest and twenty-inch biceps on a five foot, nine inch frame.
Eventually, he would add tattoos to his massive arms: a
Texas logo with two hearts on his right arm and Lady Justice
on his left. In 1962, Mese was serving in the United States
Air Force, stationed in England where he won the title of
Mr. United Kingdom. The following year he was invited to
compete in the Mr. America contest, but his commanding
officer turned down his request for leave to participate.

Back in Miami, Mese joined the accounting practice
started by his father in 1945. In 1971, at age thirty-three,
he married twenty-five-year-old Janice Hough from New
Jersey. They would have two children together, a son, John
and a daughter, Andrea. By all accounts Mese was an
affectionate father, but his accounting practice and his passion for bodybuilding were major distractions. The couple
divorced in 1981. Seven years later, the muscular accountant tied the knot once again, marrying Cheryl Ann Fernandez in Miami.

Mese was a very busy man. In addition to his accounting practice and overseeing Sun Gym, he organized and
promoted bodybuilding competitions. He was well known
and highly regarded among serious bodybuilders in the
United States and Europe, serving as the president of the
South Florida Body Builders Association and the secretary of the National Physique Committee. Now when com-
petitive bodybuilders, men and women, came to Miami to
compete, they would train at Sun Gym where Danny Lugo
was the general manager.

Lugo didn't come to Sun Gym alone. He brought his
bodybuilding buddy Noel Adrian Doorbal with him to work
as a personal trainer at Sun Gym. They met before Lugo
went to prison in 1991, when Doorbal was newly arrived in
the United States from Trinidad. At the time, Doorbal was
staying in Miami with Lucretia Goodridge, his cousin and
Danny Lugo's future wife. He was working for minimum
wage as a kitchen helper at Fiesta Taco and commuting to
work on an old bicycle. By 1994, however, he was the twenty-
two-year-old president of Sun Fitness Consultants, Inc.

Even though his visa had long since expired, he was able to obtain an American Express card. He also had a sports car and a million dollar mutual fund account at Merrill Lynch. The initial deposit of $745,000 represented the proceeds from Lugo's alleged Medicare scam. The funds had to be hidden from the prying eyes of Lugo's federal probation officer, so they were deposited into Doorbal's account. Lugo, however, had complete authority to make trades and write checks on the account. Word had gotten around Sun Gym that when it came to making money, Danny Lugo had the Midas touch, and members would routinely ask Lugo for investment advice.

Jorge "George" Delgado didn't have the Midas touch. In 1991, the Cuban-born car salesman—he arrived in Miami in 1966, a two-year-old refugee from Castro's Cuba—was living in his mother-in-laws' house. He and his wife, Linda, were in dire financial straits when Linda opened up to her boss, millionaire businessman and certified public accountant Marcelo "Marc" Schiller.

Unlike so many successful Miami businessmen, Marc Schiller was not living la vida loca in South Florida. He wasn't flashy, he didn't live in a mansion, and he didn't chase women. He was born in Buenos Aires, Argentina, in 1957, but left with his family when he was seven years old. A naturalized American citizen, Schiller grew up in the New York City borough of Brooklyn, graduated from Abraham Lincoln High School and went on to study accounting at the University of Wisconsin. From there he went to work for several big accounting firms in Texas until he took a job in South America as the comptroller of an oil pipeline company in Bogota, Colombia. There Marc met and married Diana, a Colombian-born coworker.

The couple fled the South American country in the aftermath of the 1988 kidnapping of the company's president by leftist guerillas who were in the business of abducting wealthy executives and holding them for ransom. The

man was held captive for seven months while a team of
executives from the pipeline company, including Schiller,
negotiated his ransom. They never notified the authorities.
That's because the police in Colombia and other South and
Central American countries are often in cahoots with the
guerillas, so kidnappings are handled privately to ensure
the victim's safe return.

Fearing that he was in danger of being abducted, too,
Schiller, Diana and their infant son sought refuge in Miami,
where Schiller started his own accounting practice and
a medical supply company, Dadima Corporation, which
billed Medicare for nutritional supplements and feeding
kits for patients who, because of serious digestive problems, could only be fed through tubes. Dadima, with Schiller at the helm, billed Medicare $350 to $400 per month
per patient for the supplements, and $350 per month for the
supply kits per patient. Between his accounting practice
and his Medicare business, Schiller was earning close to
one million dollars a year.

Moved by Linda's story of her financial problems and
by her tears, Schiller put then-twenty-seven-year-old Jorge
to work as his marketing representative. His job was to call
on businesses and pitch them on hiring Schiller as their
accountant. Delgado wore a suit and a tie, and he carried a
presentation folder. He would also pick up checks and documents from Schiller's clients. By all accounts, Delgado
was a successful representative for Schiller's accounting
practice. The two men became friends as well as business
associates. Eventually, they became partners.

The Schillers trusted Delgado completely. They confided in him. Delgado knew the security code to the Schiller home, which he looked after whenever Marcelo and
Diana were away. He knew where Schiller banked and
was privy to his business secrets. He knew how much
money Schiller had squirreled away in the Cayman Islands,
and where he deposited funds received from Medicare. He
also knew that his boss was scamming the government
agency.

In 1992, Schiller sold Dadima to Delgado for $250,000. Schiller even financed his friend's purchase of the company. He renamed his accounting practice D.J. and Associates, but he continued to provide accounting and billing services to Dadima, which Delgado renamed J & R Medical Investments. Schiller and Delgado launched another company, JoMar Property Investments, which they formed to buy and sell mortgages. Once again, Schiller bankrolled Delgado's interest in the business, but his involvement with the new venture was limited because he was busy with yet another venture—Schlotzsky's, a deli restaurant franchise he owned, was occupying most of his time.

Thanks to the generosity and friendship of Marcelo and Diana Schiller, Jorge Delgado's financial situation improved greatly. In a dramatic reversal of fortune, Delgado netted three hundred thousand dollars in 1993. He and his wife Linda were able to move into their own home. Delgado even bought a speedboat and joined Sun Gym, where he hired Danny Lugo as his personal trainer. The two men eventually became inseparable, so much so that Delgado brought his Sun Gym pal to Schiller's office and to his home, and it wasn't long before he proposed that Lugo join him and Schiller in a business venture.

Schiller, however, would have no part of Danny Lugo. He vehemently expressed his disapproval of the muscleman. Schiller didn't trust Lugo. He found him crude, abrasive, and menacing. Experienced in the business world, Marcelo Schiller recognized that Danny Lugo was dangerous and full of shit. What's more, he was increasingly troubled by his protégé, Jorge Delgado, whose mannerisms were becoming more and more like Lugo's.

"He wasn't the Jorge Delgado that I knew," Schiller would remember, adding, "He was trying to act tougher and crueler than before he went to the gym to work out." Since joining Sun Gym, Delgado swaggered when he walked, just like Lugo did, and he began dressing like the muscleman, too. Schiller refused to do business with Lugo, telling his former protégé, "It's either him or me, Jorge."

Delgado would choose Lugo, but the final break did not occur until January 1994, when Schiller attended a business lunch at an Italian restaurant in Miami Lakes with Delgado and a banker from Miami's Central Bank to discuss a financial backing for JoMar. But the banker kept prodding Delgado, asking him about J & R's bank accounts. Delgado became defensive and evasive. The more the banker pressed him, the angrier Delgado became. After the lunch, Schiller confronted Delgado in the parking lot.

"Jorge, what's going on?" he demanded.

Delgado snarled. "It's none of your business what's between me and Danny Lugo."

Schiller wasted no time. With his very next breath he told Delgado that they were through, and that he was ending their business relationship "immediately."

The rift was bitter, and it was engineered by Danny Lugo who persuaded Delgado to hire John Mese as his accountant and financial advisor. What's more, it wouldn't be long before the conniving ex-con convinced Delgado to join him in the criminal enterprise that would become known as the Sun Gym gang. Their first victim: Marcelo Schiller.

CHAPTER FIVE

PUMPING IRON,
PLOTTING MURDER

The plot was hatched in Sun Gym, during Jorge Delgado's workouts with his new best friend and personal trainer, Danny Lugo. To the regulars at the gym, Danny Lugo was a financial genius. Jorge Delgado thought so, too. He confided to Lugo that the Medicare-related business that he had purchased from Schiller had been involved in Medicare fraud when Schiller was the owner. Delgado feared that he might have been inadvertently involved in continuing the fraud after he purchased the business. He asked Lugo to review the company's financial records.

One week later Lugo reported his findings, telling Delgado that Schiller cheated him out of more than two hundred thousand dollars—his "rightful share" of the proceeds from their Medicare business. Lugo even convinced Delgado that Schiller had cheated him as well, even though Lugo had never done any business with Marc Schiller. Delgado vetoed any possibility of suing his former boss and one-time mentor because a lawsuit might expose Medicare fraud, which could land Delgado in federal prison.

In early October 1994, Danny Lugo decided that they should kidnap Marc Schiller and force him to return the money. At first Delgado resisted, but his willpower was no match for Lugo's charm and persuasiveness. Two weeks later, a meeting was held in Danny Lugo's office inside Mese and Associates' suite of offices in Miami Lakes. Delgado was there along with Doorbal and two other Sun Gym employees—Stevenson Pierre, an immigrant from Haiti, and Carl Weekes, Pierre's roommate.

Carl Collin Weekes was an ex-Marine from Brooklyn, New York. In September 1994, Weekes decided he'd better leave Brooklyn in order to straighten out his messed up life. He had served in the Marines for little more than year but was mustered out after threatening another marine. Back in Brooklyn and unemployed, he took up drinking and smoking crack cocaine, and he got himself into a heap of trouble by committing house burglaries and robbing drug dealers at gunpoint. But he went through rehab, found Jesus, and got sober.

Weekes decided to restart his life in Miami where Stevenson Pierre was living. Weekes' cousin was Pierre's girlfriend, the mother of his seven-year-old son. The plan was for Weekes to find a job in Florida, save some money, and bring his girlfriend and their two children to Miami. The two men had met several times at family events. Pierre was willing to help his girlfriend's cousin, but he had his doubts. Nevertheless he agreed to let Weekes move in with him. He even promised to help him land a job at Sun Gym, where he had been working since February 1994.

Stevenson "Steve" Pierre had once lived in New York City, where he worked as a credit analyst and a skip tracer for American Express. He lost his job when the credit card giant relocated its operations elsewhere. In March 1993, Pierre left New York for Miami. He began working at Sun Gym in February 1994. At five foot five and one hundred thirty pounds, Steve Pierre was no muscleman, but Danny Lugo hired him to collect overdue membership fees from the gym's clients and to man the front desk. His weekly pay was $375.

A few days after Weekes arrived in Miami, Pierre brought him to Sun Gym where he met Danny Lugo and Adrian Doorbal. Lugo wasn't impressed with the ex-Marine. At five foot eleven and less than one hundred fifty pounds, he was no muscleman either, but Lugo was polite, telling Weekes that the gym could use a janitor, but there was a hiring freeze. If anything opened up, he promised, he would give Weekes a call. It came in mid-October, when Danny Lugo phoned Weekes to invite him to his office along with Doorbal and Pierre. Jorge Delgado joined them, too.

Danny Lugo led the meeting. First he briefed the three men, telling them that a rich "scumbag" named Marcelo Schiller had stolen one hundred thousand dollars from him, and two hundred thousand dollars from Sun Gym member Jorge Delgado. Schiller and Delgado, Lugo said, had been involved in Medicare fraud. It would be their job to "take Schiller down" and get the money—and a lot more—back. They would take over ownership of Schiller's house and all its furnishings; his million dollar accounts in the Cayman Islands; his cars; his investment in La Gorce Palace, a luxury condominium then under construction on Miami Beach; as well as his Schlotzsky's deli restaurant.

Lugo also revealed his diabolical plan. They would kidnap the mustachioed accountant and take him to a warehouse Delgado had previously rented on West 77th Street in Hialeah. There they would torture him and force him to sign over his assets. Then, like a general, Lugo gave the troops their marching orders. It would be Doorbal's job to use his enormous strength to capture Schiller and rough him up once he was their prisoner. Weekes and Pierre would assist Doorbal and guard the accountant once he was inside the warehouse. Delgado was to prepare a comprehensive list of Schiller's assets and a detailed layout of his house.

The gang met again two days later. Jorge Delgado read a list that he had drawn up detailing Schiller's assets, the names of his relatives, and his cars. At first, Stevenson Pierre seemed hesitant, but Lugo reassured him that their chance of getting caught was slim to none. Lugo said that was because Schiller was scamming Medicare, and he wouldn't dare go to the police. After the abduction he would just leave town. Besides, Lugo promised, Doorbal, Weekes, and Pierre would each be paid one hundred thousand dollars. Every time they met, Lugo made it a point to remind his cohorts that Schiller was a rich businessman and that they each stood to make a lot of money.

John Mese did not attend the meeting. However, he was waiting in the wings with his notary stamp. With it he would notarize all of the documents needed to transfer Schiller's property and stock accounts to the gang. He would also use his financial expertise to launder Marc Schiller's money, for which he would take a 5 percent fee.

To prepare for the kidnapping, Lugo and Delgado drove to The Spy Shop on Biscayne Boulevard where Lugo purchased two Omega Tasers, masks, rope, walkie-talkies, handcuffs, night-vision binoculars, and duct tape. Lugo also rented a burgundy Ford Aerostar with a sliding right-side door for the takedown. Then the gang began stalking Marc Schiller.

"We didn't know his movements," Stevenson Pierre would tell investigators. "What Lugo came up with is that we were going to go on a stakeout to figure out when he left for work, and what time he came home from work, and who was actually living in that house."

During the first two stakeouts, the gang drove to the Schiller home in Old Cutler Cove, his children's schools, and the deli, but they didn't see Schiller. Delgado told the

Sun Gym thugs that Schiller drove a green Land Rover, but he had gotten a new car, which they discovered for themselves when they saw the accountant park it behind the deli.

After their second stakeout, Lugo decided that they were ready to grab Schiller. He told the gang they would seize Schiller on Halloween. Doorbal, Weekes, and Pierre would don masks and ninja outfits and go trick-or-treating in Schiller's neighborhood. They'd grab Schiller when he came to the door in response to their knock. Lugo would be waiting at the curb in the van, and the men would shove Schiller into it.

The Sun Gym thugs agreed that the plan was brilliant, yet another example of Danny Lugo's genius at making money. The Halloween abduction plot was aborted, however, when Lugo decided to participate in horror night festivities at a Miami strip club instead.

The gang made its first serious attempt to kidnap Schiller a week later. It was before dawn when Doorbal, Pierre, and Weekes, with Lugo waiting in a nearby park in the rented van, took up positions in front of Schiller's house, nervously waiting for the accountant to retrieve his morning newspaper. The gang members were in stealth mode, dressed in ninja outfits—all black. And they wore camouflage makeup, which Weekes knew all about from his Marine Corps days. They planned to pounce on Schiller as soon as he bent down to pick up his paper. When that happened, they would grab him and rush the house, taking the entire family hostage. The plan was aborted, however, when an early morning jogger frightened them. Worried that they had been spotted, the jittery thugs turned tail and sprinted to the van.

Lugo was disappointed but undeterred. By stalking Schiller the gang learned that his usual routine involved working at the deli form nine o'clock in the morning until two in the afternoon. They also learned his regular routes to and from the restaurant. That knowledge sparked yet another idea: They would ram Marc Schiller as he drove his green Toyota 4Runner. When Schiller came out to inspect the damage, Doorbal would punch him and push him back into his Toyota. Then Weekes would get behind the wheel and drive the SUV, with Doorbal and Schiller inside, to Delgado's Hialeah warehouse.

They tried to put the new plan into action a few days later. Lugo followed Schiller while the rest of the gang waited up ahead in Steve Pierre's Honda Accord. They were in position, waiting for the accountant to drive by on his way to his deli. Lugo was in constant walkie-talkie communication with Pierre. Doorbal was beside him in the passenger seat while Weekes sat in the back. The plan was for Pierre to broadside Schiller's vehicle, but Schiller blew by the Accord before Pierre could pull out.

Doorbal was enraged. "You're fucking up! You're fucking up!" He screamed at Pierre. "You're a punk! Do you know what happens when you fuck up? Something could happen to your son," he threatened. Pierre took Doorbal's threat seriously.

It wouldn't be the last time Doorbal would go ballistic. After another failed attempt, Doorbal started crying.

"He fell into a tantrum," Steve Pierre recalled. "Screaming, yelling, crying. It took a while for Lugo to calm Doorbal down, advising him 'there will be another chance.' " Besides, Lugo assured Doorbal, the failed attempt had not been a wasted effort. "Now we know exactly what time Schiller leaves for work, and we know exactly what type of vehicle he drives."

They used their new knowledge one sunny morning when they decided to park their van next to Schiller's usual parking spot at the deli and wait for him to pull in. When Schiller arrived he exited the car and started looking in the backseat for his briefcase. At that moment Doorbal and Weekes began to reach out for him. The plan was to pull Schiller into their vehicle and drive off, but just as they were about to grab the unsuspecting accountant, Steve

Pierre got cold feet. He yelled that they were being watched by a passerby. Doorbal and Weekes retreated to the van. The gang drove to a fast food restaurant to regroup.

There would be three more attempts to take Marcelo Schiller down. After the third failed attempt the gang's morale was very low, so Lugo decided to take his men to Solid Gold, his favorite strip club. He bought them drinks, and he told them that if they could capture Schiller, they would have more than enough money to party with any Solid Gold girl they wanted.

Their spirits raised, the men hatched yet another plan, and at nine o'clock in the morning on Tuesday, November 15, 1994, they were in position outside Schlotzsky's. The plan was to trap Schiller in the narrow alleyway behind the deli. Lugo was in his car, a Toyota Camry, blocking Schiller's 4Runner from driving forward. Doorbal, Pierre, and Weekes were in the van, which was parked around the corner. They were waiting for Danny Lugo to announce over the walkie-talkie that Schiller was walking toward his SUV. Doorbal would then pull behind Schiller's SUV, preventing it from backing out of the alley. As soon as Lugo spotted Schiller walking towards his vehicle, he radioed Doorbal. As Schiller attempted to drive off, blasting his horn for Lugo to clear the way so he could pass by, Doorbal's voice came over the walkie-talkie. "This fucking thing won't start," he shouted. Mission aborted again.

Within an hour, the gang rendezvoused at Lugo's office. This time it was Lugo who went ballistic. The veins in the muscleman's massive neck bulged and his usually swarthy complexion turned ashen. Lugo read the riot act to his three henchmen. He told them they were a bunch of incompetent fuckups, and he announced that he was bowing out. If they wanted to get Schiller, he growled, they'd have to get him themselves. Then he stormed out.

Adrian Doorbal rose to the challenge. He was comfortable pinch-hitting for Danny Lugo. He was the manager of personal trainers at Sun Gym, but whenever Danny Lugo was away Doorbal was in charge, and he now had a plan of his own to capture Schiller.

First, he decided to bench Steve Pierre. He would be brought back to watch over Schiller once he was captured and imprisoned at the warehouse, but Doorbal seriously doubted Pierre's enthusiasm for the kidnapping plot. Besides, the slightly built Pierre was no strongman, and Doorbal decided that if the plot were to succeed, the gang would need more muscle.

He set his sights on a replacement: twenty-nine-year-old Sun Gym weight-lifting instructor Mario "Big Mario" Sanchez, a six foot four, two-hundred-seventy pound behemoth able to bench-press four hundred seventy-five pounds. That he was licensed to carry a concealed weapon, a .45, was a big plus. What's more, Sanchez, a part-time bouncer, was an honorably discharged Army veteran who had combat training and served with the elite Special Forces.

It was around noon when Adrian Doorbal approached Big Mario while he worked out at Sun Gym. Doorbal asked the weight lifter to step outside with him so they could talk. The two bodybuilders walked to the rental van and climbed inside. Carl Weekes was already there. Doorbal told Sanchez about a deadbeat "drug dealer" who owed him money. He said he planned to collect the debt later that afternoon. "Help me, Mario, and I'll pay you one thousand dollars."

It was an offer Mario Sanchez should have refused.

"What kind of a drug dealer is this?" he wanted to know. "Is this a small-time guy or is this a big-time drug guy, because if it's a big-time dealer like a cartel guy, I'm not gonna go collect from that guy. A thousand dollars is going to land me in a morgue, with my mouth full of flies." Besides, Sanchez said, he didn't want to beat anyone up.

"Just be there as an intimidator," Doorbal replied, promising that no one would get hurt. But Sanchez had his doubts. He wanted some time to think it over. He left the gym and drove home, but before driving off he told

Doorbal to call him later; he would let him know then if he would help.

Money was tight for Big Mario. He had recently separated from his wife, and he was short on cash to buy Christmas presents for his young son. What's more, his VW Jetta needed a new set of tires. Even before he could speak with Doorbal again, Sanchez had made up his mind.

Earlier that morning Marc Schiller awoke, and, as he did every morning, he retrieved the *Miami Herald* from his driveway. A story on the front page of the business section reported that the Federal Reserve was expected to announce an increase in interest rates later that day, and financial experts were advising consumers to pay down their credit card debt.

Although not business related, another story on the front page of the local section might have caught the accountant's eye, too. The banner headline read: "Memo Puts Prosecutor on Hot Seat." A memo, filled with spelling errors, had been written by a senior federal prosecutor in Miami and leaked to the press. In it, the G-man complained about the abilities of the prosecutors in the Miami-Dade state attorney's office, charging that many of them were mediocre at best, with "bad work habits . . . bad training and bad attitudes." Needless to say, the memo created quite a stir.

Miami-Dade State Attorney Katherine Fernandez Rundle quickly fired back. "The Dade State Attorney's Office is one of the finest in the country," she declared. Then she reminded her critic that the attorney general of the United States, Janet Reno, had been her predecessor.[2]

---

[2]Janet Reno left Miami in 1993 when President Bill Clinton chose her to be the first female attorney general of the United States. Then-governor Lawton Chiles named Katherine Fernandez Rundle, Reno's protégé and top deputy, to succeed her. She was elected to the office in 1995 and has been reelected ever since.

"Look at the achievements of many former prosecutors who are in the judiciary, law firms, and the DOJ (Department of Justice)," Rundle declared. "This cannot be tainted by the ill-informed, isolated opinion of one lawyer."

But the big news in Miami that morning was the weather. The outer bands of Tropical Storm Gordon had reached South Florida the night before, after leaving more than one hundred dead across the Caribbean. The entire region, from Key West to West Palm Beach, was on a tornado watch. The late season storm, the paper said, would pound the region throughout the day, causing flooding, downed power lines, and major beach erosion. Gordon's strong winds and torrential rains put a damper on Marcelo Schiller's plans for the day: After only a couple of months in the restaurant business, Schiller realized that his deli venture had been a blunder, and he was hoping to unload it. A prospective buyer was to meet with him at the restaurant later that afternoon. The accountant worried that the storm would prevent the man from keeping the appointment. Ever the optimist, Schiller drove to his restaurant despite the rotten weather.

At about the same time, Adrian Doorbal and Carl Weekes were on the road, too, driving the rented van through the pouring rain to Mario Sanchez's apartment. Doorbal was too pumped up to leave such an important decision to a telephone call; he wanted a face-to-face answer from the muscleman. Even before Doorbal rang Sanchez's bell, the weight lifter had made up his mind. After weighing the pros and cons, Big Mario decided that if all he had to do to earn a thousand dollars was stand by looking mean and tough, he was in.

Mario Sanchez was armed with his .45 caliber semi-automatic when he left his apartment and climbed into the van with Adrian Doorbal and Carl Weekes. Rolls of duct tape, a Taser, and handcuffs were inside a paper bag behind the driver's seat. As they drove, Doorbal told Sanchez where they were going—to a strip mall near the Miami

International Airport. They would park and wait for the "drug dealer" to emerge from a restaurant, then Weekes and Doorbal would confront the man as he entered his SUV. If there was any resistance, Sanchez was to emerge from the van in his role as the intimidator.

At about 3:30 P.M., Doorbal pulled into the mall's parking lot. He drove to the rear of Schlotzsky's deli, parking the van with its rear against the fence so that they could have an unobstructed view of Schiller's 1994 Toyota 4Runner while they waited to ambush him. Meanwhile, inside the deli, Schiller's meeting with the prospective buyer had ended. It didn't go well. Schiller's asking price was much higher than the prospective buyer was willing to pay. Schiller doubted that anything would come of the meeting. Besides, he had other things on his mind. He was in a hurry to get home because the full force of the tropical storm had not yet hit Miami. In 1992, Hurricane Andrew nearly destroyed Schiller's house, and he didn't want Diana and the children to go through something like that again. Moreover, Thanksgiving was little more than a week away, and he and Diana and the children were planning on spending it with her parents in Colombia. They would stay there at least until Chanukah, the Jewish Festival of Lights, which would begin on December 18.

The sky was dark and rain clouds hung overhead when Marc Schiller, wearing a white polo shirt and jeans, emerged from the rear door of his restaurant. The rain, which had been coming down in torrents just moments before, had let up. At about 4:15 P.M., Doorbal spotted Schiller in the parking lot.

"There he is," Doorbal exclaimed.

"That's him," Weekes agreed.

With their prey in sight, the two men darted from the van. Doorbal exited from the driver's seat while Weekes emerged through the sliding side door. Sanchez stayed behind, watching from the front passenger's seat. Within seconds, Doorbal and Weekes pounced on Schiller, but the takedown was anything but easy. Schiller grabbed the steering wheel and held on for dear life as Doorbal and Weekes tried to pull him away.

"Help! Help!" Schiller yelled, but no one came to his assistance. Weekes zapped him with the Taser. It sent an electric shock—120,000 excruciating volts—through the accountant's entire body, but the painful jolt wasn't enough to subdue him. Schiller kept on struggling, so Weekes fired the Taser again, this time hitting him in the ankle. The pain was unbearable. Now writhing in pain, Schiller let go of the steering wheel. Doorbal and Weekes dragged him to the van where Mario Sanchez was still waiting in the front passenger seat.

"Pull him in," Doorbal barked. Big Mario turned around and extended his massive arms. With one swift motion he was able to haul Schiller in through the open side door. With their catch lying facedown behind the front seats, Doorbal slid the side door shut and ran to the driver's seat.

Tires squealed as Doorbal floored the accelerator. He drove the Aerostar across the mall parking lot and onto Northwest 36th Street where he turned east toward the Palmetto Expressway, taking it north to Hialeah. Because of wet weather and bumper-to-bumper traffic, the seven-mile trip would take more than fifteen minutes. Weekes put a revolver to Schiller's face.

"Do you see this?" the ex-Marine yelled as the van navigated through heavy late afternoon traffic.

"Don't move," he commanded. "If you move I will kill you." Then he wrapped tape around Schiller's eyes and threw a heavy mover's blanket over his head. On the way to the warehouse, Schiller was repeatedly stomped and pummeled; punched in the face by Big Mario Sanchez and kicked in the ribs by Weekes, who removed Schiller's wallet from his pocket and yanked two gold chains and a gold Star of David from around his neck.

"Looks like we've got ourselves a real live matzo ball," one of the kidnappers said. They had a big laugh over that. And they laughed with every punch and kick they gave

Schiller. They zapped him with the stun gun several more times, laughing loudly every time the hog-tied accountant writhed in pain. The torture and terror didn't end once they had Schiller in the warehouse. In fact, it only became worse, much worse.

CHAPTER SIX

SCHILLER'S LIST

Marcelo Schiller was nearly unconscious when the Aerostar pulled into Jorge Delgado's Hialeah warehouse. With tape wound around Marcelo's entire head, he couldn't see. His arms had been handcuffed behind his back, and his legs were bound together with tape, too. Schiller's entire body ached with pain, and he had no idea where he was or why he had been abducted, but when he heard the distinctive sound of a door rolling up he knew he had been taken to a warehouse.

As soon as the van was inside, Schiller heard one of his captors talking on a cell phone: "The eagle has landed. I have a present for you." The caller was Adrian Doorbal, and he was proudly letting Danny Lugo know that the "eagle," Marcelo Schiller, had at long last been taken down. Ten minutes later Danny Lugo was there, too. He couldn't wait to phone Delgado. "Come down to the warehouse," he said. "I have a surprise for you."

Lugo was waiting outside when Delgado pulled up. Schiller was out of the van, handcuffed, eyes and feet taped, and lying on the floor. Sanchez and Weekes dragged their prisoner from the van. They pushed him facedown onto a piece of cardboard. They removed his shoes and shackled his feet to his hands, which were already cuffed behind his back. Then they lifted Schiller up and chained him to a wall. One of them pressed a baseball bat against his face.

"Do you feel this? Do you know what this is?" he demanded.

"It's a baseball bat," Schiller replied.

"If you move, I will break your face," the thug promised.

Then they left Schiller alone in the warehouse for several hours. Before leaving, however, they tuned a radio to Miami's Y100, blasting the volume so that if Schiller yelled or screamed for help, no one would hear him. But the continually blaring radio would help Schiller keep track of the days.

While his captors were away, Schiller had time to wonder about the men who had abducted him, and why they had taken him prisoner. He had left South America to get away from guerillas who preyed upon wealthy businessmen. Had they followed him to Florida? Schiller would have to wait to find out. When the gang returned, they sat him on a chair. Still shackled and unable to see through the tape, one of them shouted, "You stole two million dollars from our family. We want it back!"

Schiller had no idea what he was talking about. "I don't have two million dollars," he replied

They demanded a list of his assets. When Schiller was evasive, he was accused of lying, which led to more slapping, punching, and kicking. Then he was zapped with the Taser again, and pistol-whipped with the butt end of a gun. When Schiller asked for a cigarette, he was burned with it on his hands and knuckles. His captors just laughed. They even burned him with his own The Sharper Image lighter, searing his arms and burning the hair on his chest. The thugs found that funny, too.

The brutality continued for an hour and a half. When it stopped, Schiller asked to use the bathroom. One of the thugs took him there but Schiller, still shackled, was unable to remove his pants, so he wet himself. He would remain in the soiled clothing for two weeks.

Every now and then, to make sure that Schiller could not see through the tape, his captors would walk or run Schiller into a cement wall. They couldn't stop laughing when the accountant crumbled to the floor. One of his captors played Russian roulette against Schiller's ear, then forced him to take the barrel of the gun into his mouth. The thug pulled the trigger, but the gun didn't fire.

It wasn't long before Schiller realized that he was being held by four men who referred to themselves in code. The one in charge was referred to simply as "The Boss," while at other times he was called "Batman." The others were "Robin," "Sparrow," and "Napoleon."

It was The Boss who issued a dire warning: Cooperate or else! The gang, he vowed, would seize Diana and their two children, David, six, and Stephanie, two. They would bring them to the warehouse where the children would be chained next to him while gang members took turns raping Diana. Schiller never doubted for a minute that his sadistic and cold-blooded captors would carry out their threat. Faced with that prospect, he agreed to cooperate fully. But it wasn't until The Boss began rattling off a detailed list of Schiller's assets that the accountant was able to put two and two together.

Marc Schiller was a secretive man. Only Jorge Delgado knew about the Swiss bank account; the account in the Caymans; Schiller's life insurance policies; his purchase of the La Gorce Palace condominium; his and Diana's jewelry, the Rolex watches and Diana's diamonds; as well as the stash of cash the Schillers kept in their safe. No one else was privy to all that information, which told Schiller that Jorge Delgado was involved.

What's more, Schiller realized that the man the others called "The Boss" was none other than Danny Lugo. He tried to disguise his voice, but the muscleman couldn't completely eliminate his distinctive lisp and New York accent. Schiller, however, never let on that he knew the identity of his interrogator, not even when Lugo put a cell phone to his ear and a gun to his temple. He ordered the accountant to phone home. Before dialing, he told Schiller to tell Diana that he had been called away on a business trip. He was to say he would be gone for a couple of days and warn her not to call the police. "If you tell her anything different, I will kill you," Lugo vowed.

Despite being bound and tortured, his body battered and wracked with pain, Marc Schiller had the presence of mind to offer Lugo a deal: "I'll you give you anything you want if you let my wife and children leave the country."

Lugo agreed. He even allowed Schiller to call his travel agent so he could arrange for their flights. Then Schiller phoned home. He told Diana that she and the children had to leave for Colombia immediately, that there would be tickets for them on the next flight to Bogota. He told his wife not to alert the authorities and to stay calm, but she became hysterical anyway. Nevertheless, Diana did as she was told and didn't ask questions. Terrified, on the morning of November 18 she and the children fled to Colombia where they would be safe at her mother's home. She never contacted the authorities. That afternoon Danny Lugo came to the warehouse. He was furious. He had been to the Schiller house expecting to find jewelry, cash, and Jet Skis, which were not there. For that, Schiller was beaten.

Over the following days Marc Schiller's captors continued to brutalize and humiliate him. The air-conditioning was never turned on, and the windows were kept tightly closed. Even in November, South Florida is hot and humid. Daytime temperatures in the warehouse exceeded one hundred degrees, and Schiller sweated profusely. His captors didn't feed him until day three of his captivity, when one of them brought him a bagel with cream cheese.

"Here, you'll like this, you're a Jew," the thug said. But Schiller couldn't eat. He was too uncomfortable, and too worried about his family's safety. A few days later they brought him some hamburgers.

At one point, Lugo's devoutly Buddhist wife, Lucretia, visited the warehouse. She was pregnant with their second child and suspicious of her husband's mysterious absences from their home. To appease her, Lugo brought her to the warehouse to show her just what he'd been up to. Detectives would learn that Lucretia took one look at Schiller, shackled, half-starved, and filthy, then left. They say she never told anyone what she had seen.

By day, the gang kept Schiller chained to a metal railing in the bathroom. At night he was stuffed, bound and shackled, into a narrow cardboard box. He wasn't allowed to wash or brush his teeth. Unable to go to the bathroom when he needed to, he urinated on himself. With no toilet paper to use, he couldn't clean himself after defecating. Schiller wasn't allowed to wash until the end of the second week of his imprisonment when Stevenson Pierre found the stench emanating from Schiller so repulsive, he brought him soap, a toothbrush, and a bucket of dirty water and allowed him to clean himself. Later, Schiller was given clean clothes and allowed to change.

Not only was Schiller brutalized, he was also terrorized and humiliated. The thugs taunted their starving prisoner with food. One morning, Lugo and Doorbal brought Schiller coffee and a plate they said contained toast, scrambled eggs, and sausages. The musclemen had a hearty laugh as Schiller, half-starved, his hands cuffed behind his back and unable to see, desperately tried to find the eggs and sausage that were supposed to be on the plate. But there was no food—Lugo and Doorbal had eaten it themselves.

Eventually, Schiller realized that the men guarding him followed a routine. Danny "The Boss" Lugo almost never came to the warehouse during the day, while Sparrow (Carl Weekes) and Napoleon (Stevenson Pierre) were generally there at night. Robin (Adrian Doorbal) could show up at any time, but he mostly arrived with Lugo.

At one point during his second week of captivity, the

man called Sparrow began talking with Schiller. He mentioned that he was black, that he had a drinking problem, and that he was a proud father of a little girl. Sparrow gave Schiller food and soda at night when no one else was around. He even told Schiller that he felt badly about his abduction and imprisonment.

It wasn't long before the duct tape that wound around Schiller's head began cutting into his skin. When the bridge of his nose began to bleed, one of the thugs just placed a hood over his head, but the pain was excruciating. When Schiller appealed to one of the gang members on the graveyard shift, the thug unwound the duct tape and put a Kotex over his nose. Then he rewound the filthy tape, covering the sanitary napkin. Schiller's pain eased somewhat, but Lugo and Doorbal couldn't stop laughing when they saw their captive with a Kotex poking out from under the duct tape.

While Schiller's suffering amused his captors, his kidnapping was also about business. Little by little, in between the merciless beatings and humiliating taunts, the Sun Gym gang forced their prisoner to sign over everything he owned. With his eyes taped tightly shut, Lugo guided Schiller's hand as he wrote his name on checks, deeds, and other documents that transferred funds from Schiller's accounts to accounts controlled by Lugo, Doorbal, and John Mese.

At the point of a gun, Lugo forced Schiller to call his Swiss banker and his banker in the Caymans, instructing them to transfer all the funds in his accounts to his bank in Miami. Overnight, $1.26 million was routed to Schiller's Sun Bank account. From there, the funds found their way into Sun Gym accounts. Meanwhile, the thugs ran up $92,000 in charges on his credit cards, purchasing clothing, electronics equipment, and sex toys. And they plundered the Schiller home.

They had been going there regularly, ever since Diana and the children fled to Colombia. First, they emptied the contents of the safe, taking ten thousand dollars in cash and jewelry as well as the deed to Schiller's house, and papers pertaining to the La Gorce condominium. Lugo went through stacks of bank documents and personal papers, poring over each one with a fine-tooth comb.

By December 10, everything the accountant owned had been taken from him; more than $2.1 million in cash, stocks, and real estate. It couldn't have happened without the help of another accountant—John Carl Mese. His notary stamp made everything seem legal. Mese laundered Schiller's cash, and he also notarized forms that named Lillian Torres the new beneficiary of Marc Schiller's MetLife policies. Upon his death, the insurance company would pay two million dollars. The gang wanted that, too, but in order to collect they would have to take more than Schiller's property and money—they would have to take his life.

From day one, Marcelo Schiller was convinced that he would never get out of the grimy warehouse alive, but he was wrong. The Sun Gym thugs were not going to kill him there—they planned to do that elsewhere. For days Lugo, Doorbal, and Delgado discussed and debated the best way to do away with their prisoner. They couldn't shoot or stab him, because that would lead to a police investigation, and it would delay the two million dollar payout they wanted from Schiller's life insurance policies. Doorbal volunteered to strangle Schiller by crushing the accountant's Adam's apple with his thumbs. Finally, Lugo decided to stage a car crash. They would get Schiller rip-roaring drunk, his blood alcohol level so high investigators would be convinced that he had been the victim of his own DUI.

With that settled, the gang's treatment of Schiller changed. They brought him a thin mattress to sleep on, and they no longer kept him stuffed inside the cardboard box during the day. Instead his captors let him sit, shackled and unable to see, inside his 4Runner. It had been driven there by Jorge Delgado sometime during Schiller's first night as a prisoner of the Sun Gym gang.

The first morning, they handcuffed Schiller to the 4Runner's steering wheel, while the next they opened the SUV's rear hatch and put him inside the trunk area, handcuffed to the door. By doing this, Schiller's fingerprints were certain to be all over the vehicle.

On Tuesday December 13, after a few days of the new routine, Schiller was told that he would soon be freed, but he had to be drunk when he was released.

"Drunk? I don't drink, why do I have to be drunk to get let go?" Schiller wanted to know.

"Don't argue," he was told. "That's the way it has to be."

Later, Sparrow explained that The Boss had a friend at Miami International Airport who worked in customs. The friend would help him stow away on a flight bound for Colombia, but Schiller had to be falling down drunk so he would be unable to identify the man. Before they could release him, Schiller would have to "train," Sparrow said, explaining that his body had to get used to the alcohol so he wouldn't vomit when they left him at the airport.

It was a ray of hope, but Schiller didn't believe him. To set the stage for his demise, and with Lugo putting the words into his mouth, Schiller was forced to phone business associates with a cover story devised by Lugo, that he had fallen head-over-heels in love with a beautiful Latina named Lillian Torres and had run away with her. He would never be seen again, he said, because he was leaving everything behind to start a new life with Lillian. Among those he called were his real estate agent and Gene Rosen, his attorney. Rosen was incredulous. He knew Marc Schiller to be a dedicated family man, someone who would never leave his wife and children, but all he could do was scratch his head and hang up the phone.

They also had Schiller call his wife in Colombia. They

forced him to tell Diana that he was wrapping up business and would be joining her and the children very soon. During the call, Diana put six-year-old David on the phone.

"When are you coming home?" the little boy wanted to know.

"Soon. I'll see you soon," Schiller answered, even though he believed that he would never see his son again.

The Sun Gym gang thought that the Lillian Torres cover story was brilliant. Everyone, especially investigators, would conclude that Marc Schiller, depressed and ashamed because he lost everything in a midlife crisis, went on a bender. Then, after a night of very heavy drinking, he climbed behind the wheel of his SUV, rammed it into a pole, and died.

The next day Lugo began plying Schiller with liquor, mostly shots of tequila followed by vodka chasers. Later, Lugo allowed Schiller to wash up. It was only the third time in four weeks that he was allowed to clean himself. The muscleman even gave Schiller a change of clothes and a pack of cigarettes. Then he began plying Schiller with liquor again, only this time the drinks were heavily spiked with sleeping pills.

A few hours later Schiller sat shackled to a chair inside the grimy warehouse that had been his prison for the past four weeks. He was ordered to keep his eyes tightly closed as his captors unwound the tape that covered his eyes. Once again Schiller was ordered to swallow shot after shot of whiskey laced with sleeping pills. He did as he was told, then he passed out.

At about half past two in the morning, after three days of forced drinking, an unconscious Marcelo Schiller was strapped into the passenger seat of his Toyota 4Runner. While Weekes and Doorbal followed in another car, Lugo drove to a deserted area in a warehouse district not far from Schlotzsky's deli. When they arrived, the musclemen moved Schiller into the driver's seat while Lugo sat down in the passenger's seat. With the vehicle aimed directly at a concrete utility poll, Lugo pressed down on the gas pedal then jumped to safety just before the crash. The gang didn't expect Schiller to die in the initial crash. For that they brought along a gallon of gasoline, and for good measure they placed a portable propane tank inside the 4Runner. They would set the SUV on fire and the exploding propane tank would blow the accountant to kingdom come.

Investigators say it was Danny Lugo who doused Marc Schiller with gasoline and splashed it around the inside of the 4Runner. Then, with Schiller's The Sharper Image lighter, he lit the blaze, certain that once it got going the propane tank would blow up. As the thugs watched the Toyota burn, they couldn't believe their evil eyes— Marcelo Schiller had extricated himself from the blazing SUV. Incredulous, the three thugs watched as Schiller staggered toward them along the deserted roadway.

"Get him" Lugo yelled.

Weekes, the wheelman, turned the Camry around and sped toward Schiller, but the gravely injured accountant managed to evade the oncoming car. Weekes made a U-turn and took aim. This time he hit his target. Schiller bounced onto the hood and rolled off. For good measure, Weekes put the Camry in reverse and hit Schiller a second time. Lugo and Doorbal wanted to run him over a third time.

"Go back, hit him again," someone in the car screamed. Instead, Weekes hit the gas and drove off, spooked by the headlights of an approaching vehicle. The Sun Gym thugs sped away, leaving Marc Schiller lying in a heap. Convinced that he was dead, the thugs exchanged high fives.

South Florida had been in a football frenzy all fall, certain that the beloved Miami Dolphins under Don Shula were bound for the NFL playoffs, and hopeful that they would go all the way to Super Bowl XXIX. It would be played in Miami on January 29, at Joe Robbie Stadium, the stadium named after the Dolphins' owner and founder. After beating the Kansas City Chiefs in a nationally televised game Monday night, the Dolphins were nine and five with only two games to go until the end of the regular season.

While Dolphin fans were hopeful, veteran private investigator Ed Du Bois was in his Miami office, busily poring over security plans for the upcoming Super Bowl. At age fifty-one, Edward Du Bois III was the head of Investigators Inc., Florida's oldest private detective agency. The firm had been founded in 1958 by his father, Edward II, a retired FBI agent. Edward III took it over when his father died in 1968.

Investigators Inc. was no sleazy gumshoe operation. Over the years it had worked closely with virtually every law enforcement agency in South Florida, including state prosecutors, the FBI, and the MDPD. Among the firm's clients was the National Football League, for which the agency provided investigative services in South Florida. For the Super Bowl, Du Bois was responsible for coordinating security for hundreds of dignitaries and celebrities who would be coming to Miami for the big game and the pre- and post-game festivities.

As Du Bois reviewed security plans to ensure the safety of the VIPs, he was interrupted by a phone call from Gene Rosen, a Miami civil attorney for whom Du Bois' firm had done work in the past. Rosen said he had a client, a local businessman who desperately needed his help. He had been abducted, beaten, and left for dead. At that very moment the man was lying in a bed in the intensive care unit at Miami's Jackson Memorial Hospital. Would Du Bois please call him? His name, Rosen said, is Marcello Schiller.

Marc Schiller awoke in the hospital strapped to a board, his head and arms wrapped in bandages. He had tubes running out of every part of his body, and he was vomiting blood. He was in and out of consciousness. He couldn't move his feet. What's more, he couldn't open his eyes—the glue from the tape left them tightly shut. Worried doctors told Schiller that he might be paralyzed.

"Your spine has been twisted and you lost spinal fluid," Schiller remembers a medic telling him. He also had a broken pelvis, a ruptured bladder, numerous cuts, bruises, and burns. Doctors had him on the operating table for six hours. They removed his spleen and left him with an incision that ran from his chest all the way down to his groin.

Schiller was brought to Jackson Memorial as a "John Doe" at four o'clock in the morning. He reeked from alcohol and his body emitted a putrid odor. At first hospital staffers thought he was a homeless drunk; they would not learn his identity until he regained consciousness. Schiller remembered absolutely nothing about the crash or having been run over, but when a doctor told him that he had been in a car accident, Schiller had no trouble recalling his abduction.

"You're wrong. I was not in an accident. I was kidnapped," he declared. "Get me a phone! Please get me a phone."

He called the only person in Miami he could trust—Gene Rosen. Within an hour Rosen was at his bedside, listening intently as Schiller filled him in on what had happened. Schiller asked Rosen to call his sister, Michelle, in New York, and he asked the lawyer to arrange for him to have a bodyguard. That's when Rosen put in a call to Ed Du Bois.

At first, the sleuth was skeptical of the story Rosen told him, and he was reluctant to get involved. It sounded to Du Bois like a drug-related kidnapping, but as he thought about it some more, he reasoned that drug dealers don't hire civil attorneys like Gene Rosen to settle scores. Besides, if the abduction really was drug related, Schiller would be dead. Moreover, Rosen vouched for the man, assuring the private detective that he was a legitimate businessman. Du Bois picked up his phone and called Marcelo Schiller.

Ed Du Bois recalls that the conversation was brief.

Schiller told him about his ordeal, and he said that he was in fear for his life, certain that once the gang realized that he had survived, they would hunt him down and kill him in his hospital bed. Du Bois told Schiller that bodyguards would cost $65 an hour, then advised Schiller to get out of town.

"I told him if the circumstances surrounding his problem were accurate, and that he was in fear of his life, then the prudent thing to do was to leave the hospital immediately," Du Bois said. He explained that the police "would send a patrolman to the hospital to take his statement that day, or the next day, or the next week, and by then Schiller would be dead." Before hanging up, Du Bois assured Schiller that he did not have to notify the police just yet.

"There is no statute requiring immediate notification to police," Du Bois explained. "Get out of the hospital now; we can call the police later."

Meanwhile, the Sun Gym gang was at Schiller's Old Cutler Cove house where they scoured the newspapers and watched every TV newscast hoping the media would report the drunk-driving death of Marcelo Schiller, but to no avail. Fatal auto accidents are not unusual events in South Florida, so Lugo began making phone calls, claiming that he was looking for his brother Marcelo Schiller. The first call was to the morgue, but Schiller wasn't there. Then he phoned area hospitals, finally learning that Schiller was at Jackson Memorial Hospital where he was listed in critical but stable condition in the intensive care unit. Lugo wasted no time. He summoned Doorbal, Weekes, and Pierre to a meeting.

The thugs put their heads together to devise yet another plan to murder Marcelo Schiller. They would kill him in the hospital. Doorbal volunteered to strangle him while Lugo and Weekes staged a diversionary fistfight in the hallway. Someone else suggested suffocating Schiller with his own pillow and murdering anyone who was in the room with him. But what if he was under police guard, one of them wondered. Unable to agree, they decided to just play it by ear; they would go the hospital and figure out what to do when they got there.

Miami's Jackson Memorial Hospital is huge, a 1,550 bed hospital twenty blocks from downtown Miami. It shares a campus with several other health-related institutions and the University of Miami Leonard M. Miller School of Medicine. The facility is so big that the Sun Gym gang, led by Danny Lugo, became lost in the maze of corridors trying to find Schiller's room. But they were confident that he wasn't going anywhere, so Doorbal, Weekes, Pierre, and Lugo decided to regroup and try again the next day. Lugo even purchased green hospital scrubs at a uniform supply store, but when he phoned the hospital Sunday morning to check on Schiller's condition, he learned that Marc Schiller had been discharged.

Schiller had taken Ed Du Bois' advice. On Saturday morning, the gravely injured accountant was strapped to a gurney and wheeled to a waiting ambulance. It took him to the airport where an air ambulance flew him to New York. The flight, which cost six thousand dollars, was paid for by Schiller's brother-in-law. By Saturday afternoon, Schiller was safe and sound and undergoing treatment at Staten Island University Hospital. He would remain there until Christmas Eve, then he would recuperate at his sister's home.

While Marc Schiller convalesced, the Sun Gym gang was living large in Miami. They had netted more than two million dollars in cash. Weekes and Pierre were paid off; Weekes took fifty thousand dollars and bought himself a BMW. Pierre settled for thirty thousand dollars. It was considerably less than the one hundred thousand dollars they were each promised, but the two men didn't make a fuss—they knew what Lugo and Doorbal were capable of. The rest of the loot went to Doorbal, Delgado, Mese, and Danny Lugo, who already had tucked away a million dollars from his Medicare scam.

Ownership of Schiller's Old Cutler Cove home was transferred to D & J International, a Bahamas corporation Lugo set up to launder money. Eventually, they planned to put the house on the market for three hundred thousand dollars, but in the meantime the gang replaced all the locks and at first told curious neighbors that the house had been purchased by a corporation for entertaining. Then Lugo decided to embellish the bullshit story. Calling himself Tom, he hinted that the house would be used by "U.S. security forces." The Schillers had been deported, he said, and the house had been confiscated by the United States government. Neighbors need not be alarmed if they saw strangers coming and going. Most of them would be diplomats and other foreign dignitaries.

Lugo even spent money on home improvements. He added lush landscaping to hide the comings and goings at the house from nosy neighbors, and he upgraded the security system by adding closed-circuit video monitoring with waterproof sensors and cameras on the outside and a twenty-five inch monitor on the inside that he purchased at The Spy Shop. From time to time the gang spent the night at Schiller's house, enjoying the Jacuzzi, the swimming pool, and the fifty-one inch television set.

By all accounts Lugo was a good neighbor, always friendly and accommodating. He introduced himself around the neighborhood. He saw to it that the homeowner's association fees were paid on time, and he even helped one couple change a lightbulb that hung two stories above their front door. Another neighbor happily accepted UPS packages when he wasn't there. When the neighbor wanted to know why the packages were addressed to Schiller, Lugo claimed that he was forwarding them to Schiller in Colombia.

Through Delgado, Lugo leased a top-of-the-line eighty

thousand dollar gold Mercedes—he was still on parole, which meant his name could not appear on the lease. Nearly every night Lugo and Doorbal would drive it to Solid Gold in North Miami Beach, where they enjoyed themselves in the Champagne Room, a plush elevated area reserved for high rollers. Drinks cost more in the Champagne Room—one thousand dollars for a bottle of champagne—and so do the dances, but Doorbal and Lugo had money to burn, and burn it they did, routinely handing out hundred dollar bills to the dancers and buying rounds for the room.

Noel Adrian Doorbal had come a very long way since Fiesta Taco, when he rode to work on an old bicycle. He had moved out of the rattrap he had been living in and into a beautiful two-story, two-bedroom, two-bath townhouse at 6911 Main Street in Miami Lakes. He furnished it with items taken from Schiller's Old Cutler Cove house. He was driving a Nissan 300Z and seriously dating an older woman, a thirty-one-year-old registered nurse from Boca Raton named Cindy Eldridge. They met at Sundays on the Bay, a restaurant in Key Biscayne. She was there celebrating her birthday with friends when they bumped into each other and started talking. Cindy, a pretty blond divorcee, was impressed when Doorbal told her that he was a personal trainer and the co-owner of a Miami gym. Despite the forty-five mile distance between Miami Lakes and Boca Raton, they managed to see each other on weekends and sometimes during the week, too.

And while Doorbal was seeing Cindy, after the Schiller kidnapping he was a regular at Solid Gold, hoping to win the heart of exotic dancer Beatriz Weiland—Michele to the men who ogled her. The Hungarian-born beauty came to the United States in 1991. With big blue eyes, full breasts, slim hips, and perfect skin, Doorbal, and many others, too, thought she was the most beautiful woman he'd ever seen. But there was a problem: Despite his bulging muscles and apparent virility, thanks to his narcissistic quest to become a he-man, Doorbal was a dud in bed. His excessive use of steroids had rendered him limp.

As for Lugo, he was smitten by Solid Gold's Sabina Petrescu, a twenty-five-year-old European beauty queen, a finalist for the title of Miss Romania in 1990. Her subsequent career path led her to Moscow where she worked as a model, then to Mexico, and finally to the swanky Miami flesh palace where she danced in a cage and called herself Beverly.

Elena Sabina Petrescu claimed she entered the United States from Tijuana, Mexico, hidden inside the trunk of a car driven by her then-husband, Constantine Petrescu. She began her career as an exotic dancer in Las Vegas. Sabina and Constantine moved to Miami in January 1994. By July, they were divorced. She met Danny Lugo on Super Bowl Sunday, 1995.[3] By then the former beauty queen had already appeared in the buff in *Penthouse*.

Sabina didn't like dancing in the nude in front of horny men. She especially didn't like friction dances, so when Danny Lugo told her he was a music mogul, and that he might have a part for her in a music video he was producing in London with Bruce Springsteen, the ice was broken. Within a week they were dating, but Sabina didn't jump into bed with him right away. When she was sick and couldn't work, he brought her chicken soup, and he wrote a check so she could pay the rent on her Bal Harbour apartment.

A month later Lugo set Sabina up in a Miami Lakes love nest. He promised to take care of her. He told Sabina that the rent was paid for a year. Sabina, he vowed, would never have to dance naked again. Soon, they were a couple, living together in a cozy apartment overlooking Main Street in Miami Lakes.

---

[3]The Miami Dolphins didn't make it to the Super Bowl. They were eliminated in the second round of the playoffs.

"You don't owe me anything," he told her. "We'll just be friends. If you get to love me later, that's okay. You don't owe me anything."

The location was a very convenient one for Danny Lugo; his pregnant wife, Lucretia—Lugo never told Sabina that he was married—lived just a few miles away, and Doorbal's townhouse was across the street.

The Romanian beauty had never met a man like Danny Lugo. He made no sexual demands on her, and he was kind and generous. To replace her broken-down Daihatsu, Lugo gave Sabina a car, a 1994 black BMW station wagon. It had been green until Lugo had it repainted, and it had been driven by Diana Schiller, but Lugo didn't tell that to Sabina. And he didn't tell her that the vehicle identification number had been changed. He recruited Dan Pace, a Sun Gym employee, to take care of that for him.

For Valentine's Day, Lugo gave Sabina a diamond engagement ring and a pearl necklace. In April, he paid for her to visit her parents in Romania. He even paid for them to accompany her back to Miami.

Meanwhile, Sabina was beginning to have doubts about her mysterious lover. She wondered about his odd hours and why he kept a pair of night-vision binoculars in the apartment. When she confronted him, Lugo told her it was all work related.

He swore her to secrecy. "Sabina," he said, "I'm with the Central Intelligence Agency, that's the bad CIA, the one that kills." Doorbal, he said, was in the CIA, too. Lugo proceeded to tell Sabina of the harrowing missions he'd been on for the spy agency. Gullible Sabina bought his explanation. She asked him no questions. The bullshit story even added to Lugo's appeal.

"I found it exciting," she admitted. She thought of her boyfriend as a real-life James Bond, which explained his sudden disappearances, sometimes for days on end. From then on, whenever he had to go away for a while, Lugo would just tell Sabina that he had been called to CIA headquarters. "I am going to Langley today," he'd say, then he'd go home to his wife. It would be another month before Sabina realized that her secret agent man had been lying to her.

Meanwhile, Marc Schiller was out of sight and out of Danny Lugo's mind, but he was making steady progress convalescing from the ordeal the Sun Gym gang had put him through. He put on weight—he had lost forty pounds from his 175-pound frame—and he was walking again, although he couldn't take a step without using a walker. It still hurt for him to urinate, but he was reunited with his family and he was determined to get his property and his money back.

In addition to severe physical trauma, Schiller suffered psychologically, too.

"I was mentally a mess," he remembers. "I hardly slept at all. I had nightmares all the time, and during the day I had crying fits. If I fell asleep, I would wake up shaking my hands, thinking I was still chained."

His wife would ask him what happened, but he couldn't bring himself to tell her. "It took a while," Schiller says.

He did talk to Ed Du Bois, however. And he stayed in touch with Gene Rosen. After New Year's, Schiller phoned Rosen and instructed him to notify the police that he had been kidnapped. The lawyer did, and he reported back to Schiller that he would have to return to Miami to file a complaint if he wanted the MDPD to investigate. That was not an option. Marc Schiller wasn't ready to return to the Sun Gym gang's stomping ground.

"I didn't know what to do," Schiller recalls. "I was deathly scared and I was on crutches, and I didn't want to stay in New York because I didn't want to put my sister in danger in case somebody came looking for me." In February, with the aid of a pair of crutches, Schiller hobbled aboard a flight for South America.

The Sun Gym gang had kidnapped, tortured, and humiliated him. They forced him to send his terrified wife and children fleeing for their lives. They took every material possession from him, and they tried to end his life in a fiery car crash. When that didn't work, they ran him over twice, then they hunted him down in the hospital. No matter what they did, however, the musclemen couldn't kill Marc Schiller. Like a phoenix rising from the ashes, he was alive, and as soon as he was well enough, Schiller vowed, he would take down the Sun Gym gang.

CHAPTER SEVEN

MEETINGS WITH MESE

A few days before he left New York for South America, Marc Schiller set in motion the wheels that he hoped would put Danny Lugo and the other goons behind bars. He put in a call to Ed Du Bois. He told the detective he wanted to hire him to investigate his kidnapping.

It was a week before the Super Bowl, and Du Bois was knee-deep in security work for the big game, but he promised to begin investigating as soon as the NFL's extravaganza was in the history books. In the meantime, Du Bois asked Schiller to send him a detailed memo, everything he could recall about his abduction and imprisonment along with whatever documentation he and Gene Rosen had managed to dig up.

One week later, a manila envelope arrived at Ed Du Bois' office. It was from Marc Schiller. Inside was the memo Du Bois had requested—four single-spaced typewritten pages—plus copies of documents that Gene Rosen was able to acquire. One was a certified copy of the quitclaim deed that transferred ownership of the Schiller home to

D & J International, a Bahamas corporation. The others were the MetLife forms that named Lillian Torres as the beneficiary of Schiller's life insurance policies. The documents had been signed by Schiller, and they had been notarized by John Mese. Du Bois put in a call to Schiller, informing him that he had known Mese for years.

"He must have been involved," Schiller said.

Ed Du Bois and John Mese weren't buddies, but they had known each other for many years. They graduated from the same high school and lived in the same community. Over the years they crossed paths many times at the Miami Shores Country Club, where they were both members, and at the Kiwanis Club. At one point their offices were across the street, diagonally, from each other in Miami Shores. As far as Du Bois knew, Mese was a pillar of the community, an honest and decent man whose passion in life was bodybuilding. Nevertheless, the detective decided that his investigation into the Schiller abduction would begin with John Carl Mese.

"I placed a phone call to him," Du Bois remembered. "We exchanged the typical greetings, and I asked if I could come by and have a meeting with him."

Mese asked the detective if he was bringing him "a big client, like from the NFL."

"No," Du Bois replied, "but I think this is a very important meeting, John, and it may be one of the most important meetings of your life."

Ed Du Bois was in John Mese's storefront Miami Shores office bright and early on Thursday, February 2. He explained he represented a client by the name of Marc Schiller.

"I don't recognize the name," the muscular accountant declared. To refresh his memory, Du Bois handed Mese the first three pages of Schiller's memo. He held back the fourth page "because it had some information that I thought that I should maintain as confidential."

Mese read the memo. "He was very nonemotional, and he had no comment," the private eye remembers. "He was not upset, was not concerned."

"Sounds like that guy had a hard time," Mese offered, as he passed the pages back to the detective.

"John, I will hand you two more documents that I'm concerned about. They have your name on them."

"*My* name?" Mese replied, seeming surprised.

"Yes. As a matter of fact, you notarized these two documents, and your wife is down there as a witness on one of them."

Du Bois then handed over a certified copy of the quitclaim deed and the MetLife change of beneficiary form, pointing out that Schiller's signature on the form was perpendicular to the signature line. Diana Schiller's signature was on the quitclaim deed, too, on the line below her husband's signature. Du Bois noticed that the document was signed, witnessed by John's wife, Cheryl, and notarized by John on November 23, five days after Diana took the children and fled to South America. Du Bois kept that tidbit to himself. As for Mese, he just glanced at the documents and passed them back.

"Ed, I'm a notary and I notarize things in my office for others all day long," he said dismissively.

"Do you know a Daniel Lugo or a Jorge Delgado?" the detective wanted to know. Mese admitted that he did, and that he had represented both men in their dealings with the Internal Revenue Service.

"John, I think these men perpetrated a pretty serious crime against my client. Can you tell me what you know about these men?"

"Well, Lugo works at my gym." As for Delgado, Mese said he was a client who has an office in the same building as Mese and Associates in Miami Lakes.

"Can I have a meeting with them?" Du Bois asked.

"Sure," Mese said. The accountant even offered to set it up. Before leaving, Du Bois had one more question for Mese: "John, please tell me how the hell on November 23 you could notarize a document, and your wife could witness it, for someone who had been out of the country since November 18?"

Mese just shrugged his shoulders, but as soon as the private eye left his office, he was on the phone with Danny Lugo. He told him that a private investigator representing Marc Schiller had been there asking questions, and he wanted to meet with him and Jorge Delgado.

A few days later Mese phoned Du Bois. They would meet on Monday, February 13, at eleven thirty in the morning. The accountant promised that Lugo and Jorge Delgado would be there.

Du Bois had no intention of attending the meeting alone. Schiller's memo was too chilling, and the private eye knew the level of brutality the Sun Gym gang was capable of. He arranged for a beefy private eye named Ed Seibert to accompany him. Seibert would sit in on the meeting with him while two other men from his staff sat outside in a parked car, their cell phones programmed to speed dial 911. Du Bois would not bring a gun into the meeting, but Seibert would—two fully loaded handguns were concealed under his jacket.

Ed Seibert had been a homicide detective in Washington, D.C. He had also worked for the Bureau of Alcohol, Tobacco, and Firearms (ATF) and, after retiring from the federal agency, freelanced as a security consultant in Central and South America. Seibert was very familiar with South American–style kidnappings, which were always accompanied by a ransom demand. He read Schiller's memo as he and Du Bois drove to the meeting. It struck Seibert that the Sun Gym gang had never demanded a ransom. To Seibert, that meant that the gang never intended to release Schiller.

The two Eds walked into the storefront office and asked for Mese. When the accountant emerged from an inner office, he greeted the private detectives, telling them that Lugo and Delgado had not yet arrived. Mese said he had business to attend to. He asked the visitors to wait in the front lobby. Later, Mese reappeared. He assured the detectives that Lugo and Delgado were on their way. Before Mese could turn and walk back to his office, Du Bois showed him a color photo of Marc Schiller.

"Was this the person you notarized the documents for?" Du Bois inquired.

Mese could not say for sure. "It may be him and it may not be," he said. "All Latins look alike to me." Then Mese laughed and walked away. The two private eyes would cool their heels for more than two hours before Mese reappeared.

"Come on back," he beckoned. He led Du Bois and Seibert to a small room in the back of his office where he introduced them to Jorge Delgado who was seated behind a desk. Danny Lugo couldn't make the meeting, said Mese, who introduced the detectives to Delgado.

Meanwhile, the two detectives had no way of knowing that Lugo never intended to show up for the meeting. According to Delgado, Lugo told him about Du Bois.

"He said that a private investigator was asking questions about Schiller's abduction, and he wanted me to show up and see what the investigator wanted; he wanted me to represent him."

As for Mese, he seemed unconcerned, Delgado recalled. He told Delgado that "he had no problem because he had covered his ass." And he showed Delgado paperwork that, he claimed, would prove that Schiller had been to his office—tax returns and passports that showed Schiller had been there to "notarize everything along with his wife."

Du Bois spoke first. "I explained the same thing that I had explained to John, that I represented Marc Schiller, and that he had been kidnapped."

Delgado asked to see Schiller's memo. Du Bois handed over the first three pages, as well as the other documents Schiller had sent him. Delgado looked them over.

"This is about a business deal," he said nonchalantly before passing the pages back to the detective.

"Is this the customary way you do business, Jorge?" Du Bois demanded, pointing a finger at Delgado. "Kidnapping? Torture? Attempting to murder and steal the assets of a business associate? Is that how you do business?"

Then Du Bois decided to close in. He became more assertive. "I've figured this all out," he recalls saying. "You almost had the perfect crime, but you left such a paper trail. It was easy for me to find and easy for me to follow."

Silence fell over the tiny office. Delgado squirmed in his chair. Du Bois decided to close in. "Had Marc Schiller died, this would have been the perfect crime. You had all his money. You had the house, and then you had a change of beneficiary on his two million dollar insurance policy. You even set up a script where he was going through a midlife crisis, but guess what asshole? Marc Schiller is alive, and we're going to put your ass in jail."

Delgado was stunned. Then he pleaded for another meeting with the private detectives. This time, he promised, Danny Lugo would be there, too, and everything would be explained. Mese suddenly reappeared and joined the discussion. The four men agreed to meet the next day, Valentine's Day, at half past nine in the morning. This time it would be at John Mese's other office, the one in Miami Lakes.

The next morning the two Eds met in front of Shula's Hotel and Golf Club in Miami Lakes at half past eight. They bought coffee at a Main Street bakery, then they drove to John Mese's office. They talked about the news that morning, which was dominated by the weather.

Much of the United States was in a deep freeze thanks to an Arctic cold front that had swooped down from Canada. It had reached Miami, too, driving nighttime temperatures below forty degrees. It also brought sixty-one mile an hour wind gusts that pushed giant airliners around the tarmac at Miami International Airport the night before. Despite the chill, the weatherman promised Miamians that the mercury would hit seventy by the afternoon.

In other news that morning, the O. J. Simpson murder trial was in its third week in Los Angeles, with gavel-to-gavel coverage on CNN. In New York, rapper Tupac Shakur headed for the Clinton Correctional Facility in Dannemora where he would serve his sentence for sexually abusing a woman in his hotel room. Shortly afterwards, his album *Me Against the World* climbed to the top of the charts. The rapper, who formed the group Thug Life in 1993, was one of Noel Adrian Doorbal's favorite performers. The two Eds had not met Doorbal, but they were about to become familiar with his name.

In phone conversations with Schiller and his Miami attorney, Du Bois learned that the kidnappers had forced Schiller to sign two checks, one for $700,000 and the other for $526,000, payable to Sun Fitness Consultants. A quick check with the Florida Department of State revealed that Doorbal and Mese were officers of the corporation. John Mese was listed as its director and registered agent, while Adrian Doorbal served as the company's president.

John Mese was not in his office when Du Bois and Seibert walked in at nine o'clock sharp. The receptionist was surprised to see them. There was nothing in the appointment book indicating that they had an appointment with the accountant. The two Eds said they would wait in the small waiting room. It contained a couch, a coffee table, two chairs, a large popcorn machine, and a chess set. The detectives played chess until Mese arrived two hours later.

"He walked up in a three-piece suit, and he seemed surprised to see us," Du Bois remembers. The accountant was sweating, and he had red blotches on his ruddy face.

"John," Du Bois, said, "we set this meeting up yesterday, and we have been waiting here for hours. Where is Lugo? Where is Delgado?"

"Let me call them," Mese replied before scurrying away. Five minutes later he returned to assure the detectives that Lugo and Delgado were on their way. Mese then ushered

the private eyes into a small office where they could wait.
Inside were two chairs and a desk. Two dirty wineglasses
and an ashtray filled with cigarette butts sat atop the desk.
The two Eds didn't know it, but Mese had led them into
Danny Lugo's office, the very room where he had planned
the kidnapping of Marc Schiller, along with Doorbal,
Weekes, Pierre, and Delgado. "I want you to look at this,"
Mese said as he handed Du Bois the bogus Schiller folder.
Then he left the detectives alone.

While Du Bois looked through the folder, Seibert rum-
maged through a trash can that he found underneath the
desk. There was nothing of significance in the folder, but
Seibert came upon a mother lode of evidence that could put
the Sun Gym gang behind bars.

"Look at this!" he exclaimed. Seibert immediately
closed and locked the office door. Then the detectives
pored over Seibert's find—bank statements, deposit slips
totaling more than $219,000 as well as two checks pay-
able to Mese totaling $55,000, and other cancelled checks
that tied John Mese to the laundering of Schiller's money.
Du Bois no longer harbored any doubt that John Mese had
been involved in the kidnapping of Marcelo Schiller. In
fact, he was convinced that Mese was the chief financial
officer, the CFO, of the Sun Gym gang.

The money trail went from Schiller's accounts in the
Cayman Islands and Miami directly to Sun Fitness Consul-
tants, and then to Sun Gym. From there, the money moved
to the Mese and Associates account at County National
Bank, where Mese purchased a cashier's check for $67,845.
He sent it to Lugo's probation officer to pay off the restitu-
tion requirement of his parole. Attached was a letter from
Mese explaining that he had bought a computer program
Danny Lugo had created for Sun Gym.

And there was more: Cancelled checks to Lillian Torres
and Carl Weekes, and to The Spy Shop and JoMar Property Investments, the mortgage business that Schiller and
Delgado were partners in until Schiller decided to get out.
The private eyes stuffed the incriminating documents into

their pockets and into their briefcases. As soon as they were safely squirreled away, Seibert unlocked the door.

It was apparent to the detectives that two people had been in the office desperately trying to get rid of the documents, but they'd made a colossal mistake—they counted on a cleaning crew carting everything away. Instead the detectives had the trash, and it could be used as leverage against the gang and as evidence in a court of law. The detectives sat back and waited for Danny Lugo and Jorge Delgado.

They wouldn't have to wait long. John Mese came in and told the detectives that Delgado had arrived, but once again Danny Lugo wouldn't be joining them. Mese invited Du Bois and Seibert to follow him to his private office where they could meet with Jorge Delgado. This time John Mese stayed for the meeting.

"I maybe got one or two words out of my mouth when Delgado puts his hands up as if to say stop," Du Bois recalled. There was no need to talk any longer, Delgado said.

"Then why are we here?" Du Bois wondered out loud.

"We're going to give you back the money that we took from Schiller."

"How much money?" Du Bois wanted to know.

"One million two hundred sixty thousand dollars," Delgado answered. He promised that he would hand over the money the next day.

"Any strings attached to this money?"

"Yes. We're going to have you and your client sign an agreement that the return of this money is over a sour business deal, and you and your client will not repeat this story and not go to the police."

Du Bois reached for a pen and wrote out the brief agreement. It said:

Jorge Delgado agrees to pay Marcelo Schiller the sum of $1,260,000 as return of proceeds from a sour business deal. Further, Schiller agrees that the incident allegedly occurring during November 15, 1994, and December 15, 1994, as described to his attorney and investigator, did not happen.

The simple and straightforward agreement was to be signed by Marcelo Schiller, Ed Du Bois, Ed Seibert, and a witness. Du Bois agreed to contact Schiller, but he knew enough law to know that the agreement would not be binding. His goal was to get the money back for Schiller, then they would go to the police. Nevertheless, on his way out the private eye said, "It looks like we have a deal."

As they drove away from Mese's office, Seibert offered an ominous warning: If the Sun Gym thugs managed to avoid going to prison for what they did to Marc Schiller, they would search for another victim, and that victim would not live to hunt them down.

CHAPTER EIGHT

PATSIES NO MORE

Danny Lugo wasn't too concerned that a team of private detectives was snooping around John Mese's office, asking questions about the Schiller abduction. For one thing he was confident that he was in the clear. He was certain that he had successfully concealed his identity from Schiller. For another, he was sure that Schiller would not go to the police—he didn't trust them and he didn't want lawmen looking into his businesses. Lugo considered himself untouchable, so for Valentine's Day he gave Sabina an engagement ring and a string of pearls, and he announced that his bosses at Langley had given him a few days off and he was taking her to Disney World in Orlando to celebrate the end of his federal probation.

Sabina didn't even know that he had been on probation, but she couldn't have been happier for her secret agent man. The couple rented a convertible and drove north to Orlando. By the time they returned to Miami, however, Danny Lugo was having second thoughts. While in Orlando, he learned that one of Du Bois' detectives had knocked on the door of his ex-wife, Lillian Torres. The former Mrs. Lugo admitted that she had signed some papers at Danny's behest.

"Daniel came in with some papers," she remembered. "He told me that he wanted me to sign them because he couldn't have them in his name because he was having trouble with his wife or something, and he didn't want her to find out. He said he would put it under my name, and I told him no problem."

Lillian explained that she trusted her ex "because he was always there for me financially, and emotionally, too." Despite the divorce, they'd remained friends, and her former husband still came around to see the kids, so she didn't bother to read the papers and she had no idea what she signed. But she did recall that there was no notary seal on them, and she was certain that she had never gone to John Mese's office to have them notarized.

In November and December, she told the investigator, Lugo began giving her money "for my children and my education, because he wanted me to go back to school." He took her to Schiller's house in Old Cutler Cove, telling her that he was house-sitting for a friend, and he took her and the kids on a short pleasure trip to the Bahamas.

Back in Miami after his Valentine's Day sojourn with Sabina to Orlando, Lugo's mood changed noticeably. If the detectives could get to Lillian, Danny Lugo reasoned, they could get to Lucretia, and Lucretia could tie him to the warehouse and Marc Schiller. He was on edge, obsessing about Schiller, and vowing that the still-convalescing accountant would not get a nickel of "my money."

Meanwhile, Schiller had heard from Ed Du Bois. He surmised that the offer the detective brought back from his meeting with Mese and Delgado was nothing more than a ploy—a stall tactic designed to buy the gang more time to hunt him down and kill him.

Schiller was right. The gang had no intention of returning the money, but he and Du Bois and Gene Rosen played along anyway. Mese faxed a revised version of the original agreement. He added a paragraph: "Marcelo Schiller agrees that he and no member of his family will ever threaten or attempt to blackmail Jorge Delgado, Danny Lugo, or John Mese."

The addition was supposedly in response to a phone call Delgado received around New Year's from Alex Schiller, Marc's brother.

"He threatened me," Delgado recalls. "He said that he knew everything I had done, and he was going to take my eyeballs out." Marc Schiller agreed to the revision and waited for his money. When it did not come, Du Bois faxed a letter to Mese. He attached a copy of the agreement that Delgado had dictated on Valentine's Day.

Meanwhile, Lugo found a lawyer, a first year attorney in Broward County, to handle the negotiations. Du Bois brought in a lawyer, too, veteran criminal defense attorney Ed O'Donnell, a former prosecutor. Nevertheless, the stalling continued through March and into the beginning of April, even though Schiller agreed to every one of the gang's demands.

At one point, Lugo tried to pull a fast one—the agreement would read that Schiller would be paid $1,260,000, but in place of a dollar sign they would substitute the sign for Italian lira and pay Schiller the equivalent, $1,200. The Sun Gym gang's lawyer nixed that idea. While the negotiations dragged on, the gang plundered Schiller's Old Cutler Cove house.

They rented a U-Haul and systematically removed all the furnishings including the fifty-inch Mitsubishi television, expensive Oriental rugs, Jacuzzi, bronze sculptures, collectibles including Waterford crystal and Christolfe silver, and every appliance and knickknack. They also took two bicycles, a stroller, all the smaller TVs, patio furniture, couches, bedroom sets, computers, office equipment, the kids' clothes and Diana Schiller's Gucci handbags. All in all $150,000 worth of stuff. Much of it wound up in the Hialeah warehouse. By the time the gang finished, nothing was left inside, not even the plates that covered the light switches.

Towards the end of February a fed up Du Bois faxed John Mese. "We are not going to be patsies any longer," the private eye wrote. "Mr. Schiller signed these agreements and is acting in good faith in his attempts to settle this outrageous situation, and Delgado offered to make restitution of $1,260,000."

Du Bois accused Mese of trying to "destroy evidence" and of purging "incriminating documents" from files. And he offered this advice to his old pal: "Buy a shredder." Then he warned Mese: "I truly don't know what it will take for you to see the light. This is for real. And if this matter is not resolved by 12:30 P.M. tomorrow, Thursday, February 23, 1995, I intend to seek state and federal prosecution both, criminally and civilly, to the fullest extent of the law."

Despite the ultimatum, the stalling continued. Mese responded with a handwritten fax denying that either he or his wife had "done anything fraudulent" with credit cards, and he vowed to "sue the pants off anyone who alleges so."

Du Bois responded with a fax to the gang's attorney:

> To all those concerned:
>
> We have tried to negotiate in good faith for the return of the items that do not belong to you and you have stalled and continue to perpetrate criminal acts during these negotiations. It would appear that you prefer to explain your acts to the authorities instead of settling this matter between us.
>
> We will no longer stand by idly and we will no longer negotiate with those who continue to act defiantly. And there are non-negotiable terms and conditions for settling this matter:
>
> Return all of the money taken from Mr. Schiller.
>
> Return all personal documents taken from him.
>
> Return of payment for the vehicles stolen from his house.
>
> Repay all fraudulent credit card purchases made from his and his wife's cards.
>
> Pay for all items stolen from Mr. Schiller's house and all damages to it.

This is non-negotiable. No more documents signed, no more negotiations. Unless these items are returned by Friday, March 24, 1995 before 11:59 A.M., we will refer this matter to the federal and state authorities and seek all remedies, both civil and criminal, permitted by law.

You decide to settle now or go to jail. This is our last intention of settling this matter. If we do not hear from you by this date and time, we will assume that you prefer to explain your actions to the authorities.

Then on March 24, O'Donnell received a fax from Joel Greenberg, the Sun Gym gang's lawyer. It accused Ed Du Bois of "once again threatening our clients with criminal sanctions." His actions, the attorney declared, "are deemed extortion and are themselves punishable as felonies under Florida law."

Greenberg added: "The tactics used by Mr. Du Bois are not within the legal standards of a private investigator. And the same would be reported to the authorities including the State Attorney's office if necessary." His clients, he said, "are interested in working out an amicable resolution to the problem but our office will no longer accept communication from Du Bois and hereby request that his involvement in the matter cease immediately. Please be advised that our clients have reviewed the original agreement and are requesting that changes be made to same. Our office will forward the changes to you as soon as possible."

Du Bois was stunned. The extortionists were accusing *him* of extortion! Du Bois fired back:

Dear Mr. Greenberg:

The purpose of these delays are [sic] *finally becoming quite clear: Your clients need time to continue their criminal acts against Mr. Schiller, and fraudulent charges against his credit cards continue to mount.*

A recent visit to his home found it to be cleaned out.

His 1993 BMW 525 station wagon has been stolen. The household furnishings totaling over $75,000 have been stolen, and these include Oriental rugs valued in excess of $15,000 and a stereo system and television valued at $11,000, a computer and printer system valued at $4,000, and a Jacuzzi valued at $10,000. And to get the Jacuzzi out of the pool area, they ripped out a section of the screen and aluminum support for the pool screen system.

You provided your agreement to us last week and Mr. Schiller signed it. Your clients did not provide the check for restitution. And now you want copies of deeds to be included in the new agreement! These were faxed to you, and how irrelevant and how absurd.

The matter had been settled in court and we have obtained a quit title judgment, and your clients chose not to defend themselves. Mr. Schiller won the suit and the return of the house, and the delays have been deliberate and well-orchestrated attempts to buy time. In short, we have been taken for fools.

On Friday, May 24, 1995, at 11:59 A.M., if the cashier's check in the amount of $1.26 million, made payable to Gene Rosen, is not in my hand, all negotiations are off. And this will probably mean that the check exchange must take place before you have the original signed agreement. I will hold the check until the originals are exchanged.

This is non-negotiable. Mr. Schiller had made it perfectly clear that in an effort to get his money back, he will sign anything. Based on your conduct over the past several weeks, I suspect the matter will not be settled, and so be it!

Unfortunately, a CPA and longtime friend of mine, John Mese, will be the focus of a serious investigation by both federal and state authorities. Unlike the excons in your group, he has a great deal to lose.

Further, regardless of either of these authorities, I

*will deliver to your clients a RICO[4] complaint so large
that it may have to be delivered in a U-Haul truck. This
is a guarantee and I am transmitting Mr. Schiller's
thoughts as we have received them today.*

*I believe that you will be able to understand his
position in spite of the typos. And I might add that Mr.
Schiller is suffering from serious health problems as a
result of your clients' blowing up his car with him in it
unconscious, so please govern yourself accordingly.*

> Ed L. Du Bois
> President

> Encl: Marc Schiller's memo

> CC: Ed O'Donnell, Gene Rosen, Marc Schiller,
> John Mese, Jorge Delgado

The March 24 deadline passed. Finally, Schiller and
Du Bois had had enough. Ed Du Bois put in a call to Al
Harper, an MDPD captain and a veteran homicide detec-
tive Du Bois knew from Miami Shores.

"I didn't want to walk in off the street with Mr. Schiller
and just knock on a door and say, 'Who should I talk to?'"
Du Bois explained. "I wanted Al Harper to tell me where
to go and who to see, and give me a little credibility."

Du Bois told Harper all about Schiller's abduction and
imprisonment, and what he had uncovered during his own
investigation, then he waited for Al Harper to get back to
him. Harper put in a call to the MDPD's Strategic Investigations Division, the SID, an elite bureau whose crime-
busting detectives investigated organized crime, drug
trafficking, contract killing, and other major crimes. A
few days later, Du Bois received a call from SID detective

---

[4]Racketeer Influenced and Corrupt Organization Act

Kevin Long. Before revealing all the gruesome details of
the Schiller abduction, Du Bois asked if SID would arrange
a polygraph for Schiller. Based on his experience, Du Bois
knew that passing a polygraph would be the most effective
way for Schiller to demonstrate to lawmen that he was telling the truth. Du Bois remembers Long telling him that he
would make the arrangements, and they agreed that Schiller would be available for the polygraph from April 18 to
20.

Schiller flew into Miami International Airport from
Colombia on April 17. He checked into the Miami International Airport Hotel at Concourse E under an assumed
name. That's where he met Du Bois face-to-face for the
first time. Schiller was understandably nervous. Miami
Lakes is just west of the airport, a stone's throw away, and
he was worried that he might be spotted by one of the Sun
Gym thugs. As far as the private eye could tell, Schiller had
recovered from his ordeal. Except for nervousness and a
purple blotch on his nose, a remnant from the tape that had
been wrapped tightly around his head during his captivity,
there were no obvious signs of his ordeal.

The next day, Du Bois and Schiller drove to the SID
office where they were met by Detective Gary Porterfield.
The lawman asked Du Bois to come into his office while
Schiller waited outside. The private eye brought a copy of
his case file, which he handed over to the SID detective.
Then he began outlining the history of the case.

Over the next hour Du Bois filled the lawman in about
the Schiller kidnapping on November 15, and how during his month of captivity Schiller was forced to sign
over everything he owned to men connected to Sun Gym
in Miami Lakes. He gave Porterfield Schiller's detailed
memo, canceled checks, a copy of the quitclaim deed,
Schiller's hospital records, and a copy of Danny Lugo's
federal rap sheet. He told the detective, who took notes,
about the brutal and humiliating treatment Schiller was
forced to endure, and how he was filled with vodka and

barbiturates then sent crashing into a poll and run over twice in a bungled attempt to murder him. Du Bois even named those responsible: Danny Lugo, Jorge Delgado, Noel Adrian Doorbal, and John Carl Mese were the main players, he said, but there were others involved, too.

When Du Bois was done, Porterfield called Marc Schiller into his office. An hour later Schiller emerged with a commitment from the lawman to begin investigating the next day, Wednesday. Schiller remembers the detective saying they would polygraph him on Thursday, and he'd have more than enough time to catch his return flight to Colombia.

"I gave them the case wrapped in a bow and on a silver platter," Du Bois says, but on Wednesday Porterfield called. The polygraph couldn't be set up for Thursday. Could Schiller stay over until Friday morning? Reluctantly Schiller said he could, and he rescheduled his flight for Friday afternoon.

At the appointed hour on Friday morning, Schiller and Du Bois appeared at the SID office for the polygraph. Porterfield met them in the lobby. He had more bad news. SID would not be taking the case after all—it was going to the Robbery Bureau instead.

Marc Schiller was devastated. Ed Du Bois was stunned.

"Robbery? Are you kidding me?" he asked Porterfield. "You're transferring a complex case like this to robbery, which is dealing with ten thousand purse snatchings and smash-and-grabs? Why are you shit-canning this case?"

Porterfield assured Schiller and Du Bois that the case wasn't being "shit-canned." Higher-ups decided that the core of the Schiller case was robbery.

Schiller spoke up. "This is kidnapping, attempted murder, torture," he said to deaf ears. The decision had been made, and it was out of Porterfield's hands. The lawman offered to escort Du Bois and Schiller to the Robbery Bureau. When they arrived, Du Bois remembers seeing a lone detective sitting in the waiting area.

"He was looking at us, and he had a shit-eating grin on his face," Du Bois recalls. And he was clapping, "softly clapping his hands together."

After Schiller went into the robbery office for his interview, Du Bois approached the bureau's receptionist. "Why was that detective clapping and smiling at us?" he wanted to know.

"Please don't tell anyone I told you," she answered in a near whisper. "SID called over here this morning and said we should expect an Academy Award–winning performance from Mr. Schiller."

From that moment on, Du Bois knew that the investigation into the Schiller abduction was doomed. It had been poisoned by SID. The cops didn't believe Marc Schiller. Meanwhile, Schiller's meeting with robbery detectives wasn't going well.

The case was assigned to Detective Iris Deegan, a seven-year veteran of the MDPD. She would describe her meeting with Schiller as "a preliminary interview." No stenographer was present, no tape or video recording was made.

According to Schiller, at least three times during the interview the detective interrupted him with a stern warning: Filing a false report is a crime; the police have neither the time nor the manpower to follow up every wild story.

"These are dangerous people," Schiller protested. "If you're wasting your time with me, throw me in jail."

Finally, an exasperated Schiller asked Deegan directly, "Do you think I am making this up?"

He remembers her answer: "Yeah, we do."

"Then give me a polygraph now," Schiller demanded. That would take some time to set up, he was told. Schiller would have to come back the following Tuesday.

Ed Du Bois recalls that Schiller looked shaken and close to tears when he emerged from his interview with Deegan. But Marc Schiller made a decision. He was done with the cops. He wanted to be with his family. He was getting the hell out of Miami—again.

*   *   *

In fairness to the lawmen, Schiller's story was bizarre, unbelievable, like nothing they'd ever heard before except perhaps as a plot on *Miami Vice*. That Schiller had been kidnapped in broad daylight from a busy shopping center parking lot, held for a month, starved, tortured, run over twice, but survived and waited four months to report it while negotiating with his abductors for a million dollar financial settlement over a "sour business deal," understandably raised their eyebrows. Add to that his Colombian connection. Even though he was an American citizen, Schiller's revelation that the money the gang took from his Cayman Islands account had been funds he was managing for his wife's family in Colombia left the cops wondering about dark-haired, dark-eyed, mustachioed, and bilingual Marcelo Schiller. After all, in Miami a Colombian connection to offshore accounts suggests something sinister— namely drug trafficking. And where had Schiller been hiding out? In Colombia! As a result, the investigation was stalled.

"Since the polygraph was not done because the victim left the county, the investigation just didn't go anywhere," said John Farrell, the MDPD's chief of detectives.

Meanwhile, just as Ed Seibert had predicted, the Sun Gym gang was on the prowl for another wealthy victim. The Schiller kidnapping had only whetted their appetite. Besides, Danny Lugo's greed was insatiable: The big-spending muscleman was supporting Sabina and paying the rent on a love nest; he had a young child and a pregnant wife, and he was helping Lillian and her family. He also had an eighty thousand dollar Mercedes to pay for and was dropping lots of cash at Miami's flesh palaces, so he set his sights on Sun Gym member Winston Lee, a prosperous auto body shop owner whose business was in nearby Opa-Locka.

He and Doorbal had already begun stalking Lee. They'd taken dozens of photos of his Miami Lakes townhouse and were familiar with his daily routines. They had even devised a plan: Lugo would get hold of a UPS delivery truck and uniform and pretend to deliver a package to Lee. When Lee came to the door, the gang would grab him and whisk him away to the warehouse. But Noel Adrian Doorbal had stumbled upon another potential victim. He lived in a waterfront mansion. He owned a boat and drove a canary yellow Lamborghini. His name was Frank Griga.

CHAPTER NINE

READY TO STRIKE AGAIN

Solid Gold stripper Beatriz Weiland was the Sun Gym gang's unwitting link to Frank Griga. Flush with cash from the Schiller kidnapping, Lugo and Doorbal spent most nights at Solid Gold, where Doorbal would regularly slip the Hungarian beauty hundred-dollar bills in hopes of winning her heart. It wasn't long before they became close, so close in fact that the muscleman confessed to her that his extensive steroid use had rendered him unable to achieve an erection. He tried, but even with the buxom Beatriz, the most beautiful woman he had ever seen, Doorbal was a dud in bed, so he made an appointment to see a urologist who specialized in treating steroid-induced impotence with hormones. He pleaded with Beatriz to accompany him.

"He told me we were starting to date, and I was a part of his life. It was a big problem for him, and he felt that I have to be next to him," Beatriz said. She walked with him into the examining room, and she watched as the doctor plunged a hormone-filled syringe into Adrian Doorbal's butt. After a few more treatments, the muscleman recovered his lost libido.

Now able to perform, Doorbal told Beatriz that he wanted her to stop working at Solid Gold. Even though he was still seeing Cindy Eldridge, the nurse from Boca Raton, he promised Beatriz he would support her, would pay the rent for her apartment. He even took her to a warehouse in Hialeah to let her pick out furniture. She chose some rugs, "handmade rugs, very expensive," Beatriz recalled. Rugs from Persia, she thought. She didn't know they had been stolen from the Schiller home.

While Beatriz and Doorbal were close and becoming closer, she had already been close to Frank Griga. They had been lovers. But their three-month relationship ended amicably, and they remained good friends.

"He was like my brother for me," Beatriz said. "We got really close." They spoke on the phone almost every day. "I was really trusting him, and he trusted me," Beatriz said. It was Beatriz who introduced Frank to Krisztina.

Doorbal and Beatriz were at her apartment one night when the muscleman began thumbing through a photo album. He stopped turning the pages when he came to a four-by-six snapshot of a middle-aged woman casually standing in front of a canary yellow Lamborghini Diablo, but it wasn't the woman Doorbal was curious about. He wanted to know about the car.

"Who owns *this*?" he asked, his eyes nearly bulging out of their sockets.

Beatriz pointed to another photo. She identified the man in it: Fellow Hungarian Frank Griga. They had dated for a few months in 1993, she explained, and they remained very good friends. Frank, she told Doorbal, had made a fortune in the phone sex business. He lived in a waterfront mansion in Golden Beach. The blond stripper innocently filled him in on what else she knew about Frank's assets.

Doorbal could hardly contain his excitement. He couldn't believe his good fortune. Not only was he with the woman of his dreams, not only had he regained his libido, but he had stumbled upon a potential victim. When Doorbal learned just how wealthy the phone sex millionaire was, Frank went from potential to next victim. Doorbal daydreamed about driving the Lamborghini on the highways, byways, and causeways of South Florida. He liked his Nissan 300ZX, but he decided that the Lamborghini would be his. He couldn't wait to tell Danny Lugo. The blueprint would be the same as in the Schiller abduction: Kidnap, torture, extort, plunder, and kill.

While Adrian Doorbal was captivated with Beatriz, the bloom was rapidly coming off the rose for her. She had become suspicious of Doorbal's unlimited income. His explanation, that he and Danny were international businessmen, didn't ring true to Beatriz. She didn't see Doorbal, or Lugo, either, as tycoons. And he was pestering her about Frank Griga, asking her to introduce him and Danny to the Golden Beach millionaire. They had a business proposition for him, something about telephones in India, she recalled, but as far as Beatriz was concerned, all Doorbal ever did was work out at Sun Gym during the day and spend his nights at Solid Gold.

Then there was the arsenal of weapons he kept in his car and in his townhouse.

"Miami is a dangerous place," he told her. When she pressed him, the muscleman offered another explanation: He told her that, like his pal Danny, he, too, was a CIA agent. But Beatriz was too smart and too savvy to believe that bullshit story. Doorbal, she decided, was shady, maybe even dangerous. She decided she'd be better off without him. She told Doorbal their relationship was over. Surprisingly, Doorbal took the breakup well. After all, he still had Cindy, and if Beatriz wouldn't introduce him to Frank Griga, her ex-husband, Attila, would.

The two men met for the first time in April 1995, in a parking lot outside Doorbal's urologist's office. Afterward, they became friends. They'd speak on the phone just about every other day. Their conversations were about "girls, cars, basic guy stuff," Weiland said. They made the rounds of South Beach hotspots one night. Attila recalls watching Doorbal hand a fifty-dollar bill to the attendant who parked his car. Afterward, Doorbal invited Attila to his Miami Lakes townhouse.

It wasn't long before Doorbal began pestering Attila about Frank Griga. Did he know him? Did he talk with him? Would he introduce Doorbal to Frank? He and his cousin Danny were in the phone business, too, and they were looking for a partner.

It was during Frank's surprise birthday party on Friday, May 19, that Attila broached the subject with the phone sex millionaire. Frank said he'd be home all weekend. "If they are going to stop by and talk about the business, let me know," he told Attila.

The next day Attila phoned Doorbal. "Frank is going to listen to you guys," he remembers telling Doorbal. "If you want to go over, go, because Frank is about to go to the movies after six thirty. If you can make it before that, you can talk with him."

Lugo and Doorbal wasted no time. They picked Attila up and drove with him to Frank Griga's Golden Beach mansion. On the way there Doorbal, a high school dropout, turned to Weiland, who was sitting on the backseat. He had some words of advice. "Adrian told me I should be there to learn the way the big guys do it," Attila recalled.

Attila introduced them then left the room so the three men could talk in private. The meeting lasted about thirty minutes. Before the musclemen departed, Krisztina took them on a tour of the house. They dropped Attila off at his apartment before heading back to Miami Lakes. When they arrived there Lugo announced that they would abduct Griga the next day, and they planned to kidnap Krisztina, too.

It was Danny Lugo who cooked up the bogus investment scheme that would get the two musclemen face-to-face with Frank Griga. Interling International, a legitimate company, was looking to expand phone service into India. It seemed like a natural for Frank Griga. Even before he had the Interling pitch down pat, Lugo was busy trying to reassemble the gang that kidnapped Marc Schiller. He knew that John Mese and Jorge Delgado would be on board, but he needed more muscle.

Lugo decided he could do without Stevenson Pierre this time around—he didn't seem to have the stomach for it, but he phoned Carl Weekes and invited him to join him for an evening at Solid Gold. It was in the Champagne Room that Lugo told Weekes about a new victim. Would he be available to help take him down?

To his surprise, Weekes turned Lugo down. He had been arrested in April on a gun charge—possession of a concealed weapon—and he was out on bond. Carl Weekes vowed that his life of crime was over. Meanwhile, Lugo and Doorbal reached out to Big Mario Sanchez. He had quit Sun Gym, but they tracked him down at Gold's Gym while he worked out. He had been paid one thousand dollars for helping with the Schiller abduction; now they had another "job." Like Weekes, Sanchez declined, too, saying he never wanted to participate in something like that again. Lugo and Doorbal raised the ante, offering him five thousand dollars to once again look mean and tough. This time Sanchez didn't think about it. He turned the Sun Gym musclemen down again.

Desperate, Danny Lugo turned to Sabina for help. He had just returned from a trip to CIA headquarter in Langley, he told her, and his chief had given him a very important assignment. After reminding Sabina that she was always asking if she could help him in his work he told her, "Sabina, I need your help now."

After swearing her to secrecy, he told her it would be a joint CIA-FBI operation. The United States government, he said, was after a man named Frank Griga, a sleazy businessman who lived in Golden Beach. He made a fortune but never paid his taxes. In broken English, the Romanian beauty queen recalled what Lugo told her: "Danny said that there is this Hungarian man and he has a lot of money and he makes money with phone sex, and FBI want him because he doesn't report the money to the government."

The Hungarian and his girlfriend would be abducted and held in a warehouse until they could be handed over to government agents. Before turning them over to the G-men, Lugo told Sabina, he would force the Hungarian to give him some money, too.

"Why the girl?" Sabina wanted to know. "What did she do?"

Lugo assured Sabina that she would not be hurt, adding that the girlfriend would be used as leverage to force the Hungarian man to pay—or else.

Despite her misgivings, Sabina was thrilled. She sincerely wanted to help her lover. She considered him a real-life James Bond, but she'd been disappointed before. In April, Lugo had enlisted her help in capturing a "Palestinian terrorist" named Winston Lee. The mission was aborted, but she never found out why. This time, she hoped, she'd get her chance to do her part for the United States of America.

Sabina remembers looking on one night as Lugo and Doorbal prepared their kidnap kit and made sure that everything was in working condition—guns, handcuffs, rope, syringes, and several vials of Rompun (generic name Xylazine), a very powerful tranquilizer used to sedate large animals, especially horses. There are no clinical human uses for Rompun. When injected it slows respiration and heart rate, causes salivation, agitation, vomiting, extreme thirst, and a burning sensation.

While Lugo and Doorbal planned and plotted, the investigation into the abduction of Marc Schiller was stalled until April 26. That morning MDPD detective Iris Deegan decided to drive to Old Cutler Cove to check out the Schiller house. There were no bad guys there. They were long gone. In fact, the house had been emptied and abandoned weeks before, so Deegan knocked on doors. One neighbor, Manuel Salgar, remembered two men who moved into the house in December.

He described one of them as about thirty, six feet, two inches tall, and well built. He drove a Toyota and called himself Tom. The other man was shorter and younger, "a light-skinned black male," Salgar said. He drove a Nissan 300ZX. Detective Deegan took notes and left. One week later, on May 3, Deegan was back in Old Cutler Cove, this time with photographs to show to Salgar, who had no problem picking Danny Lugo out of a lineup of more than a dozen photos.

At long last Iris Deegan believed that something sinister had occurred. She subpoenaed Schiller's bank statements as well as UPS delivery records to the Schiller house. She also asked American Express for statements and records regarding charges made to Schiller's account from November 1994 through January 1995, but she never questioned Danny Lugo or anyone else named by Schiller as having had a hand in his abduction. Instead, she waited.

Ed Du Bois recalls phoning Deegan to check on how the case was progressing. The detective, he says, told him she was waiting for Schiller's bank and credit card records to arrive before moving ahead.

"Why do you keep investigating my client?" Du Bois asked. "Why not go out on the street, show your badge to these guys, and ask *them* some questions before they strike again?"

"Are you trying to tell me how to do my job?" the detective snapped.

"No," Du Bois shot back, "but it sure doesn't seem like you're doing it right."

Deegan wanted to gather more evidence, and she wanted a sworn statement from Marc Schiller. Without one she didn't think she would have probable cause to obtain an arrest warrant for Danny Lugo or anyone else associated with the Sun Gym gang. Whatever the reason, and despite the efforts of Marc Schiller and Ed Du Bois, no one from law enforcement contacted anyone from the Sun Gym gang. As far as the thugs were concerned, they were in the clear, and they were poised to strike again.

CHAPTER TEN

MURDER ON MAIN STREET

Wednesday, May 24, 1995

At 10:30 P.M. Frank Griga was behind the wheel of his most cherished possession, his bright yellow Lamborghini Diablo. He had no problem keeping up with the musclemen in the gold Mercedes just ahead. Despite his misgivings about the Interling deal and the two men who had brought it to him, he never could have imagined what they had in store for him and Krisztina. The couple believed they were going to dinner. Instead they were unsuspecting lambs being led to the slaughter.

"The very last conversation I had with Frank was on the day of his disappearance," his sister, Zsuzsanna, recalled. Frank had phoned her at her home in Budapest. He mentioned that he and Krisztina would be spending the Memorial Day weekend in the Bahamas, and he told his sister that he had been approached by two businessmen who were offering him an investment opportunity in India.

"Frank had a weird feeling about those two, but he said 'I am going to give it one more shot. I am going to go out to dinner with them and I will listen to what they want to say one more time.' "

Chopin the dog must have had a weird feeling, too, because he started behaving badly as soon as the musclemen arrived on Wednesday to take Frank and Krisztina to dinner. Evil wears many disguises. It can appear in the guise of a clergyman, or a kindly uncle, or even a lawman. Humans are easily duped but, in retrospect, it appears that Chopin the dog wasn't. Before the couple left with the musclemen, Chopin ran out of the house and Frank had to chase after him. When Chopin heard them drive away, he scratched at the door and whimpered, and he kept it up all night long.

The musclemen had been fine-tuning their evil plot for weeks, ever since Adrian Doorbal had seen the snapshot of the Lamborghini in Beatriz Weiland's photo album. They made their first abduction attempt just four days before, on Sunday, May 20. That morning Lugo, Sabina, and Doorbal piled into the Mercedes and drove towards Golden Beach. Before leaving Miami Lakes, Danny stowed the suitcase containing the kidnap kit he had assembled the night before inside the trunk along with a laptop computer, a gift for Frank. It wasn't long before one of the musclemen realized they had forgotten a vital tool of their nefarious trade—duct tape—so they stopped at a Winn-Dixie supermarket in Hallandale. Doorbal was dispatched to purchase the tape while Sabina and Lugo remained in the car.

"Wait!" Lugo screamed suddenly as Doorbal walked toward the store, the butt of a gun poking out from the back of his pants. Then he took off after Doorbal who returned to the car while Lugo went inside for the tape.

"He's crazy," Sabina remembers Lugo saying. "You can't go into a store with a gun!"

From there the threesome drove to Golden Beach. While on the way, Lugo called Frank Griga from his cell phone. Could they stop by? he asked. "I am going to the Bahamas, and I have some paperwork I would like to show you before I go."

Griga must have said it would be okay because Lugo

continued driving toward Golden Beach. As he drove, he reviewed the abduction plan with Doorbal and Sabina.

"Sabina, you wait in the Mercedes," he barked. "Keep your eyes on the garage door while Adrian and I are inside. As soon as you see it opening, back up the car and pop the trunk."

Then he spoke to Doorbal who was sitting in the back behind Sabina. "Adrian, you take the girl while I take Griga. If they put up a fight we'll shoot them full of horse tranquilizer."

The diabolical plan was to stuff the couple, hog-tied and gagged, into the car's trunk. Then Lugo and Sabina would drive to the warehouse on West 80th Street in Hialeah that the musclemen rented especially for them. Doorbal would drive away in the Lamborghini. At the warehouse they would force Frank to watch while Doorbal and Lugo tortured Krisztina until Frank gave them everything. Sabina believed what Lugo had told her—that the couple would be turned over to government agents, but the gruesome truth was the couple would be killed and dismembered, their body parts scattered throughout South Florida.

When they pulled up at Griga's, the musclemen exited the car and headed for the front door. Lugo carried the laptop. Both men were armed. "Danny got out and then Adrian got out and I saw some guns in the pants, in the pants that they were wearing," Sabina remembered.

Despite being nervous and frightened, Sabina did as she was told, and she never took her eyes from the garage door while she waited behind the wheel of the Mercedes. But the door never opened. Fifteen minutes after the musclemen went inside they emerged from the house empty-handed. There were other people in the house, workmen, and Lugo wasn't willing to wait for them to leave, not while Sabina sat outside in the Mercedes. Besides they were used to aborting abduction attempts, having had to call off several Schiller kidnap tries. Doorbal, however, was beside himself, enraged.

"We should have done it! We should have done it!' he exclaimed again and again once he was inside the car.

"No, the timing wasn't right," Lugo said calmly. "I have a new plan." Once again he phoned Frank Griga. Sabina overheard Lugo inviting Frank and Krisztina to dinner later that evening at Shula's Steak House in Miami Lakes.

"Would you like me to pick you up or do you want to meet us there?" Lugo asked.

By this time Doorbal had calmed down, and Lugo revealed yet another new plan, the Russian wife plan. Sabina would remain in Doorbal's apartment while the foursome—Lugo, Doorbal, Frank Griga, and Krisztina Furton—discussed the Interling investment over dinner. Afterward, the diners would stop by Doorbal's for desert. Sabina was to pretend to be Lugo's Russian wife. Her job was to keep Krisztina occupied until he and Doorbal could lure Griga into another room where they would "take him down." By this time, however, Sabina, was getting cold feet.

"We went to bed, just took a nap," she recalls, "and that's when I told Danny. I said, 'Danny, I'm happy nothing happened today because I cannot do it.' And he said, 'Sabina, we have to be a team. If you cannot do this then we cannot be together.' "

It was a startling ultimatum, and Sabina relented. While the two musclemen dined with the couple, she waited in Doorbal's apartment for five hours, anxious to play her part. She never got the chance. Lugo appeared distraught when he returned after midnight. He told Sabina that the dinner went well but he and Doorbal had a fight. The abduction was postponed once again.

That night, Frank and Krizstina were able to go home. They had been lucky, but their luck was about to run out.

Only four people would ever know what ruse the two musclemen used to lure Frank and Krisztina to Adrian Doorbal's Main Street townhouse. Two of them are dead, and the others never revealed the ploy. However, this much is known: By the time the foursome arrived at Shula's Steak

House, the restaurant had closed. Whatever bullshit story the musclemen told Frank and Krisztina convinced them to walk across the street to Doorbal's townhouse. Investigators believe that while Lugo sat with Krisztina in the living room, Doorbal invited the phone sex millionaire to accompany him into the spare bedroom he used as an office.

Perhaps he offered to show Griga his computer setup, or his gun collection, or perhaps they were going to prepare the documents for the Interling investment. Whatever the ploy, lawmen believe that as Frank entered the room Doorbal came up from behind and wrapped his massively muscular arm around Griga's neck, then he began to squeeze. Frank fought back desperately, but the muscleman had him in a deadly chokehold and was slowly strangling him. The two men crashed against the walls. They slammed into the computers and against the sliding glass doors. Doorbal grabbed a hard, blunt object and brought it down on Griga's skull, cracking it open. Griga bled on Doorbal's shirt, the computer equipment, the walls, and the sliding glass doors. The ruckus alerted Krisztina who screamed and tried to get to the room, but Lugo tackled her and held her down. As she fought desperately to free herself, Lugo injected her with Rompun, the horse tranquilizer.

As soon as she stopped struggling, Lugo handcuffed and gagged Krisztina, then he secured her feet with duct tape. Next, the musclemen turned their attention to Frank. As blood poured from his broken skull, they carried the dying phone sex millionaire to the bathtub and dropped him into it. And just to be on the safe side they gave him a hefty shot of horse tranquilizer, too. Then they left him to die. But they still had Krisztina, and she could give them the information they needed to get at Frank's money and other valuables.

CHAPTER ELEVEN

"OH MAN, THE BITCH IS COLD."

Jorge Delgado had been on standby mode all evening, nervously waiting for a phone call from Lugo to tell him how things were going. It came at 9 P.M. Lugo wanted to know if he could drive a Lamborghini. Delgado said he didn't. Be ready anyway, Lugo told him. We're going to need you in the morning. Based on the conversation Delgado surmised that everything was going well.

Thursday morning Lugo phoned Delgado again. This time he had bad news. There had been a struggle inside Doorbal's townhouse. Frank Griga was dead. Doorbal killed him.

"He was not supposed to die at that moment," Lugo told his pal, explaining that the plan was to get all of his money and property *before* killing him. Lugo assured Delgado that all was not lost. The girl was still alive. If they could get her to reveal the security code for the house, he would be able to get at Griga's assets. Lugo asked Delgado to come to Doorbal's apartment to help out.

Delgado lived a couple of miles away, and he arrived

in a flash. He was dressed in a T-shirt and gym shorts. The first thing he noticed when he entered the townhouse was the temperature—it was cold, very cold. Coming in from the sultry South Florida air, it felt colder than a butcher's freezer. The air conditioner was on full blast. Doorbal and Lugo were bundled up, and Doorbal was at the foot of the stairs with something slung over his shoulder. On second look Delgado noticed it was Krisztina. A hood covered her head. Duct tape covered her mouth and wound tightly around her wrists and ankles. All she had on was the red leather jacket she had worn when she left Golden Beach the night before, and she wasn't moving. But she came to as soon as Doorbal dropped her at the foot of the stairs.

In heavily accented English Krisztina begged to see Frank, then she became hysterical. Lugo ordered Doorbal to give her another shot of the horse tranquilizer, which the muscleman did by pulling her up by her feet and plunging the syringe into her ankle. This time Krisztina writhed in pain. She pleaded to see Frank, then she screamed hysterically. Doorbal put his hand over her mouth to muffle her screams.

Delgado looked on as Doorbal pulled Krisztina up into a sitting position. He held her by her shoulders while Lugo spoke to her. He assured her that Frank was okay. She could see him just as soon as she told him the security code to the house. Krisztina, however, was having difficulty understanding what he was saying. Although she had been learning English since she arrived in the United States, Krisztina still had difficulty speaking and understanding. Besides, the horse tranquilizer was making her thirsty, and it was impairing her ability to breathe, which meant it was difficult for her to speak in any language. She was mumbling and drifting in and out of consciousness, so the musclemen force-fed her water, and they slapped her.

"Tell us the fucking numbers. What are the numbers?" Lugo and Doorbal demanded.

In a voice that was barely audible, Krisztina rattled off numbers. Lugo wrote them down on a yellow pad. Satisfied that they finally had what they needed, Doorbal gave Krisztina yet another shot of Rompun, this time injecting her in her thigh. Once again Krisztina screamed in pain, then she went limp. After about an hour, Krisztina began to shake and scream. Doorbal injected her again, which caused her to scream again.

Lugo was anxious to get to Golden Beach. If he could get into Griga's waterfront mansion, he'd be able to access the phone sex millionaire's computer, his bank records, and his valuables. Perhaps he could even get into Griga's safe, but first he had to figure out what to do with the couple: Griga was stone-cold dead in the bathtub while Krisztina was unconscious but barely alive.

According to Jorge Delgado, Lugo instructed Doorbal to put in a call to Sun Gym member John Raimondo, a six foot five, two hundred and fifty pound mountain of a man. He was a powerlifter, a martial arts expert, and a sworn law enforcement officer. The six-year veteran of the county corrections department spent his working hours guarding prisoners at the Turner Guilford Knight Correctional Center in West Dade where his personnel file was filled with glowing evaluations. Around Sun Gym, however, there were rumors that when Raimondo wasn't on duty at the jail or working out at the gym, he was up to no good. According to Delgado, Lugo believed that John Raimondo was an expert at getting rid of dead bodies.

Doorbal explained the problem to Raimondo. The jail guard said he would help them out, for a price—he wanted fifty thousand dollars. After consulting with Lugo, Doorbal made a counteroffer: Nine thousand dollars in cash plus a Rolex watch and a Lamborghini Diablo. Deal, Raimondo said. He was on his way over.

When he arrived at Doorbal's, Krisztina was sprawled on the living room floor and Griga was still in the bathtub. After surveying the scene, Raimondo, a sworn lawman, should have arrested his Sun Gym pals. Instead, he bent down over Krisztina and hoisted her up by her ankles. When she moaned, he just let her go.

"Shut up," he barked. Then Delgado said Raimondo stepped on her head. Doorbal and Lugo would have to kill her themselves, Raimondo declared, before heading for the door. On his way out the giant jail guard had harsh words for Doorbal and Lugo: "You guys are a bunch of amateurs," Delgado remembered Raimondo saying, but he promised to return later to dispose of the bodies.

Lugo left, too. He went to Sabina's. He instructed Doorbal and Delgado to remain in the townhouse until he returned. Sabina knew that things had not gone well the night before. In the wee hours of the morning she awoke and peered into the living room where she saw her secret agent man sitting in the dark, downing shots of hard liquor and crying. Now, in possession of what he believed to be the security code that would allow him access to Griga's house, he told Sabina that he wanted her to accompany him there. She did, and when they arrived Lugo parked in the driveway. With his notepad in hand, he tried the security code but the numbers didn't work. He tried different combinations, then random guesses, but still no luck. Even Sabina tried. They went around back, hoping to find another keypad. Again, to no avail.

Meanwhile, Griga's dog, Chopin, was barking furiously. Sabina recalls Lugo calling to the dog. "Sorry, Chopin," he said. "I can't get into the house because your parents didn't give me the keys. I can't take care of you."

Lugo called Doorbal on his cell phone. He needed Krisztina. Wake her up, he told Doorbal. Get the keypad numbers. Doorbal went to fetch Krisztina. He came right back. He was on the speakerphone so Sabina had no trouble hearing what he told Lugo: "Oh man," Doorbal said, "the bitch is cold."

CHAPTER TWELVE

A GRISLY SCENE

Danny Lugo was beside himself. The Sun Gym thugs had Griga's Lamborghini. Lugo had driven it to the warehouse the night before. They also had his Rolex watch and Krisztina's rings and diamond tennis bracelet, but that was all. Before driving away he emptied Griga's mailbox and handed the contents to Sabina.

"You open it," he said. The muscleman glanced at the pieces of mail as Sabina opened each one. "The man had good credit," he commented.

"And then we drove off," Sabina recalled.

Despite the sickening turn of events, Lugo had an appetite. The couple stopped at a Subway in Hallandale where Lugo wolfed down a sandwich, but Sabina couldn't eat. Her stomach was churning. She was scared. It dawned on her that she might be the next to die.

"I thought Danny was going to kill me because I knew too much," the Romanian beauty said.

Once back in Miami Lakes, Lugo dropped Sabina at their apartment, then he went back to Doorbal's. To while away the time, Doorbal and Delgado played video games. They were still playing when Lugo returned, and he was still fuming. He told his partners in crime that he had been unable to get into Griga's house, that all he could do was empty the mailbox. The three of them spent the rest of the afternoon and evening waiting for John Raimondo to return, but he never showed up. Finally the Sun Gym trio decided they would have to dispose of the bodies themselves, and soon.

By this time Frank Griga had been dead for at least fifteen hours. With the air conditioning at full blast, his body's decomposition had been slowed, but it wasn't stopped. Griga's body was beginning to stink, and it wouldn't be long before the stench of death would spread over the entire townhouse complex. That's because decomposition is caused by two separate processes: Autolysis and putrefaction. The former involves the breakdown of cells from within, by their own enzymes, while the latter is caused by bacteria that come mostly from a decedent's intestinal tract. In another dozen hours the putrid odor emanating from Doorbal's townhouse would be strong enough to arouse the neighbors.

But once again Danny Lugo had a plan, though the Sun Gym gang would have to wait until morning to execute it. In the meantime, Lugo instructed Delgado to go home for the night, but to return first thing in the morning with a U-Haul van and a large wardrobe box, the kind movers use to transfer clothing and other closet items. Lugo spent the night with Sabina. As for Doorbal, he stayed in the near-freezing townhouse with the rotting bodies of Frank Griga and Krisztina Furton.

On the morning of Friday, May 26, Jorge Delgado arrived early in a rented U-Haul cargo van and the musclemen went to work removing the bodies from the townhouse. But they couldn't just walk out the door with the corpses slung over their shoulders, so they decided to sneak Frank out by stuffing him into the black leather sofa they stole from the Schiller house.

First they removed the cushions. They placed Griga's body, which had been wrapped in cotton sheets, inside and covered it with the cushions, which they tied to the sofa's frame with rope. While Delgado stood lookout outside the van, Lugo and Doorbal carried the sofa from the townhouse and loaded it into the van. Next, they stuffed Krisztina's body into the U-Haul transfer box, which Doorbal was able to lift and carry out by himself. With their cargo of death now in the van, the three Sun Gym thugs headed for the warehouse to begin the gruesome task of making their victims disappear forever.

Adrian Doorbal had no qualms about cutting up the corpses. In fact, he was eager to do it; he even offered to do it himself. "Doorbal was going to do the job and would have no problem with it," Delgado remembers Lugo telling him. But he needed tools, so after unloading the sofa and the clothing box, Lugo and Doorbal hurried to Home Depot while Delgado remained at the warehouse.

The two musclemen prowled the aisles searching for what they needed. They purchased a McCulloch gas-powered chain saw, a hatchet, several knives, a couple of floor fans, two propane gas tanks, goggles, orange gardener's gloves, heavy-duty towels, several buckets and large barrels, rubber boots, a carton of Hefty bags, road tar, and a fire extinguisher. They charged the items on Doorbal's American Express Card; total cost, $666. Then they returned to the warehouse where Doorbal spread the Hefty bags across the floor.

Next, they placed the bodies side by side on the Hefty bags. While Doorbal prepared, donning gloves, a mask respirator and goggles, Lugo sprayed the corpses with Windex, then wiped them down with towels. When everything was ready, the two musclemen turned their attention to the chain saw. It had to be assembled.

Danny Lugo fancied himself a genius, but he had trouble following the simple directions that came with the chain saw. He and Doorbal conferred over the instructions several times. After much trial and error, they were finally ready to start the engine. They filled the tank with gasoline and cranked it, but the engine seized and stalled—they forgot to add oil. They didn't have any, so Lugo sent Jorge Delgado to get some as well as five more gallons of tar and a large black security grate, the kind that is seen on windows all over Miami. Doorbal planned to use it to create a homemade surgical table. The bodies would be placed on top while underneath two fifty-five gallon drums would catch the blood and severed body parts. And they didn't want to cut up bodies on empty stomachs, so they asked Jorge to bring back lunch.

When Delgado returned, the Sun Gym trio chowed down. After lunch, Doorbal tried to start up the chain saw again, but once again he couldn't get it going. Frustrated, he decided to take it back to the store. He needed to get something else. At 2:30 P.M., Lugo and Doorbal were back at Home Depot. They returned the gas-powered chain saw, exchanging it for an electric one—a Remington Power Cutter, no assembly required.

The two musclemen were back at the warehouse in less than thirty minutes. Doorbal immediately suited up: rubber boots, gloves, sweatpants, and goggles. Then he plugged the chain saw into an outlet and pulled the trigger. The Remington whirred to life.

Lugo and Delgado decided they did not have the stomach to watch as Doorbal went about the gruesome task of dismembering the bodies, so they moved to another part of the warehouse. Doorbal went to work on Krisztina first. Lugo and Delgado listened as the chain saw began slicing through her skin. Then the saw stopped.

"Come back here, Lugo. Come back!" Doorbal shouted angrily.

He'd been trying to cut through Krisztina's neck when her long hair became tangled on the saw blade, causing it to jam. This time they couldn't bring it back to Home Depot—the blade was covered with blood and hair, so they decided to use the hatchet instead.

For the next half hour Delgado sat alone listening to the

ghastly sound the hatchet made as it chopped through flesh and bones. He could actually hear the bones crack, and he heard the distinctive *thwack* the hatchet made each time it sliced into soft tissue.

"Thumps" he called them, staying put until his pals told him that it was all over, "that they were putting the pieces into the drums."

It was a grisly scene. The electric saw had sent clumps of tissue flying all over the place. Delgado saw the couple's heads, hands, and feet in buckets. Three black barrels held their arms and legs, which jutted out over the barrel tops. Two other barrels contained the couple's torsos.

Delgado described a macabre scene: "I proceeded to go back, and I saw pieces of legs sticking out of the drums. I saw Lugo pushing down on the tar, the black tar. He had gloves on, and he was pushing down in the barrel, squeezing it into the barrel."

To add weight, Lugo filled the barrels with black road tar. Thinking they were done, he stepped back to admire their craftsmanship when he realized they had forgotten about teeth, fingerprints, and faces, so the two musclemen went back to cutting, chopping, and slicing.

First, they removed the heads from the buckets. Next, they gouged out their victims' teeth with a pair of pliers. For good measure they used the hatchet to hack away at their jawbones, shattering them. With a knife they peeled away what was left of the couples' faces, tossing the skin into one of the barrels. Next, Lugo and Doorbal went to work on the couple's fingerprints, using the hatchet to chop away the tips of their fingers.

When that was done Doorbal rested. He was exhausted, so he sat down on Schiller's sofa, the one he and Lugo had stuffed Griga's body into. While Doorbal recuperated, Lugo put the lids on the buckets and barrels and soldered them shut. Doorbal, however, didn't relax for long. His cell phone rang at about half past four. It was Cindy Eldridge calling to remind him that they had a date for dinner.

Doorbal dated the nurse from Boca Raton on a regular

basis from the time they first met until after the Schiller abduction, when he was flush with cash and chasing after Solid Gold stripper Beatriz Weiland. When Beatriz dumped him at the beginning of April, Doorbal went back to Cindy exclusively, and now they were getting married. Danny Lugo would be the best man. They'd even set the date—June 26, her thirty-second birthday. Cindy was thrilled. Doorbal had proposed to her not long after they first met, but back then she told him to slow down, they needed to get to know each other a lot better before tying the knot. After almost a year of dating, Cindy thought she'd gotten to know Doorbal very well, but she had no idea how evil he was.

She had an inkling that all was not right with the muscleman from Trinidad, but she was in love, and love is blind. Doorbal had acted strangely earlier in the week. All Cindy knew was what Doorbal told her, that he and Lugo had a nasty argument. She had no idea what it was about, but Doorbal was in a deep funk, carrying on like a jilted lover. He even mentioned suicide. But he was in high spirits when she spoke to him again on Wednesday afternoon.

He was with Danny Lugo in the Mercedes, and they were both laughing and joking and having a great time. Doorbal told Cindy that he was looking forward to a business meeting later that night with a wealthy guy who might be willing to invest in the gym. Cindy was relieved, and she was looking forward to spending Friday evening with her muscleman. But his mood changed again when he phoned her in the wee hours of Thursday morning, this time to tell his half-asleep bride-to-be that the meeting had not gone well, that there had been a fight and he might be deported to Trinidad and he might even need an alibi.

Now, more than twenty-four hours later, Doorbal needed a shower and a change of clothes before he could make the forty-mile trek to Cindy Eldridge's apartment in Boca Raton. He also needed a nap. Delgado offered to drive him home. He had left his own minivan parked at the U-Haul office, and he had to return the rental van before the office closed at five o'clock. After dropping Doorbal off, Delgado returned the van, then drove to the warehouse to help Lugo, who remained behind to finish up. It was still light when Jorge Delgado arrived back at the warehouse. He remembers what he saw when he drove up:

"I saw Danny Lugo in between the garage door with a barrel, trying to light it up with propane, and I saw fire coming off the barrel . . . Smoke coming out. Fire coming out."

Curious, Delgado asked Lugo what he was doing. "He says he was burning the pieces of the body that they had cut."

With flames shooting from the barrel, Delgado peered inside. He got a close-up view of two heads and hands and feet. Delgado wasn't taken aback or sickened by the human barbecue. Instead, he was concerned about a passerby coming upon the gruesome scene. He mentioned that possibility to Lugo who immediately doused the flames with a fire extinguisher. Then he rolled the smoldering barrel through the warehouse to the back door where he restarted the flames.

The burning went on for another twenty minutes, but humans don't burn easily. High heat is needed. While the fire in Lugo's barrel was hot enough to barbecue hot dogs or chicken, it wasn't enough to turn human body parts into ashes.

At about nine o'clock, Lugo doused the flames again. Delgado helped him lock up the warehouse, then the two men headed for Doorbal's. They promised Adrian they would clean up the mess at his place—the blood and the wreckage from the Griga-Furton murders.

"We closed up the warehouse and left straight for Doorbal's apartment," Delgado recalled. "We went straight to clean up what was there—computers and the file cabinets, and the rug we took out and placed all that in my van."

They also removed a blood-covered computer monitor from the first floor bedroom; an arsenal of guns and ammunition including a dart gun and Tasers; a wastebasket full of assorted statements, bills, and letters; and the blood-soaked carpet padding. Everything was loaded into Delgado's minivan and driven a block to Sabina's apartment at 6798 Main Street. As Delgado unloaded all the items and placed them on the sidewalk, Lugo hauled them up the stairs to the one bedroom, two-bath love nest atop Richie's Swimwear. He stored most of the items in the apartment's storage closet, which could be accessed from the terrace.

Cindy Eldridge didn't wait up for Adrian Doorbal, but before she went to sleep she left her fiancé a note imploring him to cheer up and promising that she would tell whoever asked that he spent all of Wednesday with her. Doorbal was relieved when he read it. Even though he'd napped before making the long drive to Boca, he was exhausted from all the chopping and cutting. He climbed into bed and fell fast asleep as soon as his head hit the pillow.

Cindy was in for a rude awakening on Saturday morning. She was hoping her groom would accompany her as she shopped for her wedding dress, but the muscleman said he could not stay—he had to drive back to Miami.

"I've got things to do with Danny," he told her. She pressed him, but he wouldn't say more, which only made Cindy angry and suspicious. She decided to follow him to Miami to see what he was up to. When he drove into the parking lot of the Home Depot in Miami Lakes, Cindy pulled up and confronted him.

"What are you doing here?" she demanded.

Doorbal decided to tell her the truth, almost. He told her about the meeting on Wednesday, and that there was a fight in his apartment. There was blood on the walls, and on the carpet, and he was certain that he was going to be deported. But he didn't tell Cindy that he had murdered two people, or that he had spent the previous day chopping up their bodies with Lugo. Cindy vowed to help him, no matter what.

Lugo and Delgado were already there when Doorbal and Cindy arrived at the Miami Lakes townhouse. Maintenance men from the complex were there, too, to replace the rug that had already been removed. Doorbal told the property manager that a feral cat had wandered in and peed on it, and then went on a wild rampage. The smell was so bad, he said, he had to cut out several chunks of the rug and the padding. The workers promised to return in a few days with a new rug and padding. They never noticed the reddish-brown speckles on the wall, but Cindy did.

"Look at all this mess," she said. Then she rolled up her sleeves and went right to work.

"I saw her cleaning the entire apartment, going around with a sponge," Delgado remembered. "She had a brush and a roller [and] a paint can [that] she told me she had gotten from the landlady, and she was touching up, and she asked me to look for any spots of blood that she hadn't caught."

At one point Cindy noticed a foul odor coming from the garbage disposal.

"It smells like dead bodies," Lugo declared, a sly smile on his face.

CHAPTER THIRTEEN

SOUNDING THE ALARM

Six months after the Schiller abduction, and six weeks after private investigator Ed Du Bois first told the MDPD about it, lawmen began the process that would put the Sun Gym gang behind bars. On Friday, May 26, while Lugo, Doorbal, and Delgado were dismembering their victims' corpses, friends of Frank and Krisztina were beginning to think that something terrible had happened to the couple. Eszter Toth, the Hungarian housekeeper, was the first to sound the alarm.

Eszter and her daughter had been staying with them temporarily. She never heard the couple return on Wednesday night. When she awoke at seven on Thursday morning, she noticed that Griga, Furton, and the Lamborghini were not at the house. She took her daughter to school, then returned to pack and moved out as planned. Before leaving, Eszter left a note on the refrigerator thanking Frank and Krisztina for their hospitality. She phoned them in the afternoon and left a message. She phoned again on Friday morning, and once again the answering machine picked up the call. Concerned, Eszter contacted the couple's closest friend, Judi Bartusz. Judi said she thought Frank and Krisztina were in the Bahamas. Still concerned, Eszter decided to stop by the house to see for herself. What she saw alarmed her.

When Eszter peered into the window she saw Chopin the dog. He was barking furiously. Intuition told the housekeeper that something was amiss, but instead of entering the house herself she called Judi Bartusz. The women went inside together. What they found frightened them both.

They knew that Frank would never have left for the Bahamas without making arrangements for the dog. Chopin was like a child to the couple. They would have boarded him at a kennel while they were out of town, yet it was obvious that Chopin had not been fed or let out in two days. Judi opened the door for him to go into the back yard and fed him. Even though she was sure that her friends were not in the Bahamas, Judi put in a call to Frank's Freeport condo anyway. No one answered.

Fearful of what they might find, the two women began walking through the house. They entered Frank's office. Two round-trip tickets for a morning flight to Freeport the day before were on the desk. Next to them were Frank's passport, Krisztina's wallet, and U.S. re-entry forms. Judi's heart sank. It dawned on her that her friends never returned from their Wednesday night dinner with the two muscular businessmen, the ones she told her husband were "gangster-looking." Still sitting on a coffee table were the glasses the musclemen had sipped drinks from. Bartusz told Eszter not to touch them.

Now frantic, Judi phoned her husband, Gabor. He and Frank had grown up together in Hungary. They were best friends. Gabor Bartusz raced over and called the Golden Beach police. Within minutes a patrolman pulled his cruiser into the Griga driveway. He took a report, noting the last time the missing couple had been seen, who they were with, and what they were wearing. The cop then gave the report to Golden Beach Police chief Stanley Kramer, a former New York City detective. Kramer passed it along to the MDPD. Several days would pass before anyone from that department would interview Judi or Eszter, or visit the Griga house to collect evidence.

"The police department didn't take it seriously," says Frank's sister, Zsuzsanna. She learned about the couple's disappearance in a phone call from one of her brother's Hungarian friends in Miami. "They treated him as a young person who likes to run around, until they found the Lamborghini."

That would not happen for another two days. In the meantime the case was assigned to missing persons detective Mary Impolito. Judi Bartusz was too worried to sit still. It was the start of the Memorial Day weekend. In Miami and across the country, Americans planned to honor the nation's war dead and to remember the one hundred sixty-eight men, women, and children who perished in the April 19 bombing of the Alfred P. Murrah Federal Building in Oklahoma City. Judi Bartusz remembered Frank and Krisztina. She spent the weekend calling the couple's friends, hoping that someone had heard from them.

She phoned Attila Weiland and left a message. Frank and Krisztina were missing, she said. Attila called her back and spoke to Gabor who filled him in. At about eleven o'clock that evening, Adrian Doorbal phoned Attila.

"Let's go to Solid Gold," the muscleman suggested. He'd had an argument with Cindy. "I'm depressed. I want to see the girls. Maybe Beatriz can cheer me up."

They met at the Miami flesh palace. Attila told the muscleman that Frank and Krisztina had not returned home from their dinner meeting on Wednesday. Shula's was closed when they arrived, Doorbal said, so the four-some went to his place instead. The couple stayed there for a while then left, while he drove to Boca Raton to spend the night at Cindy's. Doorbal seemed unnerved. Twenty minutes after arriving at Solid Gold, Doorbal said he'd had enough. He left.

On Saturday, May 27, Frank Griga's very worried sister,

Zsuzsanna, called Attila from Budapest. She asked him to phone Adrian Doorbal again. He did. The muscleman repeated what he told Attila the night before, this time adding two more details. Doorbal claimed he went to Cindy's after Frank and Krisztina left his townhouse, and they might have gone with two other businessmen who had been with them, one of whom was a mystery man named Javier.

"I asked him, who are they?" Attila remembered.

"Business partners," the muscleman replied. "I also invested money with them,"

"How do you reach them if you have money with them?"

"They can page me. They have a boat, maybe they went together to the Bahamas."

Attila hoped his pal Adrian was telling him the truth, but he didn't believe the muscleman.

In the afternoon, Judi Bartusz decided to do some sleuthing on her own. She drove to Miami Lakes, to Shula's Steak House. Less than half a block from the restaurant Bartusz spotted a familiar-looking vehicle—a four-door gold Mercedes—parked at the curb. It looked just like the one she had seen parked in Griga's driveway Wednesday night. Judi wrote down the license plate. She gave it to Chief Kramer as soon as she arrived back in Golden Beach.

Earlier in the day, Lugo and Sabina flew to the Bahamas. They checked into the Atlantis resort on Paradise Island. While Judi was driving to Miami Lakes, Danny Lugo was trying to get money out of Frank Griga's Bahamas bank accounts, but he was unsuccessful. He and Sabina returned to Miami the next day.

On Sunday morning, May 28, Florida Highway Patrol sergeant Donna Ganz had been on routine road patrol since seven o'clock when her radio crackled at half past eleven. The dispatcher ordered her to a remote area in northwest Miami-Dade County where a county code enforcement officer checking on illegal dumping came across an abandoned yellow Lamborghini. It was found in a wooded area known to police as a staging ground for weekend cockfights and Santeria rituals.

The doors, which open vertically, were wide open. The key was in the ignition and the sound system had been torn out. Ganz noticed a blue parking sticker from Golden Beach on the windshield. She put in a call to the seaside town's police department. When Chief Kramer returned her call, he told her about the missing couple. Ganz ordered a flatbed tow truck to take the Lamborghini to the MDPD's Opa-Locka impound lot. While she waited for the tow, the ten-year veteran of the FHP searched the area. She found nothing.

Later that day Lugo contacted Sun Gym member Mario Gray, aka "Little Mario." He had been pestering Lugo for a job, and now the leader of the Sun Gym gang had one for him. Gray had turned down a job offer from Lugo once before, when Lugo offered him five hundred dollars to take a dart from a tranquilizer gun, the kind zookeepers use to subdue lions and tigers from afar. Lugo had already tested the gun by shooting a dart into a wall, but he wanted to measure the dart's effectiveness at penetrating human flesh.

Little Mario turned him down then, but now all Lugo wanted the twenty-one-year-old Sun Gym member to do was help him move three fifty-five gallon barrels out of the West 80th Street warehouse. Gray said he would.

Lugo asked the young bodybuilder if he knew of a remote location far off the beaten path where they could dump the barrels. Little Mario said he did. Lugo and Doorbal wanted to see it for themselves, so the three men drove to an isolated area on the edge of the Everglades in southwestern Miami-Dade County. The site was off a dirt road and next to a drainage ditch. The musclemen approved.

Later that night, Gray met Lugo and Doorbal at the warehouse. The musclemen loaded the barrels onto a rental truck and drove back to the dump site. Stopping alongside the drainage ditch, they unloaded the barrels one at a time about a hundred feet apart. Before driving off, the musclemen heaved the barrels into the murky water, then stood and watched as each one sank to the bottom. As payment for his help, Mario Gray received Marc Schiller's much-used and well-traveled black leather couch and one of his TV sets.

On Tuesday, May 30, the day after Memorial Day, Adrian Doorbal and Cindy Eldridge took their wedding vows at the Palm Beach County Courthouse in Delray Beach. Afterward, they celebrated at a seafood restaurant. While they were tying the knot, MDPD homicide detective Sal Garafalo was about to buy a cup of coffee, but he was interrupted by a cell phone call that sent him racing back to the Homicide Bureau in the MDPD's headquarters in Doral. It was from Gus Baez, another MDPD detective.

"Gus said that I was needed to come into the station, that we had an investigation that was being initiated by our team, and I was the lead investigator," Garafalo remembered.

In 1995, the Miami-Dade Police Department's Homicide Bureau consisted of seven teams of detectives. Cases are assigned by rotation and the team headed by Sergeant Felix Jimenez was slated to lead the next homicide investigation. Within the team, it was Sal Garafalo's turn to be the lead detective.

A veteran of more than twenty years in law enforcement, Garafalo began his law enforcement career in Connecticut, where he was a cop for more than four years before moving to South Florida. He had been a homicide detective with the MDPD since 1987. Over the years he had been the lead detective in dozens of cases.

As the lead investigator it was his job to oversee the processing of the crime scene, interview witnesses, and take overall charge of the day-to-day operation of the investigation including the interrogation of suspects. He was also responsible for maintaining the case file and writing search warrants and arrest affidavits. It's an awesome responsibility. Overlook just one clue and a case can go unsolved; violate a perpetrator's constitutional rights and a cold-blooded killer can get away with murder.

When Garafalo arrived at the Homicide Bureau, he met briefly with Sergeant Jimenez who informed him that he had gotten a call from missing persons detective Ed Bolita that there was a possible double homicide case in Golden Beach.

"Felix explained that we were assuming a missing persons case in which two people had disappeared under suspicious circumstances," Garafalo recalled. He met with Detective Mary Impolito from Missing Persons and Detective Iris Deegan from Robbery. The Griga-Furton case and the Schiller case were consolidated and handed off to homicide. Garafalo gathered the rest of his homicide team together and briefed them, sharing everything he'd learned and handing out assignments, called "leads," to detectives Gus Baez, Juan Hernandez, and Archie Moore. More manpower would be needed, so other homicide teams were called in to help. CSI detectives and criminalists were alerted and SWAT teams were notified to get ready.

Garafalo alerted the Miami-Dade State Attorney's Office. They would need prosecutors to help them draw up warrants and advise them on other legal issues that might arise during the initial stages of the investigation. Assistant State Attorney Gail Levine, a no-nonsense prosecutor and a ten-year veteran of the state attorney's office, was assigned to head the team.

While Garafalo was marshalling the forces of law and order, Doorbal and his new bride returned to Miami Lakes to find messages on the telephone answering machine from Attila Weiland. Doorbal phoned Weiland.

"I was really surprised to hear from him again because at that time I was sure he had something to do with Frank's disappearance," Attila remembered. "But he was talking to me very nicely and polite and told me, 'don't worry.' And he just got married and he did a honeymoon and that's why he didn't call me."

Attila quickly changed the subject. He wanted to know about Frank and Krisztina. He pressed the muscleman to tell him what he knew about their disappearance. At that point Doorbal's voice changed. It took on a sinister, even a menacing, pitch.

Said Weiland, "He just told me, 'Attila, you are supposed to be my friend.' The tone of his voice told me to back off."

On Wednesday morning, May 31, Ed Du Bois took a phone call from MDPD captain Al Harper, the veteran homicide detective he had turned to six weeks earlier for help with the Schiller kidnapping case. Harper told the private detective that the Homicide Bureau was buzzing with activity. They were investigating the mysterious disappearance of a wealthy Hungarian man and his fiancée. The two men last seen with the couple were two bodybuilders who worked at Sun Gym. Could these be the same guys who abducted Marc Schiller?

Du Bois needed to brief Sergeant Felix Jimenez on the Schiller case, Harper said. The two men met in Du Bois' Miami Shores office on Biscayne Boulevard. Jimenez listened intently as the private eye told him how the Sun Gym thugs snatched Schiller from the parking lot at his restaurant, tortured him, held him prisoner for a month, forced him to sign over all his assets, then tried to kill him in a fiery car wreck. Du Bois gave Jiminez names, and the sergeant phoned Detective Garafalo, who had been working nonstop since getting the case the day before. He told the detective whom to look for: Danny Lugo, Jorge Delgado, and Adrian Doorbal.

Garafalo put in a call to Marc Schiller in South America. He told the Sun Gym gang's first known victim about the young couple who had gone missing eight days ago, and he explained that lawmen believed that the thugs who abducted him were responsible. Could Schiller return to Miami?

Garafalo explained that investigators needed his sworn statement. With it cops would have sufficient probable cause for warrants that could lead them to the couple. Specifically, they wanted to search the residences and cars of Jorge Delgado, Daniel Lugo, and Adrian Doorbal. With Schiller's statement, they would also have probable cause to arrest Lugo and Delgado. Schiller agreed to return. He made a reservation for June 2. In the meantime, lawmen placed Lugo, Delgado, and Doorbal under surveillance. They hoped one of them would lead them to the missing couple.

The next day, Sal Garafalo drove to Golden Beach to interview Judi Bartusz and Eszter Toth. He met with them individually at the Griga house and showed them a photo lineup. Both women identified Danny Lugo and Adrian Doorbal as the men who left with Frank and Krisztina on Wednesday evening. Crime Scene Bureau personnel were at the house, too. A fingerprint expert lifted latent prints from the two drinking glasses on the coffee table. Garafalo also spoke with the Weilands, Beatriz and Attila. Beatriz told the detective about the photograph of Griga's Lamborghini that Doorbal had seen in her photo album. As for Attila, he told the detective all about the business meeting he set up for Lugo and Doorbal with Frank Griga, and about the conversations he had with Doorbal on Friday and Saturday concerning the missing couple.

When Garafalo left Golden Beach, he was certain that Danny Lugo and Adrian Doorbal were involved in the disappearance of Frank Griga and Krisztina Furton. While the lawman hoped he would find the couple alive, he knew that if Lugo, Doorbal, or Delgado didn't lead cops to the missing couple, police would have to hunt for them. To do that Garafalo needed warrants, and to get those he needed Marc Schiller.

CHAPTER FOURTEEN

A MOUNTAIN OF EVIDENCE

That afternoon Attila Weiland phoned Adrian Doorbal yet again. He had spoken to the police, he told the muscleman, and they were closing in. The cops, Weiland said, wanted to talk with him, too. He urged Doorbal to tell him what had happened to Frank and Krisztina. Doorbal hung up the phone without saying a word. In the evening, news of the couple's disappearance was broadcast on the six o'clock and the eleven o'clock news. They had not been seen since late Wednesday, news watchers were told.

"This is one of those cases where you get the sinking feeling in the pit of your stomach that somebody might still be alive, but we might not reach them in time," Chief of Detectives Farrell told reporters, adding, "We need help."

Cindy Eldridge noticed that her husband, who never before showed an interest in the news, had suddenly become a news junkie. Doorbal seemed especially interested in what newscasters had to say about the missing Hungarian millionaire and his girlfriend. Cindy confronted him about the fight with the wealthy businessman. Doorbal confessed that someone died, but he swore that he had nothing to do with it.

At midnight Doorbal left the townhouse, telling Cindy that he and Lugo had important business to attend to. Thirty minutes later, the bodybuilding duo turned up at Solid Gold where they sought out Beatriz Weiland, the beautiful stripper whose photo album sparked Doorbal's interest in Frank Griga.

Beatriz was frightened and intimidated as she stood between the two musclemen in Solid Gold's Champagne Room. Nevertheless, the blond stripper gathered her courage and looked Adrian in the eye. "What did you do with Frank and Krisztina?" she demanded.

Doorbal avoided the question. Instead, he wanted to know what she had told the police.

"I have to go," Beatriz said as she turned away. She made a beeline for the strippers' dressing rooms where she put in a call to Detective Sal Garafalo. She left the detective a message: Doorbal and Lugo were at Solid Gold. But the musclemen had no intention of sticking around. By the time Beatriz returned, Lugo and Doorbal were gone.

Back in Miami Lakes a very troubled Cindy Eldridge was wide-awake and thinking, finally putting two and two together. The missing couple disappeared on Wednesday night, and her husband said he needed an alibi for that night. There was blood on the carpet and on the walls, which she had painted over. At first, Doorbal told her there had been a fight, then he admitted that someone had died. When Cindy saw her husband again, she demanded that he tell her what had happened. Doorbal was silent for a moment. Then he drew a deep breath, sighed, and said, "Cindy, what you don't know won't hurt you."

As he promised, Marc Schiller arrived at Miami International Airport on Friday, June 2. Sal Garafalo was waiting for him when he landed at one o'clock. The two men shook hands and drove to the MDPD's headquarters just

Frank Griga and Krisztina Furton in happier times.
Florida State Archives

Marcelo "Marc" Schiller was the first victim of the gang.

Courtesy of Marcelo Schiller

Frank Griga's Lamborghini
Miami-Dade Police Department

Investigators from the Miami-Dade Police Department
recover the remains of Frank Griga and Krisztina Furton.
Miami-Dade Police Department

Morgue workers unload the remains of Griga and Furton.
Miami-Dade Police Department

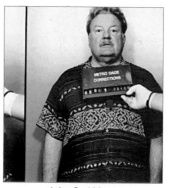

John Carl Mese
Florida Department of Corrections

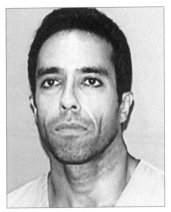

Danny Lugo
Florida Department of Corrections

FROM LEFT TO RIGHT: Stevenson Pierre and Carlton Weekes
Miami-Dade Department of Corrections

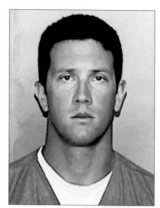

John Raimondo
Florida Department of Corrections

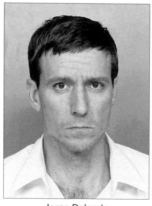

Jorge Delgado
*Miami-Dade Department
of Corrections*

Sabina Petrescu
*Miami-Dade Department
of Corrections*

Cynthia Eldridge
*Miami-Dade Department
of Corrections*

Noel Adrian Doorbal
*Florida Department
of Corrections*

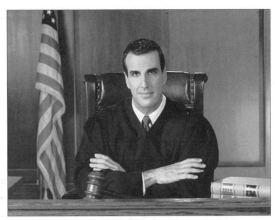

Judge Alex Ferrer
Courtesy of Judge Alex Ferrer

Danny Lugo and Noel Doorbal await their date with
the executioner on Florida's Death Row.
Florida Department of Corrections

west of the airport in nearby Doral. It had been six weeks since Schiller's last visit. Back then his story was deemed so bizarre, so far beyond belief, that the Strategic Investigations Division refused to investigate it. Instead, SID referred him to Robbery, where he was met again with disbelief and skepticism, and accusations of lying. This time, however, Marc Schiller told his story under oath to homicide detectives Felix Jimenez and Sal Garafalo, and to Assistant State Attorney Gail Levine.

Over the next two hours, while a stenographer recorded every word he said, Marc Schiller relived the painful and humiliating details of his abduction and imprisonment, and he explained how he knew that Lugo and Delgado were behind his ordeal. This time his story was believed. As soon as he was finished telling it, Garafalo drove Schiller back to Miami International Airport. Schiller didn't want to stick around. Tropical Storm Allison was heading towards Florida and Schiller didn't want to get stuck in Miami. At five o'clock he was in an airliner on the tarmac waiting to take off for Bogota.[5]

Based on his sworn statement, Levine and the detectives wrote an affidavit and drafted warrants. It was after midnight when Garafalo took them to Circuit Court Judge Alex Ferrer's house. The judge read the affidavit. It alleged that: Schiller had been kidnapped by three men and tortured into signing over all of his property; Schiller named Danny Lugo and Jorge Delgado as two of the individuals involved in the kidnapping; a person driving a car of the same make and model as the one driven by Adrian Doorbal had been seen at Schiller's home, from which Schiller's belongings had been taken while he was being held by the kidnappers; documents transferring Schiller's property had been notarized by Sun Gym owner John Carl Mese;

_____

[5]On June 4, Tropical Storm Allison became Hurricane Allison. It missed South Florida, making landfall in the state's Big Bend region south of Tallahassee.

Doorbal was employed as a trainer at Sun Gym; Doorbal associated with the individuals who had been identified as being involved in the Schiller kidnapping and had inexplicably come into a large sum of money with which he purchased a house for $150,000 in cash, and he matched the description of someone involved in the plundering of the Schiller home. The affidavits also contained facts concerning the disappearance of the Hungarian couple.

After reviewing the affidavit, Judge Ferrer signed arrest warrants for Jorge Delgado and Daniel Lugo for kidnapping Marcello Schiller, and search warrants for the homes, apartments, and cars of Delgado, Lugo, and Doorbal. Garafalo alerted the MDPD detectives who would serve the warrants, as well as SWAT teams, hostage negotiators, and CSI investigators. They were ordered to report to Miami Lakes Park on NW 67th Avenue at 7 A.M. sharp.

At the appointed hour, an army of lawmen in raid jackets and bulletproof vests assembled in the park. They were briefed by Jimenez and Garafalo and given their assignments. In order to maintain the element of surprise, the plan was to execute the warrants simultaneously at eight o'clock.

Armed with warrants, the lawmen fanned out. They went to Jorge and Linda Delgado's residence at 6193 NW 181st Terrace, Lucretia Goodridge's house at 7955 NW 188th Lane, Adrian Doorbal's townhouse at 6911 Main Street, and Sabina Petrescu's apartment at 6798 Main Street.

MDPD detective Mike Santos led the squad assigned to search the love nest Danny Lugo shared with Sabina. An eleven-year veteran of the MDPD's Homicide Bureau, Santos had been assigned to a joint local and federal homicide unit when he was called upon to lend a hand in the hunt for Frank Griga and Krisztina Furton. On the stroke of eight, Santos told MDPD detective Jerry Davenport to pound on the apartment door, but there was no response. He pounded on the door several more times, but again there was no response. Santos put in a call to the fire department.

"They have a special tool, a pry tool they use to gain entry," Santos explained.

The fire department responded quickly and within minutes the detectives were inside the one-bedroom apartment.

"We searched it to make sure there was nobody inside, and we secured the apartment to make sure it was empty," Santos said.

The cops did find a lonely cat, which was taken to the county animal shelter. The detectives combed through the apartment. They looked into every nook and cranny. Their search turned up a mountain of evidence linking Danny Lugo to the Griga-Furton disappearance: Frank's driver's license and bank documents that had been taken from his Golden Beach mailbox; items of clothing and jewelry that the missing couple wore when they left Golden Beach on Wednesday evening; Frank's crocodile boots and his Rolex watch; Krisztina's red leather jacket and red shoes; her tennis bracelet and sapphire ring.

And they found links to the Schiller kidnapping: The keys to Diana Schiller's BMW station wagon were on the kitchen table while the car was parked outside in its assigned space; a copy of a letter from La Gorce Palace to Gene Rosen with the notation "cc: Lillian Torres;" the plot survey of the Schiller home in Old Cutler Cove; a court order returning legal title of the Schiller home to the Schillers; Schiller's bank statements; a list of his overseas accounts; an angry letter from Schiller to Jorge Delgado; and several blistering faxes from Marc Schiller to John Mese. In one of them, Schiller wrote:

> Mese, how can you be so complacent about the mess you are in? I called you Friday, Monday, and Tuesday and you still have not contacted your attorney . . . If you chose to ignore it, it will only make it worse for you. You notarized my wife's signature on certain documents.

However, she was out of the country. I have her passport
with the seal on it to prove it . . .

You and your criminal pals have jacked me off for
two months promising to return what is not yours in
return for me signing an agreement. I kept my promise and signed the agreement . . . The authorities are
aware of the problem and are beginning to conduct
their investigation. If you sign the agreement, I will call
them off . . . You decide. Return what is not yours now
or face the music. Tick, tick, tick, time is running out.

The search also turned up a letter to Schiller's Swiss
banker that Marc Schiller signed while he was the Sun
Gym gang's captive. In it, Schiller requested a wire transfer of funds to his Miami bank. Other financial records
and statements linked to Marc Schiller were found, too—
bank and credit card statements and credit card purchase
receipts.

In the storage closet on the terrace, they turned up the
bloody computer monitor that had been in Doorbal's apartment Wednesday night, as well as the blood-soaked rug,
the bloody carpet padding, and a bloody pair of orange
gardener's gloves. In plastic bags they found a Taser, a vial
of the horse tranquilizer Rompun, twenty-eight syringes,
a dart gun, and rolls of duct tape. What they did not find,
however, was a clue that could lead them to the missing
couple.

Every item was photographed by a crime scene detective as it was found, then tagged, bagged, and impounded.

Across the street at Doorbal's townhouse, Cindy Eldridge
was up and about, sipping coffee when she heard pounding
on the door.

"When I knocked, I heard a female voice asking who
it was," recalled MDPD sergeant Luis Alvarez. "I identified myself as Sergeant Luis Alvarez with the Metro-Dade
Police Department."

When Eldridge opened the door, the sergeant asked if
Noel Adrian Doorbal lived there.

Cindy said he did and asked Alvarez what he wanted. He told her that he and the three detectives with him were there to search the residence.

"I had the search warrant in my hand and I asked if Doorbal was in," the detective said.

Cindy indicated that her husband was upstairs. She called out to him from the bottom of the stairway. Doorbal, bleary-eyed, bare-chested, and wearing nothing more than a pair of gym shorts, emerged from the bedroom. Alvarez read the warrant out loud. Before beginning the search, the lawman asked Doorbal if he would be willing to go to headquarters to answer some questions. The muscleman said he would. He dressed quickly and left with MDPD detectives Richard Hellman and Nicholas Fabregas.

"Just a few questions," he told Cindy as he was on his way out the door. He wouldn't be gone long, he assured her.

While at Doorbal's apartment, Sergeant Alvarez couldn't help but notice that there was no furniture in the first floor spare bedroom, and that the carpet was spotless and new. Later, after checking with the leasing office, investigators learned the carpet had been installed earlier in the week, after Doorbal reported that the carpet had been soiled by a cat. Alvarez phoned Garafalo and requested a new warrant so that he could impound the carpet.

As detectives continued searching Doorbal's townhouse, they turned up evidence linking the muscleman to the abduction of Marc Schiller: Schiller's business card, two letters from Ed Du Bois to Joel Greenberg demanding return of all property taken from Schiller, an airline boarding pass in Schiller's name, receipts for purchases on his American Express card, a receipt from the locksmith who replaced the locks on Schiller's Old Cutler Cove house, and dozens of pieces of mail addressed to the Schillers.

The cops also found documents linking the muscleman to Sun Gym owner John Carl Mese and to Danny Lugo, including corporate documents, phony passports from

Haiti and Ceylon, and identity cards with Lugo's photo attached but issued in other names, his U.S. passport, and documents regarding Lugo's federal probation.

And there was more: surveillance equipment, handcuffs, and photographs investigators would later learn were of Winston Lee's home, vials of the horse tranquilizer Rompun, and an orange dart embedded in the wall of the spare bedroom. They also found a copy of a lease for a warehouse on West 80th Street in Hialeah. It bore the signatures of Danny Lugo and Adrian Doorbal. More than two hundred items were photographed as found, tagged, bagged, and impounded.

Later, crime scene detectives sprayed the townhouse with Luminol in order to find latent (invisible) blood evidence. The chemical, which is extremely sensitive, reacts with hemoglobin in blood to produce a glowing substance that can then be photographed, creating a road map to unseen evidence. If the bloodstains are large enough, they can be collected on swabs and sent to the lab where they are checked for blood type using the ABO blood typing system. The Luminol revealed latent bloodstains and spatter in the spare bedroom where Frank Griga fought with Doorbal and in the bathroom. Swabs were taken and sent to the MDPD's lab for typing.

Meanwhile, at the home of Lugo's wife Lucretia, detectives found a Federal Express box addressed to Marc Schiller. Inside was a computer that had been shipped to Schiller while he was a captive of the Sun Gym gang. They also found Smith Barney statements addressed to Doorbal; ammunition clips for a semiautomatic firearm; bullets; a loaded .38 caliber revolver; documents related to Phoenix Trading Company, a Bahamas corporation whose officers were listed as Lugo and John Carl Mese; membership cards from the Dollhouses of America for Doorbal and Lugo; a debit slip showing the transfer of forty thousand dollars from Schiller to Doorbal; Schiller's bank statements; checks drawn from Schiller's account and paid to Mese; receipts from The Spy Shop for a pair of walkie-talkies; passport photos of

Lugo and Doorbal; and assorted pieces of jewelry. They also found Medicare-related documents—provider numbers for Vita Health Care and Palmetto Medical Supply. All the items were photographed as they were found. They were tagged, bagged, and impounded.

Jorge and Linda Delgado were at home when the long arm of the law arrived to arrest Jorge for the kidnapping, attempted murder, and extortion of Marc Schiller. As a detective read the warrant to him, Delgado laughed out loud. So did Linda. They couldn't believe that police believed Schiller's accusations. After all, Schiller had stolen from *him*. Nevertheless, detectives handcuffed Jorge, read him his Miranda rights, and led him away.

By 8:30 A.M., all the warrants had been served. Based on the information that was discovered during the searches, investigators were able to obtain additional warrants for two warehouses, Sun Gym, and John Carl Mese's home and offices. Jorge Delgado was under arrest and Adrian Doorbal was on his way to police headquarters in the company of two homicide detectives. Before days' end he would be charged too, with kidnapping, attempted murder and extortion. Cindy Eldridge was talking to detectives, too, as was Sun Gym owner and certified public accountant John Carl Mese.

He was downtown that morning at Miami's James L. Knight Center where the National Physique Committee's Florida Men's State Championship was being held. The contestants were already onstage, flexing their ample muscles at nine o'clock when MDPD detectives Gus Baez and John King showed up looking for Mese. They found him at the foot of the stage. They invited the bodybuilding impresario to headquarters for questioning. The lawmen assured him that he was not under arrest and he didn't have to go with them, but Mese left the auditorium with the cops anyway. While the bodybuilders at the Knight Center spent the morning displaying their biceps and triceps, Mese spent it in a tiny interview room at the Homicide Bureau answering questions. Most of his answers were lies, and Gus Baez knew it.

Did he know Daniel Lugo?

"Yes, yes I do, I know him," Mese replied. "He works out at the gym and has been working out at the gym for three years. I only know him from the gym and I know him as a casual acquaintance."

Did he know how Lugo earned his living?

"No."

Mese admitted knowing Adrian Doorbal, too, but only because he worked out at the gym. As for Delgado, Mese said he had done some tax work for him in 1993, and that Delgado had an office in the same Miami Lakes building as he did. As far as he knew, there was no connection between Lugo, Doorbal, and Delgado other than they were Sun Gym members.

When asked if he had ever notarized anything for Marcelo Schiller, Mese said he had, that he knew Schiller was an accountant who shared office space with Jorge Delgado. He had seen him around the building on several occasions.

Mese told the detective that in November, Schiller had walked into his office with a woman he introduced as his wife and asked him to notarize a quitclaim deed transferring title from their house to D & J International. A few days later, he said, Schiller appeared in his office again, this time with a different woman. He introduced her as Lillian Torres, his new girlfriend. Mese told the detective that he wanted to remove his wife as the beneficiary of his MetLife life insurance policies. He asked him to notarize the forms that would name Lillian instead.

As for Griga and Furton, Mese denied knowing either of them, which was true.

At noon, John Mese told the detectives that he had to get back to the Knight Center for the bodybuilding competition, but he would have time to meet with them later in the afternoon. Baez drove him back to the Knight Center. They agreed to meet at Mese's office in Miami Lakes at 4:30 P.M.

As for Adrian Doorbal, he said nothing as he was driven to the MDPD headquarters. Like Delgado and Mese, he was placed inside a windowless interview room. He was joined there by Hellman and Fabregas. It was Detective Fabregas who read Doorbal his rights, paragraph by paragraph, from the MDPD's Miranda Warning form. At the conclusion of each paragraph, Doorbal indicated that he understood by checking the "Yes" box and writing his initials.

During a break in the interview, Fabregas learned that lawmen found items addressed to Schiller in Doorbal's townhouse. He confronted the muscleman: "How you ever been to Marcelo Schiller's house or business?" he wanted to know.

Doorbal shook his head. "Never been there," he said.

"I don't believe you are telling me the truth," Detective Fabregas declared, adding that MDPD detectives searching his townhouse "found articles addressed to Schiller at the address that you say you have never been to."

Then the detective brought up the missing couple, telling Doorbal that investigators believed that he had something to do with their disappearance. "That's when he told me that he knew he was going to jail for the rest of his life," the lawman recalled. Doorbal said something else: "He didn't want to speak to me any longer." It was 1:30 P.M. Later that day, Noel Adrian Doorbal was placed under arrest for the kidnapping of Marc Schiller.

CHAPTER FIFTEEN

FINDING FRANK AND KRISZTINA

Within a little more than three hours, investigators had accumulated a mountain of evidence linking Danny Lugo, Adrian Doorbal, and Jorge Delgado to the Schiller kidnapping. They also found evidence that Lugo and Doorbal were involved in the Griga-Furton disappearance. They had pieces of the puzzle, but they were a long way from putting it all together, and they still had not located the missing couple or the Sun Gym mastermind, Danny Lugo.

He was in the Bahamas with Sabina—it was their second trip to the islands in less than a week—and his parents. They had flown there the day before and checked into the plush Atlantis resort on Paradise Island. Lugo planned to combine business with pleasure. He would file a fraudulent lawsuit against Griga in a Bahamian court that, he reasoned, he would win by default since Griga was dead and unable to defend the suit. In that way, Lugo thought, he could get his hands on the phone sex millionaire's assets in the Bahamas. The funds would then be channeled through a Bahamas corporation controlled by Lugo and Mese.

While there, Lugo also planned to have fun gambling at the resort's casino, but the jaunt to the Bahamas would turn out to be anything but fun.

On Saturday morning, Sabina was with Lugo when he put in a call to his bodybuilding buddy Adrian Doorbal. But it wasn't Adrian who answered the phone. It was Cindy, and she told Lugo that Doorbal was in police custody and that lawmen were combing through the townhouse.

The muscleman was stunned. He repeated to Sabina what Cindy had told him, then put in a call to Delgado. Jorge didn't answer either. Whoever it was that picked up the Delgado's ringing phone informed Lugo that Jorge had been arrested and taken away in handcuffs.

"I'm gonna give myself up," Sabina remembers Lugo telling her as soon as he hung up the phone. Sabina was confused. After all, Danny was with the CIA; wouldn't they help him?

No, they wouldn't, Lugo told her. "If you make just one mistake they just forget about you," he explained, adding that the spy agency "would pretend that they never knew me."

Lugo changed his mind about turning himself in. Instead, he went into hiding. He checked out of Atlantis and, with Sabina and his parents in tow, he moved to another hotel, the British Colonial Hilton, registering under Sabina's last name, Petrescu. He phoned Miami attorney Michael Haber who flew to the Bahamas to meet with him. They huddled in private behind closed doors. Sabina remembers what happened when her muscle-bound secret agent man emerged from the meeting: "He was crying."

Sabina had never seen him so distraught. Lugo wrote out a check for five thousand dollars and sent her to a bank to cash it, but the manager wouldn't hand over the cash without first verifying the transaction with Lugo. Sabina gave the manager the name of the hotel they were staying at and the phone number. The banker called, verified the transaction, and cashed the check, but Lugo was on edge, concerned that his whereabouts could be easily traced. The next morning they moved to the Montague Beach Inn.

Lugo was very worried. He talked about fleeing with Sabina to Romania. He told her that he didn't care if he never saw his family again; he just wanted to get away. But he had a problem: He didn't have a passport. All that Americans needed to travel between the United States and the Bahamas was proof of citizenship, and Lugo had brought his U.S. birth certificate. To go almost anywhere else, he needed a passport.

At Lugo's direction, Sabina flew to Miami the next day with instructions to get rid of the contents of the storage closet. It was late in the afternoon when Sabina took a cab from the airport to her Miami Lakes apartment, but she couldn't unlock the door. The cops had changed the lock. When Sabina went to the leasing office to complain, the agent there asked her to wait and walked to a back office. Within minutes, a marked MDPD cruiser pulled into the parking lot. A few minutes later, an unmarked MDPD car arrived, too. It was driven by homicide detective Archie Moore. He took Sabina into custody and drove her to the Homicide Bureau where she was read her rights and questioned by detectives. They wanted to know where Danny Lugo was hiding out. For twenty hours Sabina, believing that she was protecting her troubled lover, insisted that she didn't know. Then she broke. A detective drove her home.

Even before Sabina revealed Danny Lugo's location, the MDPD was hunting for him in the Bahamas. Detective Bobby Fernandez from the MDPD's Warrants Bureau was on the ground in Nassau on June 7. With the help of the Bahamian police, he tracked Lugo to the Atlantis resort. Then he learned that Lugo was at the Montague. Bahamian police were notified and brought the muscleman to their headquarters on Friday, June 8. Detective Fernandez took him into custody. The muscleman agreed to return to Miami voluntarily. Fernandez booked two seats on the next flight and escorted his shackled prisoner back to Miami. As their plane slowed to a stop at Miami International,

Lugo looked out the window. He noticed several MDPD cars, their police lights flashing, on the tarmac.

"Is that all for me?" he wanted to know.

"Yes," Fernandez said. "I explained to you that you're in a little bit of trouble."

The lawman led Lugo from the plane and turned him over to Sal Garafalo who was waiting for him on the tarmac. Lugo refused to talk to the cops. He was booked into the county's Pre-trial Detention Center on charges of kidnapping, attempted murder, and extortion.

Whatever hopes detectives had of finding Frank Griga and Krisztina Furton disappeared earlier in the day, when investigators made some chilling discoveries in the Hialeah warehouse on West 80th Street that had been rented by Lugo and Doorbal—an empty box that once held a Remington chain saw, and a woman's fingernail. They also found a user's manual for a McCullough gas-powered chain saw, a pair of handcuffs, hair on the floor, an empty fifty-five gallon barrel, duct tape, several knives, pliers, rope, a mask respirator, welder's goggles, solder, Windex, several pairs of gloves, several pails of Ready Road Asphalt, Frank Griga's AAA card, and a receipt from Allied Marine in Fort Lauderdale made out to Frank Griga.

They also used Luminol to look for latent (invisible) blood evidence, which was found in the bathroom. The stains were swabbed and sent to the lab for blood typing.

News of the fingernail find made the headlines in Miami the next morning. Later that night, Felix Jimenez was at his desk in the Homicide Bureau when his phone rang. Jeff Geller, a former MDPD homicide detective turned private investigator, was on the line. He was working for Jay White, one of three Miami attorneys Lugo had hired to represent him. Geller wanted to know if Jimenez would meet him and Lugo's lawyers on the steps of the Pre-trial Detention Center where Lugo was being held. The muscleman, he said, was willing to lead investigators to the bodies.

Sergeant Jimenez alerted Assistant State Attorney Gail Levine and drove to the jail with two other MDPD detectives for the rendezvous. Geller was already there. So were Lugo's three attorneys and Gail Levine.

Standing on the jailhouse steps, they discussed Lugo's offer. He would lead detectives to the bodies if the death penalty was taken off the table. Levine said no. Nevertheless an agreement was reached: Lugo would take detectives to the location of the bodies if police agreed to tell jurors of his post-arrest cooperation and helpfulness. An agreement was drafted and signed by Lugo, his attorneys, the State Attorney's office and the MDPD. At 1:00 A.M., Jimenez signed Lugo out of the jail.

"I placed him in my car," Sergeant Jimenez recalled. "His attorneys . . . wanted to accompany him in the vehicle, but for security reasons, I had two other detectives with me and I didn't have space in my car."

They returned to MDPD headquarters in Doral where the two lawmen with Jimenez picked up another car while another detective, two attorneys, and a shackled Danny Lugo took seats in Sergeant Jimenez's car. Jimenez had no idea where they were going. Under the terms of the agreement he could not ask Danny Lugo any questions; he could only follow his directions.

Lugo directed Jimenez to drive south along Florida's Turnpike toward Homestead. He instructed Jimenez to exit the highway at Allapattah Road/SW 112th Avenue. From there the muscleman directed Jimenez to a dirt road off SW 240th Street that ran parallel to a drainage ditch.

They drove several hundred feet until Lugo told the detective to stop. The cops, the attorneys, and Danny Lugo got out of the cars. The muscleman pointed to a pair of round black objects that were poking out of the murky water. The cops shined their flashlights on them and immediately saw two barrels. Lugo said that there was a third barrel nearby.

The lawman walked about fifty feet west, swatting hungry mosquitoes every step of the way, until he spotted the

third barrel. Jimenez immediately called for MDPD units
to secure the scene and guard it through the night. He also
arranged for an MDPD aerial unit to photograph the area
at first light, and he arranged for the barrels to be removed
from the murky water in the morning. He alerted the Medical Examiner's office to expect their arrival and prepare for
a double autopsy.

CHAPTER SIXTEEN

BODIES IN BARRELS

There is no glamour in being a homicide detective. Sergeant Felix Jimenez and his team had been working virtually around the clock since May 30. The hours are long and irregular. The pay is barely enough to live on and the job takes a terrible toll on family life. The reward comes when all the pieces of the puzzle come together and a killer is caught and convicted, and no piece of the puzzle is more important than the autopsy. It can establish cause and manner of death. It can also establish the identity of the deceased through facial identification if the body is in decent shape, if there are dental records, or if there are fingerprints.

The Miami-Dade County Medical Examiner's office is housed in the Joseph H. Davis Center for Forensic Pathology, a sprawling three-building facility that occupies 89,000 square feet. It's adjacent to the University of Miami/Jackson Memorial Medical Center. The state-of-the-art facility opened in 1988 at a cost to county taxpayers of more than ten million dollars.

The morgue itself takes up more than 23,000 square feet on a ground floor. There is a main morgue with twelve autopsy rooms and a separate "decomp" morgue with two autopsy rooms that handles decomposed bodies or bodies known to have infectious diseases.

Bodies brought to the morgue are stored in massive refrigerated rooms called "coolers." The main morgue has four; each has a capacity of 120 bodies, while the decomp morgue has a cooler capable of handling seventy-five bodies.

In all, the Miami-Dade County Medical Examiner's morgue can store 555 bodies, a number that the building's designers deliberately chose. They based it on the combined passenger and crew capacity of a 747 jumbo jet.

It's a very busy facility. Each forensic pathologist conducts more than two hundred postmortem procedures each year, while the examiner's office handles more than three thousand annually.

Autopsies, or postmortems, are smelly, dirty, and gruesome. They are performed by forensic pathologists—medical doctors whose specialty is pathology and whose subspecialty is medicine as it relates to the law, most often criminal law.

There is a standard protocol for autopsies. After arriving at the morgue, a body is removed from its container, usually a body bag, and placed on a stainless steel autopsy table. The container isn't discarded. Instead it's sent to the crime lab where criminalists will examine it for trace evidence—for example, fibers, dirt, hair, or paint chips that may have been transferred to it from the body.

The first phase in the actual postmortem procedure is the external examination. The pathologist will examine the corpse while it is still clothed—damaged clothing should correspond with wounds to the body. After carefully removing the clothing, the pathologist sends the garments to the laboratory for processing. After that the corpse's height and weight are recorded.

Next, the pathologist will perform a careful external

examination. X-rays may be taken in order to find broken bones or unseen evidence like bullet fragments. The pathologist will also search for additional trace evidence that may have become embedded in the body. If found, it will also be collected and sent to the lab for processing.

If there are indications that there had been a struggle, a homicide victim's fingernails will be clipped and processed because the assailant's hair, blood, or tissue may have gotten under them. If a sexual assault is suspected, the pathologist will comb the corpse's pubic hair, looking for hairs from the attacker that may have become entangled with the victim's. In addition, the pathologist will check for semen by obtaining anal and vaginal swabs.

Next, the pathologist will painstakingly examine each wound and injury, measuring them one by one for length and depth. Their locations will be precisely marked on an anatomical diagram. In addition, each will be photographed. If weapons have been found that investigators believe are connected to the corpse, they will be compared to the wounds and injuries on the body.

The second phase of the postmortem, the internal examination, is not for the squeamish or weak-kneed. It involves dissecting the corpse. The pathologist makes a Y-shaped incision on the front of the body from the shoulders in a downward direction towards the breastbone, then a straight incision down towards the pubis. Using a saw, the pathologist will cut the ribs and collarbone in order to remove the breastplate exposing the heart and lungs. They will be removed and weighed and sent to the toxicology lab for testing.

Next, the pathologist will examine the abdomen, weighing each organ and taking tissue samples for microscopic examination. The contents of the stomach will be examined along with other body fluids including urine, bile, and liver samples, all of which may be sent for toxicological testing.

The pathologist will look for brain injuries, too, by opening the skull with an incision from behind one ear, crossing over the top of the head to a point behind the other ear. Using a saw, the pathologist then removes a section of skull to expose the brain, which will be removed and weighed, and from which tissue samples will be taken.

Finally, each removed organ is returned to the body and the incisions are sutured. Once all the results are in from the toxicology lab, the medical examiner will write and file an official autopsy report.

That's the usual procedure, but the Griga/Furton autopsies were anything but usual. For one thing, corpses don't usually come into the Medical Examiner's Office in sealed barrels, but the office had been alerted and Dr. Roger Mittleman, the associate medical examiner who would perform the postmortem, had set aside an area able to receive them and remove their contents.

On the morning of June 10, Felix Jimenez was there when the barrels arrived. So, too, was Dr. Mittleman. They both watched as morgue workers unsealed the barrels and extracted their contents. Dr. Mittleman documented what he saw with his camera, as did an MDPD crime scene detective. And what they saw was unusual, too: Bodies without hands or feet, an obvious attempt to stymie identification. Jimenez was furious. It was not what he had bargained for when he met with the muscleman's attorneys on the jailhouse steps. He had expected bodies, not body parts. Jimenez put in a call to Assistant State Attorney Gail Levine. She put in a call to Lugo attorney Jay White.

"I called Mr. White and told him, 'You have no agreement on cooperation because the cooperation I contemplated was full bodies, not parts of bodies,'" the prosecutor recalled.

In his initial report, Dr. Mittleman wrote:

Three fifty-five gallon metal drums were found in an irrigation ditch at SW 112th Avenue & 240 Street (drainage ditch). There was a confession that the murders of a couple had occurred and their bodies would be found within the drums.

OBSERVATION OF SURROUNDINGS & VICTIMS:

The bodies were delivered in 55-gallon drums to the Dade County Medical Examiner's office. Three drums were delivered, two of which are sealed and one of which is open. The open drum (drum C) contains dark liquid, concrete rocks and small fragments of apparent dark stained gauze and tape.

Barrel "A" (95-1564) contains dark fluid, tar granules, and the torso of a man who has had the head, hands, and feet amputated. There is no blood extravasation at the sites of amputation. The amputation site of the head is facing upward when the interior of the barrel is examined. In addition, a few small fragments of metallic silver colored apparent solder are formed in the drum.

Barrel "B" (95-1563) has dark fluid, tar granules, and the torso of a white woman. The torso is upside-down with the legs upward at the time of this examination. No other body parts are found in the barrel labeled "B" except the torso, which has had the head, hands, and feet amputated. No blood extravasation is noted at the amputation sites.

Both bodies are in moderate stages of decomposition with mild bloating, softening of the skin, and foul odor. Neither of the bodies has any sign of rigor mortis. Rigor mortis is not observable. The bodies are of cool temperature.

The bodies are not clothed except for a pair of jockey brief style underwear (size 36-38) on the man in barrel "A".

SCENE IMPRESSION: (INCLUDING PROBABLE CAUSE AND MANNER OF DEATH):

Double homicide.

NOTE: The foregoing is of a speculative nature and subject to modification pending additional information and investigation.

Without a face, fingers, or teeth, there was no way to establish a positive identification at that time for the corpse from barrel "A." In his report of July 15, Dr. Mittleman detailed his findings.

EXTERNAL EXMINATION

The body is that of a moderately decomposed white male weighing eighty pounds and measuring five feet, nine inches. The latter measurements are obtained without the head, hands, and feet, which have been amputated at the neck, wrists, and ankles. The decompositional change is manifested by bloating and skin discoloration. The external genitalia are unremarkable. The anus is without trauma. There are a few strands of dark curly pubic hair and longer dark curly strands of anal hair. No tattoos are detected on the torso. A small, 0.5 x 0.1 x 0.2 centimeter, flat black skin blemish is on the lower left back.

At the amputation site of the head there is black grease extending into the cervical vertebral column and also in the adjacent soft tissue. Black grease is also noted on the left shoulder with a small defect of the skin. The amputation sites are characterized by sharp to irregular proximal sites of bony amputation with some fraying of the bordering bone. The neck amputation site is through the vertebral body and lamina of C6. The bone is sharply cut and is embedded with black grease. The left leg is severed 16 inches below the knee with a sharply cut tibia and fibula with slight fragmentation of the cut end of the fibula. The bone is focally blackened. The right leg is severed 14 inches below the knee with sharply cut tibia and fibula with bony fragmentation. The tibia is focally blackened. The left forearm is severed 10-3/4 inches below the elbow with sharply cut radius and ulna and focally blackened bone. The right forearm is severed 10-3/4 inches below the elbow with jagged and fragmented ends of radius and ulna and blackened soft tissue.

On the right side of the abdomen there are two small linear, parallel, horizontally situated foci of skin separation and in addition two obliquely situated parallel linear foci of skin separation measuring 3 centimeters and 4 centimeters and located below the smaller foci. Similar foci are arranged parallel to one another and horizontally situated along the anterior aspect of the lower portion of the left leg just above the amputation site. The latter skin separations measure 1 centimeter to 3.5 centimeters in length.

Except for postmortem decomposition, the internal examination revealed a normal heart, lungs, kidneys, stomach, gall bladder, and liver. X-rays revealed no bullets or other projectiles. Tissue samples were sent to the toxicology lab where analysts found traces of Xylazine, the generic name for Rompun, in the brain, liver, and kidneys.

Dr. Mittleman also detailed his findings for the corpse from barrel "B."

The body consists of a moderately decomposed white female weighing 45 pounds and measuring five feet, five inches. The head is disarticulated in the mid neck, as are the hands and feet below the wrists and ankles, respectively. All of the margins of the excision are bloodless. The body is in a moderate state of decomposition characterized by mild bloating and discoloration of the skin.

The associate medical examiner observed no trauma to either the anal or vaginal area.

He measured the amputations, noting that "the amputation site for the right leg is 13-1/3 inches below the knee . . . The left leg is amputated 12-1/2 inches below the knee . . . The right arm is amputated 8-1/2 inches below the elbow . . . The left arm is amputated 8-1/2 inches below the elbow." He noted scars that indicated breast implants.

The internal examination revealed a normal heart, lungs,

kidneys, stomach, gall bladder, and liver. Tissue samples
were sent to the toxicology lab where analysts found significant amounts of Xylazine in Krisztina's liver, kidney,
and brain, more than enough to kill several one thousand
pound horses.

Dr. Mittleman removed the breast implants, each of
which bore the name of the manufacturer and a serial
number. Investigators went to work trying to track down
the physician who had done the breast implant surgery. It
wouldn't be long before they located the doctor, a local
plastic surgeon. The doctor's records matched the serial
numbers to Krisztina Furton's breast implants, but the
breast implant serial numbers were not enough to positively establish the identity of the female corpse.

What's more, they had no forensic evidence establishing
the identity of the male corpse. They assumed it was Frank
Griga, but assumptions are not good enough, so on June
21, Felix Jimenez flew from Miami to Budapest, Hungary,
to collect DNA samples from relatives of Frank Griga and
Krisztina Furton. Through DNA matching, investigators
hoped to establish the identities of the bodies in the barrel.
Americans had become familiar with DNA through the
O. J. Simpson murder trial. They learned that DNA analysis could prove whodunit. In this case, DNA would be used
to prove who it was.

Working with a forensic physician in Hungary, Jimenez
was able to obtain blood samples and mouth swabs from
Frank's mother and Krisztina's parents and sister. Similar samples were taken from Frank's sister who arrived in
Miami the second week of June. When Jimenez returned to
the United States, the samples were sent to a DNA laboratory for analysis.

Swiss scientist Friedrich Miescher discovered deoxy-
ribonucleic acid (DNA) in 1869. It wasn't until 1985 that
two British scientists found that each individual's DNA
is unique, a combination of DNA donated by each par-
ent, which is why it can be used to establish paternity or

maternity, and it can also be used to establish a genetic link between siblings. DNA analysis would positively establish the identity of the bodies in the barrels as Frank Griga and Krisztina Furton.

Before the DNA analysis came back from the lab, the MDPD announced that the mutilated heads of a man and woman had been found in buckets in the Everglades. An anonymous tip phoned into the Homicide Bureau on July 7 sent detectives scurrying north into Broward County, to mile marker 30 on Alligator Alley, a section of I-75. The roadway, which crosses the Everglades, connects Miami and Fort Lauderdale with the Gulf Coast cities of Naples and Fort Meyers. The tipster told detectives they would find the buckets, and that they had been dumped there by Adrian Doorbal. On July 8, after several hours of searching, lawmen located four buckets, two of which contained human skulls.

"Both heads were partially skeletonized and mutilated, with the teeth having been forcibly removed from the heads," Jimenez said. A corrosive chemical had eaten away at much of the skulls. He added that the hands had yet to be found.

Although the musclemen attempted to pull all of the teeth from the heads to prevent police from positively matching them to Griga and Furton, one tooth, a molar, remained in one of the heads. Using dental records and X-rays, a forensic dentist would eventually match the tooth to Griga.

The gruesome find was brought to the Medical Examiner's office on July 8, but the MDPD withheld the information from the public. In a memo, Dr. Mittleman wrote:

Four buckets are numbered by police and submitted for examination. The heavy plastic containers have a 3-1/2 gallon capacity buckets with the brand name "Ready Road Repair." The buckets that are of concern at this time are buckets 1, 3, and 4. The other bucket contains

a knife, hatchet, and red/white mechanics rags. The lid
has been removed from the latter bucket as well as a
black plastic garbage bag, which encased the bucket.
The contents of the bucket will be processed by the
police Crime Laboratory.

Bucket 1: The encasing black plastic garbage type
bag has been removed, however, the lid is still on the
bucket. The lid is removed revealing a black plastic bag
with a small human skull.

Bucket 3: The lid for this 3-1/2 gallon bucket is still
on the top of the bucket. The encasing black plastic garbage type bag had been removed prior to my examination. It is present at the side of the bucket at the time
of this examination. When the lid is removed, another
black plastic garbage type bag is found with portions of
human extremities.

Bucket 4: This bucket is sealed within an encasing
black plastic garbage bag, which is then opened and the
lid is found on the bag itself. The lid is removed and
there is another black plastic bag with a large human
skull.

Buckets 1, 3, and 4 each have black tar granules
at the bottom of the bucket and foul smelling fluid. In
the garbage bags containing the skulls, dark hair is
found in buckets 1 and 4. Dark hair is also found in
the soft tissue surrounding the bones in bucket 3 and
along the external surfaces of both skulls (buckets 1
and 4).

Associated with the plastic bags which encase the
buckets, an 18 x 15 x 4 centimeter aggregate of dark
to white irregular soft to fine fragments of material is
radiographed. Two fragments of bone are identified and
a gold colored earring fastener.

In his final report, Dr. Mittleman ruled both deaths had
been homicides, but "by unspecified means."

*   *   *

On July 17, police arrested Carl Weekes and charged him with attempted murder, kidnapping, and extortion in the Schiller abduction. Two days later, cops arrested Sabina Petrescu. Lawmen had found Diana Schiller's BMW in her parking spot outside her Miami Lakes apartment. They also found the car's keys on the Romanian beauty queen's table. She was charged with possession of a stolen automobile and possession of a motor vehicle with an altered vehicle identification number.

Investigators had five members of the Sun Gym gang—Lugo, Doorbal, Delgado, Weekes, and Petrescu—behind bars, all on charges related to the Schiller kidnapping, but lawmen were not done with the Sun Gym gang. The following month they arrested John Carl Mese, the man they considered the gang's CFO.

"Mese was directly involved in preparing the documents that were used to take money and property from Schiller," said Felix Jimenez. "If he was not involved in the plot itself as a planner, he was involved during and after."

The bodybuilding impresario tried to talk his way out of the jam he found himself in, but every time he opened his mouth he put his foot into it.

As he promised, Mese met with Baez and Detective John King on the afternoon of June 3, during a break in the bodybuilding competition at the Knight Center. Despite official corporate documents and bank records linking him to Lugo and Doorbal, Mese repeatedly denied that he had anything more than a casual relationship with the two musclemen. On June 6, Baez and Jimenez made an unannounced visit to John Mese's Miami Lakes office. As they drove into the parking lot, the detectives spotted the accountant as he was about to get into his car.

"We explained that we still had some issues that we needed to ask him about," Baez said. The detectives invited Mese to follow them to the Homicide Bureau. Mese agreed. Ten minutes later John Mese found himself in a tiny interview room answering detectives' questions again.

As soon as Mese sat down, Jimenez read him the

Miranda warning. The warning, a staple of every TV police drama since the late 1960s, was named for Ernesto Miranda, an Arizona man who confessed to kidnapping and raping an eighteen-year-old woman after intense questioning by detectives. It's been a requirement of police procedure since 1966, when a landmark U.S. Supreme Court decision overturned Miranda's conviction because he had not been advised of his rights under the U.S. Constitution.

"We had a suspicion that he was involved in this case, and I felt that he might say something incriminating [and] that I might be able to arrest him, and I felt safe to advise him of his rights at the beginning of the interview," Jimenez explained

Said Detective Baez: "We knew that at some point during the interview we would be asking him incriminating questions, like were you involved in the abduction of Marcelo Schiller, did you normally cash checks or deposit checks into your account, were you involved in the abduction of Krisztina Furton and Frank Griga?"

At 9:45 A.M., John Mese signed the Miranda form, indicating that he had been informed of his constitutional rights. The detectives asked the accountant about a November check for eighteen thousand dollars drawn from one of Marc Schiller's bank accounts made payable to the Mese and Associates escrow account. Mese explained that it represented his fee for notarizing the quitclaim deed. The detectives were skeptical. The lawmen knew that notaries customarily charge five to ten dollars for their services.

It wasn't long before Mese terminated the interview, telling the lawmen that he had an appointment with the IRS. Even though the detectives had evidence that Mese set up offshore corporations for Lugo and laundered money for the Sun Gym thugs, neither Jimenez nor Baez believed they had sufficient probable cause for an arrest at that time, so John Mese was not taken into custody. But the Sun Gym founder and owner's freedom was short-lived. On August

10, 1995, John Carl Mese, certified public accountant, bodybuilding entrepreneur, Kiwanis Club member, pillar of the community, was arrested at his Miami Lakes office on attempted murder, kidnapping, and money laundering charges in connection with the Schiller kidnapping. In the fall, investigators charged Stevenson Pierre and Mario Sanchez for their roles in the Schiller abduction, too.

In September 1995, Mese's attorney David Dermer filed a speedy trial demand. While Lugo, Delgado, and Doorbal cooled their heels in the county jail, Mese's trial was to begin on November 14. Jury selection was to get underway that morning, but when Dermer appeared in court he asked for a postponement. Just five days before, the attorney declared that he was ready for trial, but in the interim the State filed new forgery and extortion charges against his client, and Dermer said he needed additional time to investigate and prepare. Circuit Court Judge Amy Dean granted the delay, prompting angry retorts from the prosecutor and lawmen.

"We spent all weekend preparing," Sergeant Felix Jimenez told the *Miami Herald*. He said that ten detectives worked through the weekend, costing county taxpayers more than twenty-five hundred dollars in overtime.

Gail Levine was angry, too. Marc Schiller had flown in at taxpayer expense from South America the day before, prompting the assistant state attorney to fume, "The worst part is that Mr. Schiller was not only the victim here, but his life has to be put into turmoil again by the delay."

As for John Mese, he was in serious trouble, but he had supporters who tried to help him. They sent out letters to his clients asking them to donate to his legal defense fund. The letter read: "Unfortunately, he has been the innocent victim of a tragic set of circumstances that he had no knowledge of, nor control over. As the facts of this case come to light, he feels confident that his innocence will be revealed. However, escalating legal expenses may prevent his ability to prove his innocence because he has exhausted

his savings and resources as a result of the protracted
period that this case has gone on."

One of the signatories was Janice Mese, John's ex-wife.
Neither Mese nor his supporters could know it at the time,
but his legal woes would soon take an even more woeful
turn.

CHAPTER SEVENTEEN

THE SUN GYM GANG
MEETS RICO

On March 27, 1996, nine months after Danny Lugo directed detectives to the murky ditch where he and Doorbal dumped the dismembered bodies of Frank Griga and Krisztina Furton, a grand jury returned a thirty-nine-count indictment against Danny Lugo, Adrian Doorbal, and John Carl Mese. An indictment is nothing more than an allegation. It details the charges against a defendant, but prosecutors can use it as a weapon to intimidate and frighten defendants into cutting deals and pleading to lesser charges. Five others—Mario Sanchez, Dan Pace, Cindy Eldridge, Mario Gray, and John Raimondo were also named in the indictment.

Even before the grand jury indicted him, county correction officer John Raimondo was in a heap of trouble. He had been suspended from his job at the county's detention center in January after his wife of four months, an MDPD cop, alleged that he had grabbed her by the throat, slapped her, kicked her, head-butted her, and threw her to the floor. Among the prisoners Raimondo guarded at the jail before his suspension were his Sun Gym pals Doorbal and Delgado.

In the Schiller case, Lugo and Doorbal were charged with attempted first-degree murder; armed kidnapping; armed robbery; burglary of a dwelling; grand theft (two counts); possession of a removed identification plate; first-degree arson; armed extortion; money laundering (nine counts); forgery (six counts); and uttering a forged instrument (six counts); and the following crimes related to Frank Griga and Krisztina Furton: conspiracy to commit racketeering; racketeering; first-degree murder (two counts); kidnapping (two counts); attempted extortion; grand theft; and conspiracy to commit a first-degree felony. The State of Florida, Gail Levine announced, would seek the death penalty against the two musclemen.

As for John Mese, the grand jury indicted him on two counts of first-degree murder—one for Griga and one for Furton; two counts of kidnapping, one for Griga and one for Furton; one count of attempted extortion of either Griga or Furton; attempted first-degree murder of Marcelo Schiller; kidnapping of Schiller; armed robbery of Schiller; extortion of Schiller; nine counts of money laundering; one count each of forging, falsely notarizing, and uttering a Schiller quitclaim deed; one count each of forging, falsely notarizing, and uttering a Schiller change of beneficiary form; twelve counts of forging, falsely notarizing, and uttering four identical sets of a Schiller assignment of contract; and conspiracy to kidnap Winston Lee. Prosecutors announced they would not seek the death penalty for Mese. Six months later, two new counts were added to the Lugo-Doorbal-Mese indictment: Conspiracy to commit racketeering and racketeering.

Prosecutor Gail Levine and her colleagues at the State Attorney's Office viewed the Sun Gym thugs as a band of gangsters involved in an ongoing criminal enterprise and racketeering. Their diabolical business plan: Kidnap wealthy individuals, force them to sign over all their assets, then kill them, which is why the three musclemen were charged with violating the State's RICO (Racketeer Influenced and Corrupt Organizations) laws, too.

Their crimes were "despicable and vicious crimes of organized murder and torture that were driven solely by greed . . . all planned, organized, deadly, and mean," declared Levine's boss, State Attorney Katherine Fernandez Rundle, when the indictments were announced.

"The defendants did the same thing to Schiller as they did to the couple—except he lived," Rundle explained. "We will use [RICO] to show a pattern of violence conducted by the defendants, who collectively had become a criminal enterprise that targeted unsuspecting wealthy victims."

The Sun Gym ringleaders would be prosecuted under a law that had been written twenty-five years earlier to bring down the Mafia. Written by Notre Dame Law School professor G. Robert Blakey, the United States Congress passed RICO as part of the Organized Crime Control Act of 1970. While it was originally aimed at the Mafia, Congress could not legislate against specific persons, families, or entities, so it was written in very broad language, making it illegal to take part in organized crime. If prosecutors could show that a person was part of an ongoing conspiracy and could prove two crimes from a list of typical Mafia crimes like murder, drug trafficking, extortion, gambling, and loan sharking, then they could win a conviction based on the RICO act.

As a result of the federal RICO Act, mobsters like Gambino crime family underboss Salvatore "Sammy the Bull" Gravano, John Gotti's right-hand man, turned against their bosses in exchange for reduced charges and lighter sentences. Florida was one of the states that followed the feds with its own RICO laws. Under Florida and federal law, the elements of a RICO crime are participation in a

criminal enterprise that engages in a pattern of racketeering activity.[6]

To make racketeering charges stick in the Sun Gym
case, prosecutors would have to prove that the gang was
an ongoing organization whose members were involved
in illicit activities. The organization does not have to be
a formal, legal entity. It can be "any individual, sole pro-
prietorship, partnership, corporation, business trust, union
chartered under the laws of this state, or other legal entity,
or any unchartered union, association, or group of individuals associated in fact although not a legal entity."

Under RICO, the members of a criminal enterprise had
to have been involved in "predicate" acts. As far as Miami
lawmen were concerned, the abduction and extortion of
Marc Schiller, the planned abduction and attempted extortion of Frank Griga and Krisztina Furton, and the events
surrounding the planned but never executed abduction
and extortion of Winston Lee were sufficient to meet that
requirement. What's more, individual gang members do
not need to have been involved in every aspect of an enterprise's crimes to be guilty of racketeering. Accordingly,
Stevenson Pierre, who participated in the Schiller abduction but had no role in the Griga/Furton murders, could
have faced RICO charges, as could Carl Weekes and Jorge
Delgado.

Faced with RICO, the three men agreed to do what
Sammy the Bull and other mobsters had done: They turned
against their ringleaders, agreeing to tell all and testify
against Danny Lugo, Adrian Doorbal, and John Mese.

Charged with auto theft, Sabina Petrescu, convinced at

---

[6]Florida law defines a pattern of racketeering activity as "engaging in at
least two incidents of racketeering conduct that have the same or similar
intents, results, accomplices, victims, or methods of commission or that
otherwise are interrelated by distinguishing characteristics and are not
isolated incidents, provided at least one of such incidents occurred after
the effective date of this act and that the last of such incidents occurred
within five years after a prior incident of racketeering conduct."

last that her lover was no government agent, agreed to tell all to investigators, too. She knew a lot about the Griga/Furton murders, but no one was more important to the State's case against the musclemen than Jorge Delgado. He was privy to the gang's plans and schemes. He was involved in the Schiller kidnapping and extortion, *and* the Griga/Furton murders after the fact. The tale that he could tell put Jorge Delgado in the spotlight. He was the State's star witness.

But he wasn't the first to crack. Carl Weekes was. On November 2, 1995, four months before Lugo, Doorbal, and Mese and the others were indicted, Weekes and his lawyers were in a fourth-floor courtroom in the Metropolitan Justice Center. Assistant State Attorneys Gail Levine and David Weinstein were there, too, to hear Weekes plead guilty to the kidnapping of Marcelo Schiller.

"All rise," intoned the bailiff, and Circuit Court Judge Alex Ferrer emerged from his chambers and took the bench.

Alejandro Enrique Ferrer was an infant when he arrived in the United States with his parents in 1961. His father, a business executive in Havana, didn't want to live under the Castro regime, so the family left Cuba and settled in Miami. By all accounts, Alex Ferrer was driven to work hard and excel in school. He pumped gas as a teen, became a licensed pilot at age eighteen, and a cop at age nineteen. It was while wearing a badge that he worked his way through college and law school. After graduating from the University of Miami School of Law where he made the Law Review, Ferrer practiced in Miami until 1994, when he was appointed to the bench at age thirty-four.

With movie star looks and a gregarious personality, Judge Ferrer was known around the courthouse as a fair-minded, no-nonsense judge with the patience of Job, a characteristic he would need for this difficult and gruesome case. The only complaint courthouse regulars ever

voiced about Ferrer was the chill in his courtroom; Judge
Ferrer was known to turn the thermostat in his courtroom
to sixty degrees.

"I have a high body temperature," he once explained.
"Combine that with the [polyester] robe and the french fry
lights above my head, and it gets very hot."

His hot body, however, did not affect his temper or his
judgment, and it also served another purpose—it kept jurors
awake through hours of sometimes tedious testimony.

It would be necessary for Judge Ferrer to sign off on Carl
Weekes' plea deal.

"Judge, today Mr. Weekes is going to withdraw his
previously entered plea of not guilty," his lawyer, Terence
Lennamen, announced. "[Enter] a plea of guilty to one
count attempted first-degree murder with a deadly weapon;
one count kidnapping with a deadly weapon; one count
robbery with a deadly weapon; one count burglary to an
unoccupied dwelling; and one count of grand theft third
degree."

His client, the lawyer said, would testify truthfully pur-
suant to a sworn statement he gave earlier in the week. And
he would be available whenever needed, whether for a pre-
trial conference, a deposition, or a court appearance to testify before a jury.

"Testimony to the truth that he gave to Detective Garafalo," Gail Levine declared.

Ferrer turned to Weekes. "Do you understand that?" the
jurist asked.

"Yes, sir," Weekes, in an orange jail jumpsuit, replied.

At Judge Ferrer's direction, Weekes, who had been
seated, stood and was sworn in.

"Please state your name," the judge ordered.

"Carl Collin Weekes."

"Mr. Weekes, I've been advised that you wish to change
your plea from a plea of not guilty to a plea of guilty to
the count of attempted first-degree murder with a deadly

weapon, kidnapping with a deadly weapon, robbery with a deadly weapon, burglary to an unoccupied dwelling, and grand theft third degree. Is that our understanding of what you're going to be doing today?"

"Yes," Weekes said.

Judge Ferrer turned to the prosecutor. "Ms. Levine, what is the proposed sentence?"

"At the end of the case, we will then come back and ask the court to impose a ten-year sentence upon Mr. Weekes. That's the agreement. If he testifies and complies with the terms, he will receive ten years in state prison. If he fails to testify, or testifies untruthfully, be uncooperative, he'll receive a forty-year sentence."

"Do you understand that?" Judge Ferrer asked the ex-Marine.

"Yes," he replied.

Then the judge issued a stern warning to the Sun Gym kidnapper: "If you do not abide by the agreement, that is if you testify other than truthfully, or if you do not cooperate when you're required or requested to do so by the state attorney's office, then you are agreeing at this time that your sentence will be forty years in state prison. Do you understand that? "

"Yes," said Weekes.

The judge then asked if he was taking any medication; if he had ever been treated for mental illness; if he was satisfied with his attorney's representation. Weekes answered yes to each question.

"You have a number of constitutional rights," Ferrer instructed Weekes. "You can plead not guilty and proceed to trial. If you were to do that the State would have to prove the charges against you to the exclusion of every reasonable doubt.

"You would have the right to trial by judge or by jury. You would have the right to testify. You have the right to compel the appearance of any witness that might testify favorably for you, if such witness existed. And you have the right to appeal. Do you understand your rights?

Weekes said he did, then the judge asked if he was pleading guilty "because you are guilty and for no other reason?"

Again, Weekes replied "Yes."

Turning to Levine, Ferrer asked for a proffer from the prosecutor.

"Judge, if this case were to have gone to trial, the State would have proven that on or about November 15, 1994, Mr. Weekes, along with others involved in this case, abducted Marcello Schiller in front of Schlotzsky's deli, took him to a warehouse leased by Jorge Delgado, and kept him for a period of weeks."

The prosecutor then summarized Schiller's month-long ordeal and the gang's attempt to murder him. Ferrer pronounced sentence.

"Mr. Weekes," he said, "I find that you're alert and intelligent and that you understand the nature of the charges and possible consequences of this plea. I also find that your plea has been freely and voluntarily entered.

"Accordingly, the court accepts your plea of guilty to the charges of attempted first-degree murder with a deadly weapon, kidnapping with a deadly weapon, robbery with a deadly weapon, burglary to an unoccupied dwelling, and grand theft third degree."

Weekes would get credit for time served. Before the proceeding ended, Gail Levine declared that the detectives involved in the case, Jimenez and Garafalo, agreed with the plea arrangement. What's more, she said, Marc Schiller had been apprised of the plea and agrees with it, too. With that, the hearing was over. Two corrections guards led Carl Weekes away.

Stevenson Pierre was the second Sun Gym kidnapper to plead. He appeared before Judge Ferrer in an identical proceeding on January 12, 1996. Like Weekes, if he testified truthfully and cooperated, he would serve ten years in prison instead of forty.

On July 2, 1996, it was Big Mario Sanchez's turn to plead. The muscular weight lifter had been charged with kidnapping Marc Schiller, first-degree attempted murder, and armed robbery. For his cooperation and testimony, prosecutors agreed to allow him to plead guilty to kidnapping. Ferrer sentenced Sanchez to two years in prison and two years of house arrest. Before the proceeding ended, Sanchez asked if he could be released so that he could get his affairs in order before beginning his sentence.

"Denied," Judge Ferrer declared. "Nothing personal," he said, "because here you are being held on no bond when I didn't know if you are guilty or not. Now that I know you are guilty, it makes absolutely no sense to let you out."

Months later, Jorge Delgado cut a deal, too. He gave a sworn statement to Sergeant Felix Jimenez and Detective Sal Garafalo, and a confession to Assistant State Attorney Gail Levine. Delgado revealed how the plot to kidnap Marc Schiller came about, how it was planned, and how it was executed. He was not in Doorbal's townhouse when Frank Griga was murdered, but he could testify as to what he saw there the morning after the slaying and at the warehouse. He could also testify to everything Lugo told him about what had happened to Frank and Krisztina. His testimony would not be barred by the hearsay rule, which generally prohibits a witness from repeating in court what he heard others say. As a coconspirator, Delgado's testimony about what he was told by fellow conspirator Danny Lugo in furtherance of the conspiracy would be admissible at trial.

Delgado agreed to plead guilty to the attempted murder, kidnapping, and extortion of Marc Schiller, and to being an accessory after the fact in the Griga-Furton murders. For his role in the Sun Gym gang, Jorge Delgado ran the risk of being sent to death row or sentenced to life in prison. Instead, for cooperating with investigators, he would be sentenced to fifteen years in state prison.

CHAPTER EIGHTEEN

TOO MANY LAWYERS

It was a very complicated case, with multiple defendants who faced multiple counts. Extensive legal wrangling and scheduling conflicts slowed the march to trial. Squabbling among the lawyers was heated at times. At one point, Judge Ferrer admonished them: "This case is going to be hard enough to try without you guys fighting about every issue tooth and nail."

In an attempt to keep the case moving, the judge scheduled bimonthly status conferences.

At a June 7, 1996 hearing, Lugo's lawyer, veteran Miami criminal defense attorney Ron Guralnick, complained about the slow pace of the pre-trial phase.

"The reason is because we have so many lawyers," Guralnick declared. "They've got their own calendar. Some of them are in trial when depositions are set . . . It's a perplexing problem."

In court, the State was represented by three attorneys. Lugo, who was initially represented by three lawyers, would be defended at trial by Guralnick while John Mese at various times had two working in his behalf. Doorbal and John Raimondo each had two lawyers defending them. The Sun Gym gang's associates were represented by attorneys, too. The lawyers sat through hours of depositions. They filed dozens of motions and attended dozens of hearings. In one of them, Ron Guralnick argued that Lugo was entitled to have three separate trials—one on the RICO counts, a second on the Schiller counts, and the third on the Griga/Furton counts.

Regarding the Schiller abduction and the Griga-Furton murders, Guralnick contended that trying the cases together would "create egregious and extra prejudice to Mr. Lugo." The two cases, Guralnick argued, were very different. They "occurred five to six months apart" and were "not based on the same set of transgressions."

He explained: "In the Schiller case, there was an attempt to allegedly kill Schiller . . . by way of creating a phony auto accident, whereas that's not the case in the Girga-Furton matter."

In the Schiller case, Guralnick said, there was an alleged attempt to extort property and money from Schiller, but that wasn't the case in the Griga-Furton case.

"There was no attempt to extort from these two individuals and certainly not the girl, because she didn't have anything anyway. It was Mr. Griga that had the sizeable funds. So they're different in that regard."

They were different in other ways, too, Guralnick declared. "Some defendants that are involved in one case are not involved in the other case, but they're all being tried together."

In the Griga-Furton case, the bodies were hidden and dismembered and put into barrels and left in the Everglades. "And that's totally different than the Schiller case. And so they're not related in any way."

Judge Ferrer didn't agree. He denied the motion, concluding that there was a "relevant relationship" between the Schiller and Griga-Furton cases. He also denied Guralnick's motion to sever Danny Lugo from Doorbal and

Mese. At the time of their arrests, Doorbal and Lugo made statements implicating each other. Concerned that testimony during the trial about those statements could taint the jury, Judge Ferrer opted to impanel two juries—one would decide the guilt or innocence of Danny Lugo, while the other would judge Doorbal and Mese. The two juries would sit in the courtroom during the entire guilt phase of the trial, separating only to hear testimony from witnesses to whom post-arrest incriminating statements were made.

"The choice was to impanel two juries or try them separately, splitting Lugo off," Judge Ferrer recalled. "The [two jury] procedure is infrequently used. Some judges flat-out refuse to do it. It can be very complicated at times and fraught with the possibility of error."

Mese's lawyer filed motions to sever his case from his codefendants, too, arguing that the Schiller abduction and the Griga-Furton murders were separate, and that there was no evidence that Mese had any involvement in the Hungarian couple's murder.

In response, prosecutors argued that there was ample evidence that the Sun Gym owner was a key participant in the ongoing criminal conspiracy to kidnap, torture, and kill wealthy victims. While his specific role was limited to laundering assets once Lugo and Doorbal had acquired them, they argued that Mese had blood on his hands, too. Judge Ferrer denied Mese's motions for severance, too.

Representing Doorbal, veteran criminal defense Anthony Natale fought to have all the evidence detectives seized from his client's Miami Lakes townhouse and from his car declared inadmissible, claiming that lawmen lacked sufficient probable cause for their search warrants. Judge Ferrer denied that motion, too. Had he ruled otherwise, the items police seized when they searched Doorbal's townhouse linking him to the Schiller abduction and the Sun Gym gang could not be admitted into evidence at trial. Among the items were the letters and faxes Schiller and private investigator Ed Du Bois sent to John Mese, the receipt from the locksmith who changed the locks at

Schiller's home, the Hialeah warehouse lease signed by Lugo, the photos of Winston Lee's home, and the vials of Rompun.

In June, John Mese changed attorneys. His new lawyer, Bruce Fleischer, needed time to get up to speed. Mese himself seemed detached from the pre-trial proceedings. Rather than attend the hearings, the bodybuilding impresario opted to remain in his jail cell. Judge Ferrer had him hauled into court to get him on the record.

"Your attorney has indicated to me that in the future you don't want to be present at any judicial proceedings or hearings unless they are either evidentiary in nature where witnesses are going to be testifying and sworn in, or that relate to issues that are directly related to your case," Judge Ferrer told Mese.

"That's correct," Mese replied, nodding his head as he spoke.

"As far as I am concerned every hearing that we have directly relates to your case. Are you talking about something that is just related to you individually?"

"My case, your honor. A lot of stuff is not related to my case at all."

Ferrer warned him: "What you need to understand is if you miss a hearing and ultimately if you are convicted in this case, you are not going to be able to come back and say, 'Gee, I wanted to be at some of them here and my attorney, he waived my presence at that hearing.' You are going to be bound by the fact that you have indicated to me that you really didn't want to be present at these hearings unless they are evidentiary, unless there is a witness testifying. Is that what you want to do?"

Mese said he did, and he agreed to waive his attendance at every hearing with the option to attend if his attorney told him his presence was necessary. Before deputies led Mese away, Judge Ferrer issued a final warning: "You have to understand, you are losing control. You are letting your attorney decide what hearings to bring you to."

"I will leave it for his discretion," the muscleman replied.

By the late fall of 1997, the end of the pre-trial phase of the case seemed to be in sight. Ferrer announced that he wanted to begin jury selection in December or January. On November 12, Cindy Eldridge, the nurse who married Doorbal in May 1995, appeared before him to plead guilty to a charge of accessory to a felony after the fact, a first-degree misdemeanor. She had cut a deal with prosecutors, too: One year of probation provided in exchange for her cooperation and testimony.

Before adjudicating Eldridge guilty, the judge asked if she understood the terms of the plea deal, if she was under the influence of drugs, if she had ever been treated for mental illness, and if she was satisfied with her lawyer's efforts in her behalf. Eldridge answered no to the first two and yes to the third.

"Listen carefully," Ferrer ordered Eldridge, whose divorce from Doorbal would not become final for another month. "You don't have to plead guilty. You can plead not guilty and proceed to trial. If you do that, the State would have to prove the charges against you beyond and to the exclusion of every reasonable doubt." After reminding Eldridge of her rights to confront her accusers and present witnesses in her behalf, Ferrer asked if she understood that she was giving up her rights to a trial.

"Yes," she replied emphatically.

"Anybody force you to plead guilty?"

"No."

"Are you pleading guilty because you are guilty and for no other reason?

"Yes."

"Do you also understand that the maximum penalty for the charges filed against you is a year in jail? That means if you violate your probation that is what you are exposing yourself to?"

"Yes."

The judge asked Assistant State Attorney Gail Levine for a factual basis for the plea. "The State," she said, "would have shown that if this case had gone to trial, that between

May 24 and May 29 of 1995, Ms Eldridge assisted in cleaning blood in the home of Adrian Doorbal under the impres-
sion that Danny Lugo and others were involved in a violent
fight which resulted in the bleeding of someone and she did
that to assist Mr. Lugo and Mr. Doorbal [to avoid] possible
criminal charges."

Judge Ferrer declared Cindy Eldridge guilty and called
a recess. Two days later an issue arose that threatened to
derail Ferrer's timetable for getting the trial underway.

Even though he had been in custody since June 3, 1995,
Cindy Eldridge's soon-to-be-ex-husband, Noel Doorbal,
had been involved in a romantic relationship that threatened to undermine his legal team's efforts on his behalf.

The object of his affection was Sachi Lievano, a single
mother of two daughters who worked as a secretary in
attorney Penny Burke's office. Burke was one of two attorneys on Doorbal's defense team. While Tony Natale handled the guilt phase of the trial, Burke would handle the
punishment phase if Doorbal was convicted.

Under Florida law, death penalty trials are bifurcated. That
means defendants are tried in two phases—a guilt phase
and a punishment phase. To convict in the guilt phase,
the jury's decision has to be unanimous, which is not the
case in the penalty phase. If a jury in a capital case finds
a defendant guilty, it meets again to consider the penalty. Its decision, however, is not binding on the judge,
but Florida judges have rarely failed to follow the jury's
recommendation.

Despite their clearly delineated responsibilities, Natale,
the lead attorney, and Burke worked closely together as the
case headed for trial.

On the afternoon of Friday, November 14, Penny Burke
appeared before Judge Ferrer. She revealed that Lievano
became acquainted with Doorbal via the telephone whenever the muscleman called from his jail cell to speak with
Burke. The phone calls quickly blossomed into something

more, with Lievano surreptitiously visiting Doorbal in the county jail. The relationship, Burke said, had undermined her ability to effectively represent Doorbal. The attorney wanted to withdraw from the case.

Burke told the judge that when she learned of the relationship, Lievano was "terminated from my office." That didn't sit well with Adrian Doorbal, who was very unhappy that his sweetheart had lost her job. In open court, with Doorbal seated at the defense table, Ferrer summarized the situation: "Mrs. Lievano apparently has developed a romantic relationship with the defendant, Mr. Doorbal. And the concern that counsel has is that Mrs. Lievano intentionally or unintentionally may be undermining your effective representation of your client, because if he is emotionally involved with her, he may decide what she suggests. She is not a lawyer, she is a secretary. She may misunderstand strategies that you have. She may convey things to him differently and end up causing him to make decisions that could effectively cost him his life. Does that about summarize it?"

"Yes, your honor," Burke replied, adding that she had spoken to Doorbal. "We have discussed the situation and he agrees that the relationship has been affected and he is uncomfortable with me. Our relationship is now, for lack of a better phrase, [like] walking on eggshells."

Burke said Doorbal had not phoned her since Lievano had been fired the previous Friday. "This behavior is completely contrary to what it was before, when Mr. Doorbal was calling my office virtually every day. I never refused a collect phone call from him."

After listening to Natale, who supported his cocounsel's motion to withdraw, the judge told Burke, "This is not grounds to allow you to withdraw." He was concerned about the possibility of yet another delay. "I have to look at the harsh reality, and in and of itself I don't think this is grounds to withdraw," he said.

Burke protested, concerned that her credibility and her ability to prevent Doorbal from being sent to death row had been compromised.

"I find myself blindsided and strait-jacketed right now," she said. "He has heard things, and she has told him things that have jeopardized the trust that he has for me. And now I am being asked to save his life, and I am telling the court that I can't do that now." Doorbal, she said, is telling the court that he is not comfortable with her as his attorney. Leaning back in his chair, Judge Ferrer was silent for a moment. Then he leaned forward to explain his decision.

"You are a specially appointed public defender for the purpose of the case. Your client's desire to fire you based upon a circumstance that he in part created and not on your competency is not really grounds to replace you in this case."

Then he turned to the muscleman. "I don't know anything about [Miss Lievano], and I don't know anything about your relationship with her. She is not a lawyer, and people who are not lawyers often make huge mistakes as to what the law is, and strategies. If you chose to follow the instructions of somebody else instead of your lawyer's advice, you do it at your own peril. I am telling you that woman was not acting in a capacity as a representative of the law firm. She was not giving you legal advice, she is not giving you anything that you can rely on . . . If you end up getting sentenced to death, you are not going to be able to come back and say, 'My lawyer was ineffective because this woman from her office came over and gave me bad advice.' "

Ferrer sternly told Doorbal that he wanted him to proceed "with your eyes open, wide open, because if I have to make a tough decision in this case and it goes against you, I want to be able to sleep with it, too, and I want to know that you knew every possibility along the way. Do you understand that?"

"Yes, sir," Doorbal replied.

Gail Levine addressed the court. She wanted it on the record that as far as the State of Florida was concerned if convicted, Doorbal's jury would definitely be called upon to deliberate over the death penalty. "There is no possibility of a guilt phase plea to life," she declared. "It is just not happening for Mr. Doorbal or Mr. Lugo from the State at this particular time. It is not on the table, it hasn't been on the table, and as far as I can see it is not going to be on the table."

One of the most bizarre hearings was held on the afternoon of December 19. Among the issues discussed that day was the agreement prosecutors had entered into with Danny Lugo's lawyers on the jailhouse steps back in June 1995, the gist of which was that the muscleman would take detectives to the location of the bodies and police would testify to his helpfulness and cooperation.

Lugo attorney Ron Guralnick wanted Judge Ferrer to require detectives to testify at trial that his client had "cooperated" when he led them to the murky drainage ditch and the barrels containing the partial remains of Frank Griga and Krisztina Furton.

"They are not going to be able to say that he cooperated because they spent the next month looking for heads, hands, and feet," Gail Levine argued. "That's not cooperation by any stretch of the imagination. You know, he gave us some information. He participated" but "torsos were found."

"We are splitting hairs here," Ferrer interjected.

"Exactly!" the blond prosecutor responded. She added, "I never expected to pull out torsos from barrels. I thought Mr. Lugo was dealing in good faith, and he wasn't."

"We are, in a sense, arguing over the definition of 'bodies,' " Judge Ferrer observed. "If you take my example of a head, and I take out the teeth, skin, and hair, and I give you a skull, did I give you a head? It may be for all practical purposes useless if you want it for identification. If I take a body and I sever the hands, feet, and head, and then I don't have any fingerprints, footprints, or tooth impressions, it may be totally useless. If I cut it in half, is it still a body or is it half a body? I don't think the agreement is entirely clear. And your client obviously knew whether the body was whole. The State certainly didn't."

"The agreement is clear," Guralnick said. "It says 'lead

them' to the bodies. If they wanted to be more precise, they should have been. 'Lead them' to is exactly what he said he would do."

In the end, Judge Ferrer denied Guralnick's motion, telling the defense lawyer that he could argue to the jury that Lugo had cooperated, but the court could not "order specific words into the police officer's mouth."

But Guralnick stuck to his guns. "This agreement is signed by Ms. Levine. Paragraph one says that his coop-eration would be . . . in helping them locate bodies. That's exactly what he did. If they want to be more specific, they should have been more specific about it. They said 'bod-ies.' That's exactly what he led them to."

The judge stuck to his guns, too. "Your client obviously knew whether or not the bodies were whole. The State cer-tainly didn't." Motion denied.

CHAPTER NINETEEN

Let me tell you why you're here.

—CIRCUIT COURT JUDGE ALEX FERRER

Jury selection got underway in Judge Alex Ferrer's fourth floor courtroom on the afternoon of February 2, 1998. It's difficult enough to impanel one jury in a death penalty case, let alone two. The first group of twenty-five prospective jurors was summoned from the jury pool on the seventh floor for the Doorbal and Mese jury. The judge began by introducing himself: "My name is Alex Ferrer. I am the circuit court judge that asked you be brought down for the purpose of jury selection in the case of State of Florida versus John Carl Mese and Noel Doorbal." Then Judge Ferrer introduced the bailiff, the court clerk, the court reporter, the attorneys, and defendants Doorbal and Mese. Then he addressed the jurors.

"Let me tell you why you're here," the judge began. "You're here because an indictment has been filed charging the defendants with various crimes. An indictment is not proof that any crime occurred. It's merely an allegation. The document is a charging document that sets forth what the accusations are against the defendant. And the purpose of the trial, the reason you're here, is to bring a jury down so the State can proceed to present evidence in an effort to convince you that the crime committed, or the crimes alleged, did in fact occur, were committed, and the persons accused of the crime were the ones who committed the crime." Next, he gave the potential jurors a brief overview of the case.

"In late May of 1995, a Hungarian couple was reported missing from their Golden Beach home. Ultimately, the alleged bodies of these individuals were found in barrels in southern Dade County. At about the same time, it was reported in the media that a Colombian or Argentinean man had been kidnapped and held for ransom."

Ferrer told the twenty-five men and women that he was hoping to jog their memories, so that when voir dire[7] got underway the next day, they would be able to discuss with him and the attorneys what they had heard or read about the case in the media. He also explained that they would be called upon to judge guilt or innocence and then, if they found a defendant guilty of first-degree murder, they would be called upon in the penalty phase to recommend either life in prison without the possibility of parole or death.

Judge Ferrer explained the penalty phase. "When we get to the penalty phase, if we get there, if the defendants are found guilty of first-degree murder, the State's burden is to prove to you beyond and to the exclusion of every reasonable doubt, that the aggravating factors, the ones that weigh in favor of the death penalty, outweigh the mitigating factors. So if they prove that to you, the death penalty is the recommendation the jury should give. If they don't

[7]To speak the truth. The phrase refers to the preliminary examination that the court conducts of those presented as prospective jurors or witnesses.

convince you beyond a reasonable doubt that the aggravating factors outweigh the mitigating factors, the appropriate recommendation would be life in prison."

In the meantime, the judge instructed the jurors not to discuss the case with anyone. "I'm going to ask you to do several things. First of all, when you go home today, you can't talk to any family, friends, or relatives about this case. If anybody asks you what case you are a juror on, tell them that the judge instructed you that you are not to talk to anybody about the case."

He also told them to avoid news coverage of the case, and not to discuss the case among themselves. Before they left, Ferrer issued two warnings: It's going to be boring— "We will be speaking to you each individually so please bring your patience."—and bring a jacket because "the temperature in here, I've heard said by rumors, sometimes gets a little chilly."

After the prospective Doorbal-Mese jurors were ushered out of the courtroom, a new group of twenty-five Miami-Dade citizens was brought in for the Lugo case. With some minor changes, Judge Ferrer repeated what he said to the first group.

Beginning the next day, the potential jurors were questioned by the judge and the lawyers. They wanted to probe attitudes regarding the death penalty, and they wanted to be certain that the jurors selected for the case would be able to serve for two or three months without it causing hardship for themselves or their families.

Anyone who said they were opposed to the death penalty was excused, as were those who claimed it would be a financial hardship to be away from work for a month or more, as well as anyone who seemed too eager to mete out the death penalty.

Day after day, prospective juror after prospective juror for more than two weeks, Judge Ferrer repeated the mantra: "My name is Alex Ferrer. I am the circuit court judge that asked you be brought down for the purpose of jury selection," until the two juries were impaneled. Thirty-four men and women—twelve jurors plus ten alternates—were plucked from the seventh floor jury pool to sit in judgment of the Sun Gym gang's ringleaders.

On Tuesday, February 24, 1998, in a fourth floor court-room in the Richard E. Gerstein Justice Building, the mas-sive and bustling but un-majestic nine-story, gray stone courthouse, the trial was about to get underway. But the Sun Gym case wasn't the only legal matter creating buzz at the courthouse that day. In fact, it was overshadowed by a sex scandal emanating from the State Attorney's Office and a voter fraud trial that revealed the seamy side of Miami politics.

In the voter fraud case, Mayor Xavier Suarez was defending his November election victory against charges that he had stolen the election. In that contest, Joe Carollo won a majority at the polls, but lost when absentee ballots favored Suarez by a two to one margin. An investigation revealed that among the absentee voters who tipped the election to the mayor were voters who were dead or lived outside the city, while others were convicted felons who had lost their right to vote. Investigators also found ballots that were outright forgeries.[8]

As for the phone sex scandal, the *Miami Herald* reported that two secretaries in the state attorney's major crimes division had been suspended without pay over allegations they had engaged in phone sex with a jailed witness. His name was Jorge Ayala, a confessed hit man who was a key witness in the triple murder trial of the notorious Griselda "The Godmother" Blanco. She was awaiting trial on triple murder charges stemming from the cocaine trafficking violence that gripped Miami in the 1980s. Ayala pleaded guilty to one of the killings. He was

---

[8]The judge tossed the results because of absentee-ballot fraud. An appeals court invalidated the election declaring Joe Carollo the winner.

in the county jail waiting to testify against Blanco. Investigators, the *Herald* reported, had turned up evidence in Ayala's jail cell including love letters and photographs, and had tape recordings of the explicit phone conversations. Prosecutors feared that the scandal jeopardized the Blanco prosecution. Despite the outrageous news emanating from their office, lead prosecutor Gail Levine and her team were undaunted, and they were ready to try the case.

New Jersey–born Gail Levine joined the state attorney's office in June 1985, one year after graduating from law school. When she was hired, Janet Reno, the first woman state attorney in Florida, was the state attorney for Dade County. She had been appointed by then-governor Reubin Askew in 1978 when her predecessor Richard Gerstein, for whom the courthouse is named, resigned before completing his term. The six foot, two inch Miami native was very popular with voters—they returned her to office four more times.

Reno left Miami in 1993, when President Bill Clinton chose her to be the first woman attorney general of the United States. Then-Governor Lawton Chiles named Katherine Fernandez Rundle, Reno's protégé and top deputy, to succeed her. She has held the office ever since. In 1998, the Miami-Dade State Attorney's office employed more than one thousand paralegals, investigators, support staff, and assistant state attorneys, more than half of whom were women.

With a long history of women in the top job, there is no glass ceiling in the Miami-Dade State Attorney's office. Like every new prosecutor, Levine began her career working on misdemeanors, but her talent and ambition propelled her into more serious cases. Over the years the blond prosecutor proved again and again that she's a tough litigator with the guts to confront evil and the confidence to send cold-blooded killers to the death house.

Assisting Levine were David Weinstein, who joined the state attorney's office in 1989 after two years as an associate at a Miami law firm, and Joel Rosenblatt, who became a prosecutor in 1982 after spending eleven years at the Department of Legal Affairs in Miami.

Everyone was in place. The two juries were seated along a wall to the prosecutor's left, while seated to their right were Danny Lugo and his attorney, Ron Guralnick. To their right at a second table were Adrian Doorbal and his two attorneys, Tony Natale and Penny Burke. To their right and on a ninety-degree angle so that they were facing the juries, were John Mese and his attorney, Bruce Fleisher.

For the first time in a long time, the defendants were not wearing the jailhouse jumpsuits they were issued when they were arrested. Instead, Lugo and Mese wore dark suits and ties, while Doorbal wore a sweater. Their shackles had been removed.

Before breaking for lunch, Judge Ferrer apologized for the condition of the courtroom: "This courtroom, as you can see, was undergoing construction. It's still undergoing construction and the seats are all piled in the corner, but it's the only one in this courthouse big enough to house all of you." Construction workers would be in to fix the seats, he promised. They and the trial would get underway after lunch.

"When you come back, I will read to you the indictment, and the opening statements will start at that time," the judge said. He instructed the juries to remain apart: "One of the benefits of having two juries is we can try everything at one time. The downside is that you jurors for Mr. Guralnick, who is counsel for Mr. Lugo, have to be kept separate from the jury for Mr. Natale and Mr. Fleisher, and that's for defendants Doorbal and Mese. So please do not mingle with each other."

With those instructions ringing in their ears, the jurors

were excused. More than three years after Marc Schiller's kidnapping, and nearly three years after Frank Griga and Krisztina Furton were murdered and dismembered, the trial of Danny Lugo, Noel Doorbal, and John Mese was about to begin.

CHAPTER TWENTY

Heads cut off. Hands and feet chopped away.
Remains covered in gasoline and set on fire.

—ASSISTANT STATE PROSECUTOR GAIL LEVINE

At promptly one thirty in the afternoon, Judge Alex Ferrer took the bench. He instructed the bailiffs to bring the juries into the packed courtroom. As soon as the jurors were seated, the judge addressed them. He reminded the jurors and the spectators that they were about to hear opening statements from the lawyers, but first he would read the indictment verbatim.

Before turning to the indictment, Judge Ferrer admonished the jury: "Since there will be two juries in this case, you are instructed that during the pendency of the trial the members of the two juries are not to communicate with each other. You are not to go anywhere with the members of the other jury and you are to remain absolutely separate from each other. Further, you are not again to discuss the facts in this case amongst yourselves on this jury and on the other jury. I am now going to read you the indictment filed in this case and I will ask you to please give me your attention." Then Judge Ferrer read from the indictment:

In the name and by the authority of the State of Florida, Count One: The Grand Jurors of the State of Florida duly called and impaneled and sworn to inquire and in true presentment make in and for the body of the County of Dade upon their oath present that Noel Doorbal, also known as Adrian Doorbal, Daniel Lugo, and John Carl Mese, John Michael Raimondo[9] and other persons known and unknown to the State Attorney beginning on or about October, 1994, and continuing through June, 1995, in the County and State aforesaid employed by or associated with an enterprise as defined by Florida Statute 895.02(3) to wit, a group of individuals associated in fact although not a legal entity did unlawfully and knowingly agree, conspire, combine or confederate with one another and with other persons whose identities are both known and unknown to the State Attorney to violate Section 895.03(3), Florida Statutes. That is to conduct or participate directly or indirectly in said enterprise through a pattern of racketeering activity as that term is defined in Section 895.02, Florida Statutes. Said pattern of racketeering activity consisting of at least two incidents of racketeering activity enumerated in Section 895.02(1), Florida Statutes, including murder and violation of statute 782, Florida Statutes and/or kidnapping in violation of Statute 787, Florida Statutes and/or robbery in violation of Statutes 812, Florida Statutes, and/or extortion in violation of Statute 836.05, Florida Statutes, all of the aforesaid conduct being in violation of Section 895.03(4), Florida Statutes, contrary to the form of the statute in such cases made and provided and against the peace and dignity of the State of Florida.

Count two: The Grand Jurors of the State of Florida duly called and impaneled and sworn to inquire in true presentment make in and for the body of the county

---

[9]Jail guard John Raimondo's case had been severed, but Judge Ferrer read the indictment verbatim anyway.

of Dade upon their oaths present that beginning on or about October of 1994 and/or continuing through May of 1995 in the County and State aforesaid Noel Doorbal, also known as Adrian Doorbal, Daniel Lugo, John Carl Mese, and other persons known and unknown to the State Attorney, were employed by or associated with an enterprise as defined by Florida Statute 895.02(3) and did unlawfully and knowingly conduct or participate, either directly or indirectly, in such enterprise through a pattern of racketeering activity as defined by Florida Statutes 895.02(1) and 4.

Counts three through ten were the Griga-Furton counts, while the remaining counts referred to the abduction of Marc Schiller, the plundering of his possessions, and the attempt to murder him. It took the judge more than one hour to read through the entire indictment. When Judge Ferrer finished, he turned his attention to opening statements.

Looking toward the jurors who were seated to his right, the judge warned: "What the lawyers say is not evidence . . . The best example that I have heard given by lawyers of what an opening statement really entails is that an opening statement is like the picture that's on the box of a jigsaw puzzle, and if you ever built a jigsaw puzzle, you can imagine how difficult it would be to build it if you didn't know what the picture is going to look like when it's finished." Without opening statements, the judge explained, the jurors would not know where the pieces fit. He urged them to pay careful attention to the statements, then he looked down from the bench at Assistant State Attorney Gail Levine.

"Miss Levine," the judge said.

The packed courtroom was silent as the prosecutor rose slowly from her chair. She began politely and respectfully. "May it please the court, counsel, and members of the jury." Then, facing the jurors, she launched one of the most graphic and gruesome opening statements ever heard in the Richard E. Gerstein Justice Building.

"Heads cut off. Hands and feet chopped away. Remains covered in gasoline and set on fire. Set on fire so that skin and fingerprints would disappear. Stuffed into buckets and barrels, left to decompose in the grueling midsummer heat."

Her opening wasn't subtle, but Gail Levine was not known for subtlety. She was painting a vivid picture, laying out the State's theory of the case.

"Frank Griga and Krisztina Furton were kidnapped, tortured, and murdered for their money. A cold, calculated crime of greed. These are the criminal acts of those men," she declared, gesturing toward the defendants, "and those they engaged to help them. A planned series of awful crimes that started with choosing sufficiently rich victims, kidnapping them, torturing them, and taking everything they had, murdering them and then dismembering them to hide the evils of their crimes."

Levine lowered her voice as she told the jurors about Griga and Furton and the painful deaths they suffered. "On May 24, 1995, Frank Griga was a thirty-two-year-old self-made millionaire from Hungary. He died, murdered painfully by these men. Krisztina Furton was only twenty-three, and she was also Hungarian, and she had her whole life ahead of her, but these men pumped her one hundred and five pound body with horse tranquilizers until she could take no more."

The musclemen were motivated by insatiable greed. Lugo she said, looking directly at him, "presented himself as a well-educated man, but he had no intention of conducting real business, legal business." Instead, the muscleman intended to steal "so that he could play the stock market, invest, and live in the lap of luxury."

Next, Levine turned to John Mese. "He was a certified public accountant, but accounting was not what he liked. It was weight lifting, and bodybuilding, and he owned a gym, Sun Gym." But the gym was losing money, draining his assets. "Reason enough for him to join Mr. Lugo in these evil crimes."

As for Doorbal, "He was less educated, but certainly no less determined. He was an avid bodybuilder, not the man you see here today, almost three years later, an avid steroid user who was known as king of the gym. He spent his time bodybuilding and working on his body and he didn't have time for a regular job."

He was from the Caribbean, Levine said. "He grew up poor in Trinidad. He felt that the rich owed him." He didn't want to work. Danny Lugo's "ideas were good for him."

Turning to the jury, the proescutor continued. "These three men committed these crimes, not on a whim. They were planned and premeditated. They never intended to work at a job again. They set their sights on finding victims, preying on them, and they did it by working in Mese's gym"

Sun Gym, Levine said, was a fertile recruiting ground for Danny Lugo's evil schemes. That's where Lugo found Jorge Delgado, "a skinny mousey guy" who impressed Danny Lugo because he was making a lot of money. Delgado led Lugo to Marcelo Schiller. He owned property. He had money in bank accounts in the United States and the Cayman Islands. Lugo wanted everything Schiller had. So he hatched a plan: "Kidnap Marc Schiller, torture him and he gives up everything, and he writes his own ransom note, and then kill him."

Lugo, Levine said, was "the boss—they all listened to him." Doorbal "was the first assistant—Danny's main man."

Accountant and notary public John Mese was "waiting in the wings." He knew how to "file papers to make thinks look legal and to launder the money so that they could use it." Lugo knew he couldn't use just any notary, the proescutor said. "No notary is going to go with you to a warehouse, see a man tied up, chained to a wall, and authorize a signature. They had to have somebody who was in it for a piece of the action, and that was John Mese."

Mese, Levine said, "was able to switch the money around and do creative accounting to launder the money.

They enlisted others like Carl Weekes, Stevenson Pierre, and Mario Sanchez to help them."

After outlining the structure of the gang, Levine proceeded to tell the thirty-four men and women about the abduction of Marc Schiller. He was, she said, born in Argentina, educated in the United States, worked for an accounting firm in Colombia where he married a Colombian woman before moving to Miami. He was, said Levine, a wealthy man. She pulled no punches describing the torture and humiliation he suffered, how he was grabbed in broad daylight, how he "became a human lightning rod—they Tasered him and shocked him until he could not move, nor could he walk; until he basically became Jell-O.

"For four weeks, like an Iranian hostage, days without food or water. Eyes taped so tightly shut that he could feel blood dripping down his face. Never seeing light. Chained to a wall, forced to urinate on himself. Beaten by Doorbal just for the fun of it." She told the jurors about Schiller's family—how his wife and children were forced to flee the country; how the gang forced him to sign over everything they owned, including their house; and how they tried to kill Schiller by filling him with liquor over four days and staging a car crash.

"By December 14, they were done. They had everything," Levine said. But Schiller survived. He woke up in the hospital "looking like a human zipper," Levine said. Then he fled to New York where he recuperated.

Meanwhile, Lugo and Doorbal were living large on Schiller's money, relaxing at Solid Gold where they were known as high rollers. "The girls liked them, and they liked the girls," Levine declared, but not all the money was spent on strippers and champagne. Lugo sent some of the money—more than $67,000—to the Federal Government as restitution for his previous conviction. John Mese posed as his employer, claiming that he had funded the purchase of a computer program Lugo had developed. John Mese paid off his own debts, too.

And the gang searched for its next millionaire victim. They didn't have to search for long. Even while they were negotiating with Du Bois and spending Schiller's money, the Sun Gym gang had set its sights on Frank Griga and Krisztina Furton.

"They were living the American dream," Levine told the jurors. Griga came to the United States and sold cars until he took a chance and bought phone sex phone lines, with girls on the end of the line and callers paying for "harmless phone sex." The business "may not be something that you like, or I like, but it is absolutely legal and incredibly lucrative."

According to Levine, Lugo and Doorbal plotted and planned. They lured the couple to Doorbal's apartment where they would subdue Frank then torture Kirsztina in front of him "so that he would give up everything." But their plan went awry.

"Frank was hit with a hard, blunt object. It cracked his skull and blood poured out of his head, and Krisztina began to scream, but Lugo and Doorbal were ready. They had needles, syringes filled with horse tranquilizer, and they injected Krisztina and they injected Frank."

Levine admitted that the medical examiner could not say for sure what killed Frank. "He was bashed so hard in the head, [we don't know] if that caused his death, but he died there in Doorbal's apartment in his own pool of blood." Krisztina died from a massive overdose of horse tranquilzer, "enough to kill maybe one thousand horses."

What happened next, Levine said, "would have remained a mystery had it not been for Jorge Delgado." He agreed to cooperate and testify truthfully for a reduced sentence—fifteen years in state prison.

"Jorge is not a good person," the prosecutor declared. "He is a horrible person, a murderer, but without him, and without his testimony, we would not have known what happened to Krisztina Furton." She reminded the jury that the case "is not about Jorge Delgado—it's about Lugo, Mese, and Doorbal." They had the idea, the know-how, and the plan. They were the ones who "actually did these horrible crimes."

Then she told the jurors what the musclemen did next: They removed the bodies to the rented warehouse where they were supposed to be held. It was not far from the warehouse where they held Marc Schiller prisoner. Lugo and Doorbal powered up a chain saw, starting with the heads. But when the saw became jammed on Kirsztina's hair, they picked up axes.

Levine described the gruesome scene, outrage and disbelief in her voice: "*Whack, whack, whack*, until the spinal cord was cut in two and the heads were separated." Then they took off the hands. "*Chop, chop, chop*," she said, while gesturing with her hand. "Then the fingers to eliminate fingerprints."

The grisly picture the prosecutor painted caused several jurors to wince, and others squirmed in their seats. Onlookers among the spectators in the courtroom gasped. One of them was Frank's sister, Zsuzsanna. She sat in the first row, directly behind the prosecution's table.

Levine went on: "But that was not good enough. Teeth. Oh, teeth. Eyes. Ears. Noses. Their faces, chopped out through the mandible . . . and then they separated those parts, because they were going to make a human barbecue."

They assumed that "they could burn the parts like chicken" and then "just get rid of the skin, that the skin would disappear" and all they would have to do is "stuff little bones into a barrel . . . but humans don't burn like chicken." Without high intensity heat, "a body causes a lot of smoke, so Lugo and Doorbal stuffed the torsos into barrels, while the other body parts went into buckets, and they saw to it that they were discarded at various locations around South Florida."

"This is going to be somewhat of a lengthy trial," the veteran prosecutor warned, promising the jurors that after they've seen all the evidence, they will "have no doubt" that the three defendants are guilty of participating in a criminal enterprise, racketeering, and conspiracy. And even though John Mese wasn't in Doorbal's apartment when Frank and Krisztina were murdered, their blood is on his hands, too.

"It doesn't matter who actually killed Frank," Levine said, "and it doesn't matter who actually pumped injections into Krisztina. They are each guilty of kidnapping, robbing, and attempting to murder Marc Schiller, and guilty of the murders in the first degree of Krisztina Furton and Frank Griga . . . cold, calculated crimes of greed and murder. Thank you."

Next it was the defense's turn. Three lawyers stated their theories of what happened and who was to blame. With a mountain of evidence linking their clients to the Schiller abduction and the Griga-Furton murders, their job was not to disprove the allegations against their clients. Instead, their job was to sow enough doubt in the minds of the jurors so that they would vote to acquit.

First up was Lugo's attorney Ron Guralnick. He began practicing law in Miami in 1968, and he was no stranger to high profile murder cases. In 1988, Guralnick represented ex-lawman Manny Pardo Jr., who was found guilty of murdering nine drug dealers. "Instead of nine, I wish it could have been ninety-nine," the killer cop said.

He also represented fifteen-year-old Ronny Zamora in a post-conviction appeal. Zamora's case made national headlines when it went to trial in 1977. Zamora's lawyer then was Ellis Rubin, who offered a unique defense—the television intoxication defense, arguing that his teenage client was not guilty by reason of insanity after watching violence on television for years.

The Sun Gym case, Guralnick said, does not qualify as a racketeering case because the kidnapping of Schiller and the murders of Griga and Furton were not sufficiently similar. And he placed the blame squarely on Adrian Doorbal's shoulders, claiming that all Danny Lugo did was help dispose of the bodies, at most "an accessory after the fact." Danny Lugo, he said, was not involved in either the

murders of Frank Griga and Krisztina Furton or the kidnapping of Marc Schiller, who, he said contemptuously,
delayed reporting the kidnapping in order to protect his
shady business dealings. "Mr. Schiller is not a person wor-
thy of belief," Guralnick declared.

In his opening statement, Doorbal's attorney Tony
Natale, a veteran criminal defense lawyer from West Palm
Beach, urged the jurors to look outside the courtroom for
the real killer. Natale had been retained by Cindy Eldridge
when her then-husband Adrian was arrested on June 3,
1995. Since then, he had been traveling almost daily between Miami and West Palm Beach for depositions and
motion hearings. Natale began his opening statement talking about deceit, and pointing his finger at someone who
was not even in the courtroom.

"Oh, what a tangled web! Oh, what a dramatic web! Oh,
what a wonderful web they weave when first they practice
to deceive!" A trial, Natale said, "is based on the evidence
that comes in and that's what it's about, but who will tell
you? It's like what actors do, they are called to the stand,
and who are these people? What will they say, and how
do they know each other?" Then he blamed all the ghastly
crimes Gail Levine described on someone who wasn't even
in the courtroom—the prosecution's star witness, Jorge
Delgado.

"Deceit, dollars, and death are the dealings of Mr. Delgado, and the main witnesses in this case are all connected
to Mr. Delgado." Referring to the lengthy indictment,
Natale declared that "the criminal conduct that took so
long to read all begins and ends with Mr. Delgado."

He described Delgado as "shrewd," with "a very sharp
and devious mind," a mind "dedicated to dollars and deceit
to make his money,' a man, the lawyer said, who "deals in
deceit, dollars, and death. And his name is Delgado." And
it is based "upon his testimony that [the State] seeks the
death of Adrian Doorbal?" he asked sarcastically.

Marc Schiller, the lawyer said was "secretive . . . sneaky
to some, maybe sleazy, because he was concerned more

about protecting his medical businesses than reporting his plight to police." He never identified Doorbal as one of his kidnappers—"he does not directly or indirectly put Adrian anywhere near what he said happened to him," Natale declared emphatically.

He described Danny Lugo as a leader, "the boss," "very smart," "very wealthy," someone Doorbal, a poor boy from Trinidad, admired and wanted to emulate. It was Lugo, he said, who opened bank accounts for Doorbal and continued to control them. He even acquired the Miami Lakes townhouse for Doorbal. The phone in the apartment, Natale said, was listed to a business that was owned and operated by Delgado and Lugo.

"Adrian did not kill Ms. Furton. Adrian did not kill Mr. Griga. And he did not kidnap Mr. Schiller." The case, Natale promised, "is going to come full circle. It starts with Jorge Delgado, and it will end with Jorge Delgado."

Finally, John Mese's attorney Bruce Fleischer took his turn. "I don't really have much to say to you this afternoon," he said. And "I probably won't have that much to say to you during the course of this trial because the evidence against John Mese, you could call it slim to none."

All Mese was guilty of, Fleischer said, was signing his wife's signature as a witness on one of the documents he notarized for Marc Schiller.

"John Mese admitted to the police that he forged his wife's signature. I believe that's count twenty-nine." Why did he do it? Because it was close to Thanksgiving, and "there was nobody else around, and he signed his wife's name—no harm, no foul."

He implored the jurors to listen carefully to the evidence and to all the testimony. "When you digest it, and you get to the end of however long this trial is, and you apply the facts of this case as they have been presented to you, and you listen to the law that the court gives you, then you will have no other verdict in this case but not guilty to every count except count twenty-nine."

At 5:35 P.M., opening statements were out of the way.

Judge Ferrer told the jurors that testimony in the complicated case would begin the next day, at eleven o'clock. He
ordered the bailiffs to escort the jurors from the courtroom.
The lawyers remained and the three defendants remained
for a few more minutes to discuss procedural matters with
Judge Ferrer. Ten minutes later, the judge declared court
adjourned for the day. Department of Corrections personnel led the three defendants back to the county's Pre-trial
Detention Center. It's connected to the Richard E. Gerstein
Justice Building by an enclosed skyway, which means prisoners can be brought directly into the courthouse without
having to walk outside.

While the defendants changed from their court clothes
into their jailhouse jumpsuits, the jurors headed home.
More than one left the courthouse with Gail Levine's
graphic and gruesome opening statement ringing in their
ears, visions firmly planted in their minds of "Heads cut
off. Hands and feet chopped away. Remains covered in
gasoline and set on fire." But it was nothing compared to
what was to come.

CHAPTER TWENTY-ONE

Frank's dealing with some bad people.
Those were my exact words.

—JUDI BARTUSZ

The second day of the Sun Gym trial began on time. The two juries were brought into the courtroom by the bailiffs, and Judge Ferrer greeted the jurors. "Good morning, ladies and gentlemen," the judge said from the bench. "Yesterday we had the opening statements from the attorneys. Today we'll start with the presentation of the evidence. The State is going to begin by calling its first witness." Then he turned to the prosecution table. "Okay, State, you may proceed."

Gail Levine decided to begin the trial with the Griga-Furton murders. "The State calls Judi Bartusz," she announced, then the prosecutor walked to an easel that had been set up just to the right of the witness stand. She placed a poster-size photo of Frank and Krisztina on it. It had been a source of conflict a few days before, during a heated pre-trial discussion. Defense attorneys objected to its size, but they were overruled. The full color photo brought the couple to life. It showed Frank and Krisztina side by side, happy, radiant, and beaming, obviously enjoying themselves and each other.

While Levine adjusted the photo, the first of ninety-eight witnesses entered the courtroom and walked confidently to the witness stand. Judi Bartusz, a pretty woman, tall and slim with brown hair and big brown eyes, had been waiting a long time to testify against the men she believed had brutally murdered and dismembered her good friends. At long last she would have her chance to confront them. Levine turned her attention away from the photograph to the witness. She stood by while Bartusz was sworn in by the clerk, listening as Judi vowed to tell the truth, the whole truth, and nothing but the truth.

"Please tell the jury who you are," Levine commanded.

Bartusz stated her name and her age—thirty-one. She currently lived in Broward County, she said, with her husband, Gabor, and their baby.

"Where did you live before you lived in Broward?" Levine asked.

"In Golden Beach."

"What country is Gabor from?"

"Hungary."

Her husband, she said, was in the phone business in November 1988, when she first met him.

"Tell the jury a little bit about that business. Did you get involved in the business and run it for your husband?" the prosecutor asked. "Tell the jurors how it is to call a 900 phone number."

Turning toward the jurors, Bartusz said, "When you call a number it goes to a certain area, and there are people there that you can talk to, or the call can be transferred to some other place where you can talk to a woman."

"The business that Frank was in, did it have a pool of women?" Levine asked.

"Yes."

"How much was a call to Frank's business?"

"Anywhere from three dollars a minute to five dollars a minute"

"Did you know whether Frank did well in the business?"

"Yes, he did very well."

"Did you and your husband share information with Frank?"

"Yes."

"How much do you think Frank earned in 1994?"

"Three million dollars," Bartusz said.

But Judi Bartusz wasn't there to testify about Frank Griga's phone sex business. She was there to identify the two men she encountered at Frank Griga's home the night of May 24, 1995. Bartusz recalled that she was walking her dog when she decided to stop at Frank's.

"Did you notice any cars in the driveway?" Levine asked.

"A gold Mercedes."

"What did you do once you noticed that?"

"I went up to the front door with my dog." Frank, she said, invited her in.

"Who else was in the house?"

"Adrian and Danny. Adrian introduced himself and shook my hand."

"How do you know the other person was Danny? Did you hear somebody calling his name?

"I must have."

"Did you get a good look at these people?"

"Yes."

"Do you see them in the courtroom?"

"Yes."

Instead of waiting for Bartusz to point to his client, Tony Natale rose and stipulated that Bartusz identified Doorbal.

"Do you see the other person?" Levine asked.

"Yes."

"Describe an article of clothing he is wearing."

"A blue suit."

"Let the record show that the witness has identified Mr. Lugo," Judge Ferrer interjected.

"When you were talking to Mr. Doorbal, did you get a good look at him?"

"Yes."

"What kind of look?"

"Something about him struck me as strange. I said it bothered me."

"You looked him in the eye?" the prosecutor asked.

"Yes," Bartusz answered.

"How about the man you called Danny? Did you get a good look at him?" Levine wanted to know.

"I got a good look at him, but I did not look him in the eye."

Then one by one, Bartusz identified the items of clothing her friends wore the night they disappeared. There was Krisztina's red leather dress and jacket, her red pumps and red purse. "We bought them together in Las Vegas," Bartusz remarked. She also identified Frank's crocodile boots and silk shirt, his Rolex watch and Krisztina's diamond tennis bracelet and her rings, all of which were recovered by police when they executed the search warrants on June 3.

With each item, Levine asked if they were in "substantially the same condition as when you saw them on Wednesday, May 24, 1995?" Bartusz answered "yes" again and again. Responding to Levine's questions, Bartusz testified that her friends were going to have dinner with the musclemen at Shula's in Miami Lakes. She related how she watched as Frank and Krisztina drove away from the house in Frank's yellow Lamborghini Diablo, following behind the gold Mercedes with Danny Lugo behind the wheel. She never saw the couple again, Bartusz said, fighting back tears as she reached for a box of tissues that had been placed on the railing next to the witness stand and dabbed her eyes.

Bartusz said she was aware that Frank and Krisztina had plans to leave for the Bahamas on Thursday, May 25, for the Memorial Day weekend. She called them in the morning and left a message. When Frank didn't return the call she assumed that he and Krisztina had gone to the Bahamas.

"What happened on Friday, May 26?" Gail Levine asked.

"Eszter called me on the telephone and told me that she thought something was wrong at Frank's house. She asked if I would come to the house with her because she did not want to go inside alone." But Judi wasn't dressed, so she asked the housekeeper to come to her house first, then they would go to Frank's together. Inside, they found Chopin the dog running wild. He was acting crazy, Judi remembered. Right away she knew something was wrong because Chopin was there. "If Frank was in the Bahamas, he wouldn't have left the dog in the house," Judi declared. "In the house things were torn up, paper towel rolls. I let him out to go to the bathroom. He must have been in the house since Wednesday."

As they made their way through the waterfront mansion, Bartusz and Eszter also noticed drinking glasses on a coffee table, where they had been left the night of May 24. They found plane tickets for the Bahamas on a desk along with Griga's passport and Furton's wallet. Judi knew right away that the couple had not gone to the Bahamas, and she surmised that they had never returned from their dinner date with the two musclemen. Alarmed, Judi called her husband, Gabor, who notified the Golden Beach police. Gail Levine's direct examination of Judi Bartusz ended at 12:40 P.M. Judge Ferrer excused the jurors for lunch, but the attorneys remained in the courtroom. There were two issues that needed to be discussed out of earshot of the juries. One involved whether or not jurors should be permitted to take notes during testimony. Several jurors had asked the bailiffs if it would be allowed.

"This is a long enough trial. I would have no problem with them taking notes," Judge Ferrer said, but he wanted to know what the attorneys thought. Gail Levine had no objection, neither did Tony Natale, but Bruce Fleischer, Mese's lawyer, and Ron Guralnick, Lugo's lawyer, objected, explaining that note-taking would divert jurors' attention from testimony. Ferrer decided: No note taking.

The second issue concerned a journalist who was covering the trial for a Miami weekly. Prosecutors complained that he was sitting directly behind them making strange noises and gesturing while Judi Bartusz was testifying.

"He is an annoying person," Gail Levine said. "His condition is annoying us, and it's distracting."

Judge Ferrer said he would instruct the bailiff to seat the man farther back, and to advise him to refrain from making sounds and gestures during testimony. With that out of the way, the judge declared a recess.

When court resumed later in the afternoon, Judi Bartusz was still on the witness stand waiting to be cross-examined. Lawyers for Doorbal and Lugo tried to poke holes in her testimony, but they could not shake her identification of the two musclemen as the men she saw at Frank Griga's house the night the couple disappeared.

Natale questioned Bartusz about her intuitive feelings that her friends were in danger. "I think that you said something on direct that you had a strange feeling or a funny feeling, something like that, what did you say?" he asked.

"That night I went home, and the first thing I said to my husband when I walked in the door was 'Frank's dealing with some bad people. They were gangster-looking.' Those were my exact words."

"You didn't call the police that night, did you?"

"No."

"When you had these feelings, you didn't ask Krisztina, could you come over here for a second?"

It was too late, she said, "They were gone."

"So you had the feeling after they were gone?"

"Yes."

"While you were at the house seeing these people you didn't have these feelings?"

"No."

"When you were talking to Adrian in the driveway, you didn't have these feelings?"

Again, Bartusz said "No."

Lugo's lawyer Ron Guralnick probed Gabor Bartusz's

involvement in the phone sex business. "Miss Bartusz," he began, "I think that you indicated that your husband is in the phone [sex] business?

"He was," she replied.

"And was Mr. Griga?"

"Yes."

"Was it mere coincidence that two people in the same type of business lived so close to one another?"

"My husband and Frank grew up in Hungary together and they were best friends. They wanted to live near each other."

Guralnick asked her to explain how the phone sex business works. "Do you know if they are sexually explicit conversations?"

Levine objected to the question. "Irrelevant," she said. Her objection was sustained.

Guralnick persisted. "Is it only women that answer the phone?" Levine objected again, and again Judge Ferrer sustained the objection. Guralnick changed the subject. He succeeded in getting Bartusz to admit that on the night of May 24, when she met Lugo and Doorbal, neither man made any threatening or menacing gestures.

Mese's attorney had no questions for Bartusz, who left the witness stand, her testimony clearly linking Lugo and Doorbal to the murdered couple the night they disappeared.

Next, Gail Levine called housekeeper Eszter Lapolla to the stand. She had remarried since May 24, 1995, when her last name was Toth. With the help of an interpreter, Eszter testified that she met two men at Griga's house the evening the couple disappeared. Adrian Doorbal was one of them, and she pointed him out in court. Griga and Furton left with the two men, she said, and they did not return the following morning.

"Did you sleep well that night?" Gail Levine asked.

She didn't, Lapolla said, "Because the dog was scratching at the door all night."

"Was that unusual?"

"He never did it before."

She never heard Krisztina and Frank come home that night, Eszter said. She awoke at five in the morning, her sleep disturbed by Chopin's scratching. She looked in the garage and noticed that the Lamborghini was not in it. Eszter went back to sleep until seven when she awoke again, took her daughter to school, and returned to pack her belongings. Before leaving the house that morning, she left a note on the refrigerator thanking the couple for putting her and her daughter up. On Friday, Eszter returned to the house, and what she saw alarmed her. She phoned Judi Bartusz. Later, the two women entered the house together. Eszter's testimony corroborated Judi's.

Sparks flew between Gail Levine and Tony Natale during the defense attorney's cross-examination, which began with what seemed like harmless banter.

"Good afternoon, ma'am," Natale said. "We never had a chance to meet before, have we?"

"No."

"We never talked on the telephone?"

Levine was on her feet. "Objection, irrelevant," she shouted angrily.

"Move on," Judge Ferrer said, seeming to ignore the prosecutor's objection.

"You had the opportunity to speak to Ms. Levine before, haven't you?" Natale asked.

Levine was on her feet again, fuming. "Judge, irrelevant! She is supposed to speak with me," the prosecutor declared. "May I come sidebar?"

"I don't think there is anything inappropriate about the questions I am asking," Natale said defensively, but Judge Ferrer saw it differently, and he was angry, too.

"What you are doing is you are implying that the prosecutor has coached this witness, and that's an inappropriate, improper implication," he told Natale. "And there is no other reason to ask her if you have spoken to her before other than to imply that. You cannot stand up there and imply to the jury that the witness has been coached."

Ferrer sustained Levine's objection. "Don't ask that anymore," he sternly warned the defense attorney.

Bruce Fleischer, Mese's attorney, had no questions for the housekeeper, but Ron Guralnick did. "From what you observed, did it appear that Frank and Krisztina and the other men were friendly to one another?" he wanted to know.

"They were not yelling at one another," Lapolla answered.

"Did they appear to be pleasant?"

"They looked normal."

On that note the cross-examination of Eszter Lapolla ended. She was followed to the witness stand by thirty-one-year-old Attila Weiland, the man who unwittingly arranged the bogus investment meeting that brought Adrian Doorbal and Danny Lugo together with Frank Griga. Weiland testified that he was part of a tightly knit Hungarian social circle in South Florida, which was how he met Frank Griga.

"Did you become friends with Frank Griga?" Levine asked. Weiland said he did, and while they socialized only occasionally, they often spoke on the telephone about business, and making money, and life in South Florida.

"Did you seek advice from him?" the prosecutor wanted to know.

"I always asked him if he knew any way to start here, and he said making the first thousand dollars is the hardest thing. After that, if you have the money, the money makes more."

Attila said he became acquainted with Noel Doorbal through his ex-wife Beatriz, a stripper at Solid Gold who came to the United States with him in 1991. They separated in 1993 and divorced in 1995, Weiland said, and he admitted that he was in the U.S. illegally. Levine wanted to know if Doorbal ever told him how he earned his living. Weiland remembered Doorbal telling him that he was doing work for the CIA.

Doorbal mentioned to him that he was looking for partners for a phone business in Asia, and he asked Weiland to arrange a meeting with Frank Griga, which Weiland did, testifying that he arrived at Griga's home with the two musclemen. He was there when they met with Griga to pitch the investment. The meeting lasted less than an hour. As they drove away, Weiland said, Doorbal was in very high spirits, gushing that "the meeting was good and the future looked bright." Weiland didn't have the heart to tell his muscle-bound pals what Griga said to him in Hungarian—that he had no interest in investing his money with Danny Lugo and Adrian Doorbal.

Levine wanted to know if Danny Lugo was in the courtroom. After pointing him out, the prosecutor asked if Adrian Doorbal was in the courtroom, too. This time, Tony Natale didn't stipulate to his presence, so Weiland pointed him out.

"Let me ask you something, Mr. Weiland," Levine continued. "Does Mr. Doorbal look the same as he did in May 1995?"

"No," he responded. "He is different. He definitely lost weight, at least thirty pounds. His face is thinner, and his hair is shorter."

The Sun Gym muscleman had been off steroids since June 3, 1995, the day he was arrested. As for Danny Lugo, he had gained weight, Weiland said.

Weiland testified that he phoned Frank Griga early on the evening that Griga and Furton disappeared. He recalled that Frank told him, "The guys are here, and we're talking some business." Three days later Weiland spoke with Doorbal, this time to tell the muscleman that the couple was missing. He phoned him again on May 31, and this time Doorbal spoke to him in a menacing tone that frightened him.

"He just told me, 'Attila, you are supposed to be my friend,' " Weiland recalled, adding that "The tone of his voice told me to back off."

On cross, Natale tried to establish Danny Lugo's domination of Doorbal, that he led the business talks with Frank Griga while Doorbal remained mostly silent, and that Adrian Doorbal was always a gentleman.

When Ron Guralnick took his turn cross-examining Weiland, he asked, "It was Mr. Doorbal you felt threatened by, correct?"

"Yes," Weiland said. A few minutes later he was excused. Judge Ferrer declared a ten-minute recess, after which Attila's ex-wife Beatriz was slated to be the prosecution's next witness.

It was late afternoon and Beatriz Weiland had been patiently waiting outside the courtroom since eleven when Gail Levine stood and announced, "At this time the state calls Beatriz Weiland." Heads turned when the stunning blonde entered the courtroom. She never looked at Adrian Doorbal as she walked to the witness stand and swore to tell the truth, the whole truth, and nothing but the truth. Then Beatriz sat down and waited for the first question.

"Good afternoon," Levine began. "Please tell the members of the jury your name."

"My name is Beatriz Weiland."

Responding to the prosecutor's questions, Weiland stated that she was born in Budapest, Hungary, and came to the United States in 1991 with her then-husband, Attila. They married in 1990 and divorced in 1995. She had arrived at the courthouse with Attila, and despite the breakup of their marriage, they remained very close, "best friends," she said.

"Do you have a trade?" Levine asked.

"I am a facialist. I work in a beauty salon," Weiland answered.

"Have you ever worked anywhere else in Miami besides a beauty salon?"

"Yes, in Miami I worked at Solid Gold. I was a dancer," she said, adding that she worked there for five years.

"Tell the members of the jury, did you dance with your clothes on or off?"

"Yes, it is strip, and we take off the dress."

With that out of the way, Levine zeroed in on the Solid Gold stripper's relationships with Frank Griga and Adrian Doorbal, and how the muscleman came to target Frank Griga.

She said she dated Griga for three months after she met him in the early 1990s. Their relationship ended on good terms, and they remained close. "He was like brother to me," Beatriz said in accented English.

"Did he ever give you money?" Levine asked.

"Yes, lots of times. He was very generous guy."

As for Doorbal, she met him at Solid Gold sometime around Christmas 1994, and they began dating in early 1995. Doorbal, she said, usually came in with his friend Danny. They were big spenders, Beatriz said. Doorbal was sweet and considerate.

"Look around the courtroom. Do you see Adrian Doorbal?" the prosecutor asked.

Beatriz said she did, and she pointed him out. Then she did the same for Danny Lugo.

"Let the record reflect that the witness has identified Noel Adrian Doorbal and Daniel Lugo," Gail Levine said.

Weiland testified that Doorbal told her that he was investing money for global computer businesses, that he and Lugo owned a gym, and that Lugo worked for the CIA. Doorbal, she said, told her that he occasionally helped Lugo with his CIA missions.

Beatriz testified that before she ended the relationship with the diminutive muscleman, she showed him her personal photo album. Three photos were of Griga's yellow Lamborghini, and there were others of Frank Griga. The photos were introduced into evidence. Doorbal, Weiland said, wanted to know all about the car, and about the car's owner. Never suspecting that he had anything sinister in mind, Beatriz told him about Frank and his wealth. A few weeks later, Doorbal phoned the Hungarian beauty and asked her to introduce him to Frank Griga. He had an investment opportunity in mind and he wanted to offer it to Frank.

"Did you talk to Frank Griga about that?" Levine asked.

"No," Beatriz answered.

"In May 1995, did you go to Frank Griga's for a party?"

"Yes, he had a birthday party," Beatriz answered.

"You were there?"

"Yes."

"And Attila was there?"

"Yes."

"Did you ever see Frank alive again?"

"No," she said, then she lowered her head and began to cry. After a brief pause so she could compose herself, Beatriz recalled that on May 27, 1995, she learned from Attila that Frank and Krisztina were missing, and four days later she was interviewed by MDPD homicide detective Sal Garafalo. On June 1, she saw Doorbal and Lugo at Solid Gold. They tried to find out what she had told detectives, but Weiland left them in the middle of the Champagne Room to alert police. After leaving a voice mail message for Detective Garafalo, Beatriz said she returned to the Champagne Room but the musclemen were gone.

Under cross-examination by Tony Natale, Weiland stated that as far as she could tell Danny Lugo held sway over Adrian Doorbal; Lugo, she said, was definitely "the boss."

"Based on what you could see between the interaction [sic], it would be Danny who would be the one who would come up with the ideas, and Adrian would then follow and go along, right?"

"Yes."

On cross, Ron Guralnick was able to get Beatriz to temper her statement that Lugo was "the boss."

"You don't talk about boss when somebody is really two good friends," she explained.

Guralnick continued. "You told us how nice Mr. Doorbal was, and that he had done nice things for you, remember"?

"Yes."

"And was there a time that he did something or asked you to do something that really freaked you out?"

"No," Weiland said.

Frustrated, Guralnick said he had no further questions. Mese attorney Bruce Fleischer had no questions at all for the Hungarian stripper. Beatriz Weiland left the witness stand and walked out of the courtroom. On her way out she never looked at her former paramour, Noel Adrian Doorbal.

The first day of testimony in the State v. Daniel Lugo, Noel Adrian Doorbal, and John Carl Mese had been a very good one for the prosecution. Gail Levine and her team had indisputably tied Lugo and Doorbal to Griga and Furton on the last night of their lives. What's more, testimony from Judi Bartusz, Eszter Lapolla, and the Weilands brought Frank and Krisztina to life for the jurors. They came to know Frank Griga as a smart, successful, and generous young man, someone highly respected and loved by all who knew him. As for Krisztina Furton, she was revealed to be a gentle young woman who never had a harsh word for anyone. She loved her dog, her life in Miami, and Frank Griga.

In the days ahead prosecutors would try to show that the abduction of Marcelo Schiller and the Griga-Furton murders were part of an ongoing criminal enterprise, and they would have to prove that the Sun Gym ringleaders were behind the shocking crimes. Even though court was over for the day, the prosecution team went back to their office where they would burn the midnight oil preparing for the next day's testimony.

For the rest of the week, jurors would hear from a steady stream of cops. The first was Donna Ganz, the Florida Highway Patrol trooper whose dispatcher sent her to a remote area in northwest Miami-Dade County on the morning of May 28, 1995 to investigate a report of an abandoned yellow Lamborghini.

"Could you tell the members of the jury what the land is like there?" Gail Levine asked.

"It is wooded. There is no housing. Just a lot of land, dense brush," Trooper Ganz replied. It's an area known for cockfights and dumping of garbage and old cars, she added, but never a car like a Lamborghini.

"Is it an area that can be easily seen from the road?" the prosecutor wanted to know.

"No."

Trooper Ganz testified that she located the pricey automobile, looked inside, then called for a flatbed tow truck to take the car to an impound lot in Opa-Locka. Gail Levine showed her several photos.

"Do you recognize what's in those photographs?" the prosecutor inquired.

"Yes, that's the car," the trooper answered.

Ganz was followed to the witness stand by police officer Agnes Sarisky Duncan, an MDPD police officer assigned to the Crime Scene Bureau. She had been sent to Frank Griga's house on May 29, 1995 to process it for fingerprints. Under direct examination by Assistant State Prosecutor David Weinstein, Duncan testified that she lifted prints from two drinking glasses that were on a coffee table.

"You said you lifted these latents. How do you do that?" Weinstein asked.

Duncan explained: "I use fingerprint powder and the brush, and I dust the surface that I suspect has the ridge detail on it. If I see anything I put something like Scotch Tape on and I rub it out and lift it, put it on a latent card, and I affix it and I back it with a case number, the date, my initials, my badge number, and the item that I lifted the fingerprint from, and where the item was located at the time that I picked it up and dusted it."

Weinstein then showed Duncan several latent fingerprint cards and asked if they were the ones she used at the Griga house on May 29. She said they were. She collected them then left to process the Lamborghini at the impound lot. At the end of the day, Duncan turned the cards in to the Crime Scene Bureau's identification experts, one of whom would testify later in the trial.

The next day jurors heard from lead detective Sal Garafalo. The veteran lawman testified that he interviewed Judi Bartusz, Eszter Lapolla, and the Weilands on June 1.

"After speaking with them did you have suspects in mind?" Gail Levine inquired.

"Yes, I did."

"Who?"

"Mr. Daniel Lugo and Mr. Adrian Doorbal."

Under further questioning Garafalo recalled that after receiving information from Detective Iris Deegan of the robbery unit, he contacted Marcelo Schiller in Colombia and asked him to come to Miami. When Schiller arrived on June 2, Garafalo showed him a photo lineup.

"Did he pick anyone out from the pictures?" Levine asked.

"Yes," the detective answered. "Danny Lugo and Jorge Delgado."

Marc Schiller did not get his day in court until March 9. In the week preceding, jurors heard testimony from lawmen and leasing agents; the lawmen testified to dozens of items they found during searches of the Sun Gym gang's homes and offices, while the leasing agents identified Lugo and Doorbal as the men who signed leases for the Main Street apartments and the Hialeah warehouse where Frank Griga and Krisztina Furton's bodies were dismembered. But when he was called to tell the jury his story, Marc Schiller walked briskly to the witness stand, eager to finally confront Lugo and Doorbal, two of the men accused of kidnapping him and trying to kill him, and John Carl Mese, the man who investigators said helped them steal his money and his house.

Under questioning from Gail Levine, Schiller revealed his background; how he came to the United States with his parents as a young boy, grew up in New York, studied accounting at the University of Wisconsin, and became a CPA. Fluent in Spanish, he went to work for a company in Bogota, Colombia, where he met and married his wife, Diana. They moved to Miami in 1988, after the president of the company had been kidnapped by leftist guerillas. In Miami, Schiller launched his own accounting firm and a Medicare business. He hired Jorge Delgado, the down-and-out husband of his employee, Linda Delgado.

The business did well, Schiller said, earning one million dollars a year working from home. In 1994, he opened a Schlotzsky's restaurant. Through Delgado he met Danny Lugo.

"Take a look around the courtroom. Tell us if you see the person you knew as Daniel Lugo," Levine commanded.

"He's sitting right there in the gray suit, glasses, gray and black necktie," Schiller said, pointing his finger at the muscleman.

Schiller related how Jorge Delgado's demeanor and behavior changed when he began working out with Danny Lugo at Sun Gym. "He was trying to act tough and cruel. He wasn't the Jorge Delgado I knew," Schiller said.

Then the questions turned to John Mese. "Mr. Schiller," Levine began, "there is a saying about lawyers, that we shouldn't represent ourselves, but do they do their own taxes?"

"I've always done my own," Schiller replied.

"Did you use the services of John Mese in any way?"

"Never," Schiller declared resoundingly.

"Did you ever see a person named John Mese?"

"Never, not that I recall. I never heard of him."

After a lunch break, Schiller returned to the witness stand. This time he would answer questions about November 15, 1994, the day he was abducted from outside his restaurant.

"Tell the members of the jury what you were doing and what happened." Levine said.

Schiller recalled working late that day. He usually went home by three o'clock, he said, but he stayed late to meet a potential buyer for the delicatessen. At about four thirty, he left the restaurant through the back door.

"As I approached my car, I noticed some people walking towards me. I didn't get a good look at them. I opened the door and they grabbed me from behind. They had a Taser and they kept applying it. I yelled help but nobody came, and they dragged me into a van."

"Tell the members of the jury what it felt like."

"It was like getting an electric shock through the whole body. Very painful."

"How many times did you feel that electric shock through your body?"

"So many times I couldn't count them."

Over the next month, Schiller told how he was repeatedly tortured with a stun gun, pistol-whipped, burned, beaten, threatened, and forced to sign over all of his assets. "They slapped me, they hit me, they shocked me," he said. At all times he was kept blindfolded and handcuffed inside a warehouse. His face bled from sores that developed as a result of having duct tape covering his skin from his forehead to his cheeks. For nearly two weeks after his capture, Schiller recalled, he was not allowed to bathe or brush his teeth. During the day, he was kept handcuffed in an oppressively hot bathroom. In addition to his physical torture, his captors tortured him mentally throughout his captivity. He was told that if he did not cooperate his wife would be captured, brought over to the warehouse, and raped in front of him, and that his children would be handcuffed right next to him. He was forced to urinate on himself and to wear those clothes for two weeks before being allowed to change. During his captivity, Schiller had a gun put to his head for a game of Russian roulette. The cylinder was spun and the trigger was pulled twice. By the end of his captivity he had lost forty pounds.

But it wasn't long before he realized who was behind his abduction. He recognized Lugo's voice, Schiller said, and he realized that only Jorge Delgado could have provided his captors with the information they had about his assets and his house.

"There was nobody else," Schiller declared.

Once they had stolen all of his property, his captors attempted to murder him by drugging him, making him drink large amounts of alcohol, crashing his vehicle, and setting it on fire with him inside, but Schiller survived thanks to the skilled surgeons at Miami's Jackson Memorial Hospital. Instead of going to police, Schiller hired private investigator Ed Du Bois.

"How come you didn't call the police?" Levine wanted to know.

"I didn't know what to do at that time," Schiller explained, speaking haltingly, trying to remember. "It was a very tough period. I knew I had to do something but I was mentally a mess in those days."

He had just been through a month in a warehouse, ten days in two hospitals, and had lost forty pounds. He explained that he was not in the best of shape. He couldn't talk to anybody. His wife would ask him what happened and he couldn't even tell her. And, he added, he had no money, no house, no furniture, and no clothes. He couldn't sleep, he said, because of night terrors stemming from his month-long imprisonment.

Marc Schiller would be on the witness stand for three days as Gail Levine showed him photographs of his house and items that had been stolen from it—the quitclaim deed transferring ownership of his house to D & J International, cancelled checks drawn on his accounts but made out to Sun Gym Consultants or D & J International, the change of insurance beneficiary forms for his MetLife policies and other items that he had been forced to sign while blindfolded, as well as other documents that were found at Doorbal and Lugo's apartments and John Mese's office.

Showing him a photo of a black leather couch, Levine asked, "Mr. Schiller, did you ever give [Mr. Doorbal] this furniture?"

"No." And she asked Schiller if he ever knowingly signed the documents—the quitclaim deed, the cancelled checks, and the life insurance change of beneficiary forms. Again and again, he said no. Next, she showed him a gold chain and a Cartier bracelet.

"That's my chain," he said. And "that's the bracelet I was wearing on November 15, 1994. They took everything I was wearing that day."

"You mean you didn't put this in 6911 Main Street, Apartment 224, or give this to Noel Doorbal?" Levine asked sarcastically.

"I have never been to that apartment," Schiller replied.

Anticipating that defense attorneys would hammer him for not going to the police immediately, Levine brought Schiller back to his mental state in the days and weeks after he left Jackson Memorial Hospital. She asked him to tell the jury about his physical and mental condition between January and April 1995.

"That was a really difficult period of time," he began. "My physical condition was terrible, and I could hardly walk. I was still recuperating from my surgery, and physically I was very limited for a long time. I couldn't walk. I walked on crutches finally in February.

"I had problems with my bladder, and mentally it was a devastating period for me. I was depressed all the time. And sometimes I would get in a catatonic state, a very debilitated state, and stare out the window a long time. I was lost and confused and I had been completely displaced. One day you're in your house and the next day you're not. And it was just a total state of being lost. Nothing belongs to you, and you belong nowhere. I had nothing to show who I was. Basically what was taken away was my whole person, the essence of who I was. And it was really difficult for me during that time."

Tony Natale was the first to cross-examine Schiller. Instead, he focused on Schiller's inability to identify Doorbal as one of his kidnappers.

"You had no photographic array identification of Mr. Doorbal, did you?"

"No."

"And no voice identification of Mr. Doorbal?"

"No."

"But you identified Mr. Lugo?"

"Yes, I did."

"By voice and photographs?"

"Correct."

Then Natale shifted to Jorge Delgado. "Mr. Schiller, is it fair for us to say that this whole ordeal of yours began with Mr. Delgado?

"I think that it's a good possibility," Schiller agreed.

"And that during your captivity, Mr. Delgado was the one providing all the detailed information?"

"There would be nobody else."

"And he was deceitful to you?"

"Yes."

"And he attempted to deal in your death, correct?"

"It appears that way."

Ron Guralnick, however, zeroed in on Schiller's failure to go to police for four months, and that when he did, police were skeptical. And he tried to discredit Schiller's voice identification of Danny Lugo.

"Mr. Schiller, you indicated that you could not physically identify Mr. Lugo as one of your abductors, I mean by the way he looks, correct?"

"Correct," Schiller answered.

CHAPTER TWENTY-TWO

He better get his butt out of Dodge right now
if he wants to live.

—ED DU BOIS

As he stepped away from the witness stand, Marc Schiller glanced over his left shoulder toward Danny Lugo. He felt good about his testimony. He felt vindicated. He had confronted the leaders of the Sun Gym gang, told his story, and survived cross-examination. He was confident that the jury believed him. After a five-minute recess, Gail Levine called her next witness, private investigator Edward Du Bois III.

The prosecutor introduced the lanky private eye to the jurors by asking questions about his professional background—president of Investigators, Inc., the detective agency founded by his father when he retired from the FBI in 1955; licensed private investigator since 1960; Florida State University graduate; outside contractor over the years for virtually every law enforcement agency in Miami-Dade and Broward counties; investigator in South Florida for the National Football League; investigator for attorneys: "We do surveillance and background investigations, we locate assets, we find witnesses, and we take statements," Du Bois said.

He testified about the telephone call he received from attorney Gene Rosen in December, 1994, and the subsequent phone conversation he had with Marc Schiller who was in an intensive care unit hospital bed the day after he underwent six hours of surgery.

"What did you tell him?" Levine asked.

"I told him if the circumstances surrounding his problem were accurate, and he was in fear of his life, then the prudent thing to do was to leave the hospital immediately."

He heard from Schiller again in January, Du Bois said, and he agreed to investigate. He asked Schiller to send him a memo detailing his ordeal along with a copy of a quit-claim deed and a change of beneficiary form for Schiller's MetLife policy.

"Did you receive this?" Levine asked, showing Du Bois a document.

"Yes, I did."

"And that's a quitclaim deed?"

"Correct."

"And you received a life insurance change of beneficiary form, was it from MetLife?

"Yes, ma'am."

"And who did it change the beneficiary to?"

"To a woman named Lillian Torres."

He had no idea who Lillian Torres was, Du Bois said, but he did recognize the name of the man who notarized the document: John Carl Mese.

"Take a look around the room," Levine directed. "Do you see John Mese in the courtroom today?"

"Yes, I do. How are you doing, John?" Du Bois asked as Mese rose from his chair and waved.

"Let the record reflect that the defendant stood up and waved," Levine declared.

Du Bois recalled phoning John Mese to set up an appointment, and he recounted the series of meetings he had with Mese and Jorge Delgado. He testified that while waiting for a meeting to begin in a room inside Mese's accounting office, his associate, private investigator Ed Seibert, discovered dozens of documents linking the Sun Gym gang to the plundering of Marc Schiller's assets in a trash can.

"Did you watch Mr. Seibert retrieve items from the garbage?" Levine asked.

"Yes, I did."

"And did he start handing them to you?

"Yes."

"And did you start looking at them?"

"Yes."

"After you looked at them, what did you do with them?"

Du Bois said he and Seibert began stuffing them into their pockets and their briefcases.

The documents, Du Bois said, were a road map that went from Schiller's accounts in the Cayman Islands and Miami directly to Sun Fitness Consultants, and then to Sun Gym. From there, the money moved to the Mese and Associates account at County National Bank. There were even checks for thousands of dollars made payable to Doorbal, Lillian Torres, and John Mese.

After they stuffed their pockets with the documents, Mese entered the room and escorted the private detectives to another room where Jorge Delgado was waiting. Du Bois began speaking when, suddenly, Delgado threw up his hand signaling him to stop. He declared that Schiller's money, $1.26 million, would be returned. Schiller, however, would have to sign a statement that the money was returned because of a "sour business deal," and he had to agree not to report the matter to the police. Delgado, Du Bois said, dictated an agreement that the private eye took back to his office where it was typed.

"What were you thinking about the agreement?" Gail Levine wanted to know.

"Take the money and run, then go to the police," he replied.

"Why is that?"

"In my mind, I am not a lawyer, but I did not think that a victim could be coerced into signing an agreement like that."

But it soon became apparent that the Sun Gym thugs were stalling, that they had no intention of returning anything to Marc Schiller. Again and again, they revised the agreement that had first been dictated by Delgado. Finally, Schiller and Du Bois concluded that they were not going to get any money from the Sun Gym gang; they decided to go to the police. Du Bois recounted how he contacted MDPD captain Al Harper. He had Schiller prepare another memo and arranged a meeting with police and Schiller, but to his dismay, lawmen were skeptical and seemingly uninterested in investigating Schiller's allegations. In late May 1995, Du Bois said he became aware of the disappearance of the Hungarian couple from Golden Beach. On June 1, he met in his office with Sergeant Felix Jimenez, and he filled the lawman in on his investigation of the Sun Gym gang and the abduction of Marc Schiller.

"While Sergeant Jimenez was in your office, he started making some phone calls pretty frantically, didn't he?" Levine asked.

"Yes, ma'am," Du Bois responded.

Jimenez was phoning his homicide team, getting them ready to hunt for the missing couple and to take down the Sun Gym gang.

Levine was almost finished with her direct examination of Ed Du Bois, but she had one more avenue to pursue.

"I am showing you what's been marked 904," the prosecutor said, referring to a document that had been marked for evidence. "Is this the copy of the quitclaim deed? The copy that you showed John Carl Mese the very first day in February that you saw him?"

"Yes."

"And he never once said that he did not notarize that document, is that correct?"

Before Du Bois could answer, Mese's attorney was

on his feet. "Stipulated that Mr. Mese had notarized that document in opening statement, and we admitted to that," Bruce Fleischer declared.

"We will accept that stipulation," Levine said. "No further questions for this witness."

Under cross-examination, Tony Natale elicited testimony from Du Bois that at all times he was negotiating with Jorge Delgado or John Mese.

"Did John Mese ever say that he was representing Jorge Delgado?" Natale inquired.

"Yes," the private eye said.

"Did John Mese ever say that he was representing Mr. Lugo?"

"Yes."

"Did John Mese ever say that he was representing Mr. Doorbal?"

"No."

"During the course of your investigation, do you know of any evidence that would link Mr. Doorbal to any specific actions, as it relates to Mr. Schiller's kidnapping?"

"No."

Ron Guralnick, Lugo's attorney, wasted no time trying to discredit Ed Du Bois by impugning his motives.

"Isn't it better for the police to get right on top of the case, right when it happens, rather than letting four or five months go by before they are even told about it?" the defense attorney asked.

"Usually, yes.

"Why is this case different than that?

"Because the police are not reactive. The police would not have come out to see Mr. Schiller on December fifteenth."

"How do you know they weren't going to do that?

"Because I dealt with police all my life, and I know that if Mr. Schiller, his life was in jeopardy and if he felt that these guys were coming to kill him like they planned to do, then he better get his butt out of Dodge right now if he wants to live. The crime had been perpetrated against him.

He had plenty of time to go to the police. He was in harm's way and he was going to die if he stayed at that hospital, and the best advice was for him to get out of that hospital."

"Well, let me ask you a question. He named certain individuals that he felt were involved in this crime, did he not?"

"Yes."

"Supposing by not going to the police these certain persons took off for parts unknown and whatever, the police would have lost them, wouldn't they?"

"Well, at least he would still be alive. If I called the police that day and told them about my plight with my client, Marc Schiller, and they would have sent a note-taker out to interview him in the hospital and take a lot of notes, go back to the police department and talk to their sergeant and discuss the case. Then, three or four days later would come back out there, by that time Marc Schiller would have been dead at Jackson Memorial Hospital."

"This is your interpretation?" Guralnick asked.

"Yes."

"Okay, sir. You are earning a fee from Mr. Schiller, correct? You were?"

"No, no, no, not at first.

"Did you not ask him for a retainer before you were doing this?

"In January, yes."

"How much did you ask him for?"

"I asked him for a thousand dollars."

"Okay. Wasn't it fifteen hundred dollars?"

"I thought that it was fifteen hundred, but it was a thousand."

"So that was a mistake at your deposition?"

"Yes."

"So, it was a thousand dollars and how much has he paid you so far?"

"Mr. Schiller paid me six thousand dollars and change, I think."

"And he owes quite a bit, doesn't he?"

"Yes."

"How much?"

"Seven thousand dollars more."

"Sir, isn't it a fact that if you had directed the police to this immediately you wouldn't have been earning a fee, would you, sir, because the police would have taken over the investigation?"

"Well, I wouldn't have earned a fee because he would have been dead."

"And let's say he would be alive, you wouldn't have earned a fee if the police investigated this case from the beginning because you notified them in the beginning, would you, sir?"

"Fees were not my concern when I told Mr. Schiller to get out of the hospital and go to his sister's house. I didn't think that I had a case. I didn't really care. The fees were not the consideration. His well-being and his life were my consideration."

"We can't say that you did not have some vested interest in this as far as not reporting it to the police?"

"That's true," Du Bois said, adding, "My business is similar to yours. If I take a client, I want to get paid."

Despite the tough questions, Du Bois remained unflappable, and he held his own, so Guralnick tried another tack.

"You never had any conversations with Danny Lugo, did you?"

"No."

"You never even met Danny Lugo?"

"No, sir."

"Danny Lugo never signed any of those documents?"

"No."

Referring to the meetings at Mese's office, Guralnick asked if Lugo ever attended any of them. He didn't, Du Bois conceded.

"But Mr. Delgado always showed up to the meetings, correct?"

"Yes."

"And it was Mr. Delgado who gave you the conditions that were necessary before he said he would return the money to Mr. Schiller, correct?"

"Yes."

"It was Delgado who said that you can have the money?"

"Yes."

The defense attorney tried to create doubt about Lugo's involvement in the Schiller kidnapping, but in the days that followed, other key witnesses would take the witness stand, and their powerful testimony would irrefutably tie Lugo to the Schiller kidnapping.

The first key witness was Danny Lugo's ex-wife, Lillian Torres.

"Lillian, have you ever met anyone by the name of Marcelo Schiller?" Gail Levine wanted to know.

"No."

"Were you ever the girlfriend of Marcelo Schiller?"

"No."

"The fiancée of Marcelo Schiller?"

Again, Torres answered, "No."

She did recall signing some papers that Lugo had brought to her home one day, testifying that she just did as he asked without reading them because she trusted him. And she remembered going to John Mese's offices once, but while there she never signed any papers. She also recalled going to a warehouse in Hialeah where Lugo allowed her to select various items of furniture, and she testified also that beginning in late November 1994, Lugo began giving her thousands of dollars.

"He said it was for my children and my education because he wanted me to go back to school," Lillian remembered. At Christmastime he took Lillian and the children to the Bahamas.

Big Mario Sanchez tied Lugo and Doorbal to the Schiller kidnapping. Sanchez testified that he helped abduct Marc Schiller on November 15, 1994, and he was at the warehouse when Lugo arrived there after Doorbal's "the

eagle has landed" phone call. Sanchez, who worked as the
Sun Gym weight lifting instructor, also testified that Doorbal approached him in April 1995, offering him five thousand dollars to participate in a similar kidnapping. He did
not know who the target was, but he clearly remembered
Doorbal saying that he wanted a yellow Lamborghini.

Stevenson Pierre, the Sun Gym front desk manager, testified that he was in on the planning of the Schiller kidnapping from day one. He recalled the first meeting at Danny
Lugo's office inside Mese and Associates in Miami Lakes.

"Tell the members of the jury what happened when you
went into the office," Gail Levine directed.

Lugo led the meeting, Pierre said, "more or less telling us
about this individual and letting us know that he owed [Lugo
and Delgado] money. And they were all involved in some type
of medical fraud, Medicaid fraud, and this individual treated
them bad. He went on saying that this individual treated Jorge
Delgado bad, and he had a baby coming, and they needed the
money. And at the same time he offered us over a hundred
thousand dollars each to participate."

He even went to The Spy Shop with Danny Lugo, where
they purchased handcuffs, Tasers, walkie-talkies, and bat-
teries. On the day of the abduction, Pierre said, he was
called to Delgado's Hialeah warehouse where he saw Schiller tied up. He looked on as Schiller was zapped with the
Taser and beaten, and he watched as Schiller was forced by
Danny Lugo to sign dozens of documents. He also testified
that Doorbal wanted to kill Schiller from the very beginning, but Danny Lugo wavered before finally deciding that
Schiller had to die. In the wee hours of December 15, 1994,
Lugo phoned Pierre and asked him to drive to an industrial
area on NW 36th Street. When he arrived, he saw Schiller's smoldering Toyota 4Runner. Firemen were on the
scene, extinguishing the flames. A cop directing traffic at
the scene told Pierre that a drunk driver had hit a pole and
then was run over by another vehicle.

Immediately afterward, he drove to the warehouse
where Doorbal, Lugo, and Weekes were laughing about

what they had done to Schiller, and they were imitating how Schiller staggered down the road when he escaped from the burning SUV. Two days later, Pierre was part of the group that went to Jackson Memorial Hospital to murder Schiller in his hospital bed, but they couldn't find him.

"How were you going to kill him?" Levine asked.

"By any means necessary," Pierre answered.

"Any ideas as to how?"

"Suffocate him."

Sabina Petrescu was a key witness, too. Despite a grant of immunity, she was visibly nervous when she took the stand.

"Take a deep breath and tell the members of the jury your name," Gail Levine directed.

"Elena Sabina Petrescu," she whispered.

"One more time, Sabina, state you name nice and loud," the prosecutor prodded.

"I'm sorry."

"Nice and loud, tell the members of the jury your name."

"Elena Sabina Petrescu," she said loudly.

"How long have you been in the United States?"

"Seven years."

"And where did you come from?"

"Romania."

"Can you tell the members of the jury why you are so upset?"

"I cannot help it. I'm sorry."

After a few sips of water, the Romanian-born stripper composed herself and was able to continue with her testimony. In response to the prosecutor's questions, Sabina recalled that she met Danny Lugo on Super Bowl Sunday in January 1995, while she was working as a dancer at Solid Gold. She also met Adrian Doorbal and Carl Weekes. "Do you see Danny Lugo in the courtroom today?" Gail Levine asked.

"Yes," Sabina answered, then she became unnerved once again.

"Just point to him and tell me what he is wearing."

"He's wearing a suit, navy blue suit," Sabina said.

With that out of the way, Sabina recalled asking the muscleman, "Do you like me to dance for you?"

"What did he say?" prosecutor Levine asked.

"He said no, just sit down. And he was paying me twenty dollars quite often. And he was telling me about a video that he was sponsoring with Bruce Springsteen in London, and maybe he could use me for that."

Lugo pursued her, she said, and they began dating. He offered to set her up in an apartment that he would pay for. Eventually their relationship became sexual and they began living together in an apartment in Miami Lakes. He gave her a car, a BMW station wagon, and he told her he was a stock trader, and that he worked for the CIA.

"What did you think when he said that?" Levine asked.

"I found it exciting. I believed him. I thought the CIA, they're the agents, they go after the bad people, they're heroes."

Lugo even showed her surveillance equipment. On one occasion, he told Sabina he was going on a mission to catch a terrorist. Lugo pointed out the house of the terrorist to her and explained he was going to capture and beat him.

Levine wanted to know if Lugo ever mentioned Marc Schiller. "Did Danny tell you that he got involved in a disagreement between George Delgado and Marc Schiller?"

"Yes," Sabina replied. "Danny didn't like what Marc Schiller was doing to George, stealing from him. Danny found out that Marc Schiller was stealing from George, and he fixed it [so] that he wouldn't steal from him anymore."

"Who fixed it?" Levine asked.

"Danny."

"Did Danny tell you what he had to do to fix it?"

"No."

"Did Lugo ever discuss with you Marc Schiller's kidnapping?"

"He didn't tell me that he was kidnapped."

"What did he tell you?" Levine asked.

"He just told me, as far as I remember, he mentioned an accident, and he said he should have run that bastard over. He should have run that bastard over with the car, but he couldn't do it because he had a family, and somehow he was out of the country. I couldn't understand because he was just giving me bits of information. He would not give me the whole story.

Under questioning from Gail Levine, Petrescu testified that she accompanied Lugo to an attorney's office in Fort Lauderdale where she overheard a conversation about the payment of one million dollars to Marc Schiller; that Lugo told her about a Hungarian man who made a lot of money from phone sex and who was wanted by the FBI for not paying his taxes; that the man drove a yellow Lamborghini or Ferrari, and that Lugo explained that his mission was to capture the man and turn him over to the FBI. A few days later, Lugo and Doorbal showed up at their apartment with handcuffs, syringes, and tape. The musclemen, Sabina said, were getting ready for their mission. The plan was to tie the couple up, stuff them into in the trunk of Lugo's Mercedes, and, with Sabina behind the wheel, drive to a warehouse where they would be held. Sabina recalled driving to the Hungarian's Golden Beach home and waiting for the musclemen to emerge with their prey, but the abduction plot was aborted.

"We should have done it," she remembered Doorbal declaring angrily. Later, Lugo made plans to meet with the Hungarian man in the evening. Eventually, Lugo told her that the couple was at Doorbal's apartment. Lugo told her Doorbal's apartment stunk and it was cold. A day or two later, Petrescu drove with Danny Lugo to the Golden Beach house, but they were unable to enter it. On the way back to Miami Lakes, Sabina said she overheard a phone conversation Lugo had with Doorbal. "The bitch is cold," Doorbal said. Petrescu did not call the police because she believed that Danny Lugo worked for the CIA, and she was afraid that he would kill her.

Afterward, Lugo and Doorbal came to the apartment with a rug that they put into the balcony storage closet. They placed some computers on the floor. Later, Petrescu noticed blood on the computers. The next day, Lugo came to the apartment again, this time with Jorge Delgado and more items. Lugo and Petrescu then flew to the Bahamas. While there, Lugo learned that Adrian Doorbal and Delgado had been arrested. Lugo mentioned alternatively that he wanted to surrender or escape. He told her that bloody clothes were hidden in the bags in the apartment and he sent her back to Miami to dispose of them.

Sabina flew back to Miami. She was taken into custody at her apartment and eventually arrested. At first she lied to police, telling them that she didn't know where he was. She wanted to protect Danny, she said, because she was afraid he would be accused of something he had not done. Later she learned that Lugo had been arrested, too. She visited him in jail and on one occasion Lugo told her that police would not be able to identify the Hungarian couple because their fingers had been cut off and thrown into a canal and, she said, he mentioned something about teeth but she didn't understand what he meant.

"Is everything you testified to what you remember?" Levine asked.

"Yes."

"Not anything anyone suggested to you?"

"No."

"Even me?"

"No."

"By the way, do you still ask me every time you see me whether I'm going to arrest you?"

"Yes."

"Oh, by the way, did I tell you I'm only going to arrest you if you tell a lie?"

"Yes."

By the time Levine finished her direct examination, the Romanian beauty queen had calmed down. She even seemed relaxed. And it was a good thing, too, because she was about to undergo a withering cross-examination from Lugo attorney Ron Guralnick, but before that she had to endure Tony Natale's questioning.

"Danny didn't just cater to your physical needs or material needs, he was really able to get into your heart, wasn't he?" Natale asked.

"Yes," she answered.

"Is it fair to say there came a point in time when you believed you loved Danny?"

"Because he was very sweet and he cared for me. I felt I loved him, yes."

She trusted him, and he promised to teach her the stock market, Sabina said. He promised to care for her and to protect her.

"And Danny was very good at getting you to believe what he wanted you to believe, wasn't he?"

"I think that now," Sabina said.

"He deceived you, correct?"

"Yes."

"He betrayed you, correct?"

"Yes."

"And he led you astray?"

"Yes."

"Now there came a time, and I believe Miss Levine mentioned that you and she have spoken on several occasions?"

"Yes."

"And there came a time when you felt that, based on the actions of the prosecution by giving you immunity, that you were now protected, right?"

"Yes."

"They even provided money for you to get an apartment, right?"

"They loaned, yes, sure."

"And they discussed with you and prepared you for what was going to happen as this case went on, right?"

"Yes."

"Now you felt from your dealings with the prosecution that they were smart?"

"I think yes, sir, they're smart people."

"Objection, judge," Gail Levine shouted. "Can we have a sidebar?"

At sidebar, a fuming Gail Levine declared, "I object to this, whether I am smart, whether my team is smart. Whether we handled the case appropriately is not evidence for the jury. It shouldn't be considered by the jury the way the attorneys act. It is not evidence. I don't know where this line of questioning is going."

But Judge Ferrer knew. Speaking to Natale, he said: "There is an undercurrent there. You make Lugo out to be strong and smart, and now all of a sudden the state attorney is smart and strong. It seems to me that you've replaced Mr. Lugo with the state attorney's office as the ones she depends on."

After calling the defense attorney's line of questioning "some kind of psychobabble," Ferrer said Natale was "suggesting that the state attorney is in league with Lugo." He added, "You already represented to the jury through her [that Lugo] manipulated her, has lied to her, has done all these things. Now you are saying, 'All the qualities that he has, the state attorney has,' so by implication the state attorneys lie and manipulate, and she is being led like a sheep to the slaughter. If you have evidence of that, great, it's not a bad faith argument. Otherwise it is."

Ferrer sustained Levine's objection and Natale concluded his cross-examination. Ron Guralnick attacked Sabina's credibility, and he didn't waste any time.

"When you testified yesterday, didn't you say that when you first entered the United States it was in the trunk of a motor vehicle?" the defense attorney asked.

"Yes."

"So you entered the United States illegally?"

"Yes."

"Before you ever entered the United State illegally, you planned to enter illegally, isn't that correct?"

Sabina responded by claiming that she did not plan it, she just did what her ex-husband suggested.

"Did your husband force you into the trunk?" Guralnick asked.

"No," she replied.

They went back and forth on whether she planned to break the law, with Sabina insisting "I was not planning to break the law, but it was breaking the law. It was the only way."

Once in the United States, Sabina said she went to work as a stripper, but she was not proud of her chosen profession even though she would earn three to four hundred dollars a night in cash.

"Was that because you had to take your clothes off?" Guralnick asked.

"Yes."

Referring to the photos of her that were taken for *Penthouse* magazine, Guralnick asked, "So you had no embarassment of being published naked for everyone in the world without your clothes on?"

She hemmed and hawed, then Sabina asked a question: "Can I please not answer the questions anymore, this kind of questions?"

Immediately, Gail Levine objected to the defense attorney's question, declaring that it was irrelevant. Guralnick fired back. "First, she said she was embarassed, she didn't want to be a stripper because she had to take her clothes off. Now it comes out that she was trying to get into the centerfold of *Penthouse* magazine, which is worldwide, so she can't be too ashamed. This goes to her credibility." Nevertheless, Judge Ferrer sustained the prosecutor's objection, but Guralnick was undeterred; he hammered the Romanian-born stripper's credibility regarding other matters: She lied to customers at Solid Gold, telling them that her name was Beverly and that she came from France; she lied to police until she was offered immunity; and, he suggested, she was lying when she claimed that Danny Lugo told her he worked for the CIA.

"Did you ever ask him for an identification card or a badge?"

"No sir, I trusted him."

"Besides you and Mr. Lugo, was anyone else present when he told you about his CIA adventures?" Guralnick asked.

"No sir, never."

"Are you telling us that you want us to believe that you knew enough to get into this country illegally in the trunk of a car, that you've worked as a striptease dancer in New York, Las Vegas, and Los Angeles, and you want us to believe that you are so naïve that you would believe that Mr. Lugo is in the CIA?"

"Sir," Sabina began, "I know what I believed and I believed he was innocent, until I had facts from other people and they were telling me facts tied to him, to all this misery, to those clothes, those guns," she fired back, referring to the bloody clothes and firearms that detectives found stored in her apartment.

Sabina Petrescu was a key witness for the prosecution, but she was not the state's star witness. That designation belonged to Jorge Delgado. Only five feet, six inches tall, and scrawny and soft-spoken, there was nothing about Delgado that would cause anyone to think that he was a dangerous criminal, but he was the only one, other than the defendants, who could testify to everything the Sun Gym thugs had done or planned to do. For his appearance in the courtroom, Delgado was escorted by two beefy MDPD detectives, his hands were cuffed, and he wore a jailhouse jumpsuit. Over the next two days he would tell all, from the beginning of the plot to kidnap Marc Schiller to the dismemberment of Frank Griga and Krisztina Furton.

As soon as he arrived at the witness stand, Judge Ferrer

directed his police escorts to remove his handcuffs. Delgado raised his right hand and swore to tell the truth, the whole truth, and nothing but the truth. Then he sat down and began answering questions from Gail Levine.

Jurors learned that he was born in Havana in 1966 and came to Miami that same year. He had a degree in architecture, was thirty-three years old, his wife's name was Linda, they were the parents of a three-year-old daugher, it would be okay to call him George, and he once worked for Marc Schiller as a marketing representative before becoming his partner in a medical supply business that served Medicare recipients called Dadima Corporation.

"Did there come a time when Marc Schiller offered to sell you the medical supply portion of Dadima?" Gail Levine asked.

Delgado replied that he and a partner bought the business from Schiller and kept the name Dadima for a while, eventually changing the name to J & R Medical Investments. Schiller stayed on, however, as their accountant and also to handle the billing of Medicare.

"During this time did you start to make money?" Levine wanted to know.

"Yes"

"And did you join Sun Gym?"

Delgado said he did, both he and his wife in 1992, and he began training with Danny Lugo, working out at Sun Gym every other day. He also said that he knew Adrian Doorbal from the gym, too. At Levine's direction, Delgado pointed out Lugo and Doorbal, and his identification of the two musclemen was noted for the record.

"During this time did you have questions about the medical supply business and the legality of it?" Levine asked.

"Yes," Delgado responded, "at various times."

"Prior to that, did you question the legality of the medical supply business?"

"No."

"It was only after you purchased it and after you were in business for a while?

"Yes, four months," Delagado said.

"Did you discuss that with Marc Schiller?"

"Yes."

"Did you discuss it with defendant Danny Lugo?"

"Yes."

Asked if he and Lugo became friends, Delegado said they did, best friends, and he trusted him. Delegado also said he became friends with Doorbal, and he met John Mese, too. He even retained the accountant to do his accounting work. Asked why he would hire John Mese if Marc Schiller was his accountant, Delgado answered that Lugo suggested it.

"Did there come a time in late September or early October when defendant Lugo told you that there was a problem with the way Marc Schiller had done business for you?" Levine inquired.

"Yes," Delagado answered. "He brought it to my attention that Marc was cheating me when he did the billing on the Medicare business, and he showed me some paperwork dealing with that." Schiller, Lugo told Delgado, owed him two hundred thousand dollars.

"What happened next?"

"Lugo said that we should do something about it and try to get the money back, and then he wanted to make sure he can kidnap him and take the money back."

"What was your reaction?"

"I said just do whatever you've got to do and leave me out of it. I told him . . . do whatever you need to do to get the money."

"Now, George, did you think kidnapping someone for the money was wrong?"

"Yeah."

"So did you advise defendant Lugo that it is against the law to do that, that maybe you should have a lawsuit?"

Delgado said he didn't because "I knew the money wasn't legal," and because he feared that Schiller "could retaliate and kill me."

While he would not be involved in actually grabbing Schiller, Delgado testified that he provided information about Schiller's assets, his home, and his daily habits. Schiller would be held at Jorge Delgado's Hialeah warehouse, 22248 West 77th Street, and Delgado agreed to be available to keep an eye on him once Schiller was captured.

"Did you want Schiller to be physically hurt?" Levine asked.

"If that's what it took, yes," Delgado replied matter-of-factly.

"Who planned the kidnapping?" Gail Levine asked.

"Lugo."

"What was Lugo's job?"

"He was going to instruct everybody what to do and be involved in basically everything that dealt with the kidnapping. Stevenson Pierre and Carlton Weekes were going to help capture Schiller, then watch him while he was in the warehouse." Doorbal, Delgado said, was assigned to "bring Schiller down" and "get him to talk" and "rough him over."

"Was each person's job discussed in front of you?" the prosecutor asked.

"Yes."

"Who was in charge of giving out the jobs?"

"Lugo."

Delgado recalled receiving a phone call from Danny Lugo at about 4:30 P.M. on November 15, 1994. "I have a surprise for you," Delgado recalls Lugo saying. When he arrived at the warehouse he saw Marc Schiller hog-tied and blindfolded and lying on the floor. Lugo, Doorbal, Weekes, and Pierre were there, too. They agreed to take turns watching Schiller and prepared a schedule. Delgado watched as Marc Schiller was interrogated. He confirmed that Schiller was threatened at gunpoint, beaten, and burned with a cigarette.

"Did you care that any of this was happening to your old friend?" Gail Levine asked.

Delgado replied, "No."

The gang ordered Schiller to sign over real estate he owned, insurance policies he owned, and financial documents that would transfer money out of his bank and brokerage accounts. Documents that needed to be notarized were taken to John Mese by Danny Lugo, Delgado said.

"Did you become aware of John Mese's involvement concerning Marc Schiller?" Levine asked.

"Yes."

"Did John Mese, to the best of your knowledge, ever come to the warehouse?"

"Yes, he was there once, I think."

"Did you ever have a conversation with defendant Lugo where defendant Lugo explained to you how the money was going to change hands and how the property was going to be properly recorded?"

"Yes. He told me he was going to use Mese. He was going to cooperate with him because he had business dealings with him from before, and he was willing to cooperate."

When everything Marc Schiller owned had been taken from him, the decision was made that he had to die. Delgado later learned from Lugo that Schiller had been placed in his car and it had been set ablaze, and that later he had been run down. When they found out that Schiller survived and was in the ICU at Jackson Memorial, Delgado testified it was Lugo who decided to kill him at the hospital.

Delgado admitted to taking some big-ticket items from Schiller's house—stereo equipment and a color television. Lugo, he said, took a variety of items including cameras and furniture, while Doorbal took furniture for his new apartment. Everything else wound up in the warehouse. The gang also used Schiller's credit cards to order thousands of dollars of merchandise from department stores and mail-order catalogues.

Delgado testified that in February 1995, Mese called him and told him that a private investigator working for Marc Schiller had come to see him about the kidnapping. "Mese told me that he wanted me to speak to the investigator,"

Delgado recalled. But first he had to speak to Danny Lugo, who ordered him to deny it all.

"Lugo said he would take care of everything," Delgado remembered. As for Mese, he told Delgado that he was in the clear, that he had "covered his ass," but it was Danny Lugo who instructed Delgado on how to negotiate the return of the money, and it was Lugo who hired an attorney to draft a contract.

Delgado testified that he participated in the attempted kidnapping of Winston Lee. "Lugo told me that he wanted to take this guy down because he was a bad guy. He wanted to beat him up, take his money."

"Did he live at 7023 Crown Gate Court?" Gail Levine asked.

"Yes," Delgado replied.

"Did you ever go there on surveillance?"

"Yes."

Then the prosecutor showed Delgado photos of the residence that had been seized at Doorbal's townhouse on June 3, 1995.

"Is that Winston Lee's townhouse?"

"Yes."

"Is that his car?"

"Yes."

"Were you willing to participate in this as well?"

"Yes."

"Would the plan be the same—kidnap, take the money?"

"Yes."

"Kill."

"Yes."

But Lee was never abducted, Delgado said, because he proved to be an elusive target. "He was always out of town." But then in April, during lunch at a Miami Lakes restaurant, Adrian Doorbal announced that he was looking into the kidnapping of a wealthy Hungarian man named Frank Griga. Delgado said he heard nothing more about the plot until the day it happened, when Lugo phoned to ask if he knew how to drive a Lamborghini.

' "I told him, no I did not, never driven one, never been inside one," Delgado recalled. Before hanging up, Lugo told him to forget it, he would take care of the Lamborghini himself.

"Prior to this telephone conversation, did you have any idea that the Hungarian couple was going to be kidnapped that day?" Levine asked.

"No."

"The next day, did you go and meet with defendants Lugo and Doorbal?"

"Yes."

Delgado said he met them at Doorbal's townhouse, 6911 Main Street, apartment 224, in Miami Lakes.

"Tell us what happened when you went into the house," Levine commanded.

"I went in, Lugo opened the door and he told me to have a seat on the couch that was right in front. And he proceeded to explain to me what had happened the night before. He told me that Doorbal had got into a scuffle with Mr. Griga, and he had killed him. He had strangled him. They were fighting inside the room, in the back room where the computers were and inside his apartment. He also told me that the man was dead and he was inside the bathroom. They had him wrapped up and he was inside the tub.

"He told me that also they had a girl there and he had to take care of the girl. And when he was sitting down watching TV with the girl in the living room, he heard the noise and proceeded back to the back room where the computers were, and he opened the door and already Mr. Doorbal had him in the headlock, twisting his neck, and he was killing him. The girl screams, started to scream, and he told me he just grabbed the girl and stopped her from screaming and held her down and then proceeded to tie her up. And he explained to me that all the commotion was happening and he had to sedate her, had to take her out. They had syringes and vials of horse tranquilizer, and they were injecting her to keep her calm and they had her tied up with tape and had a hood on over her head. She was taped to her ankles and also her hands were wrapped behind her."

"Was the plan supposed to be that the man would immediately die?" Levine asked.

"No," Delgado explained. Lugo and Doorbal were "supposed to extort money from him, but Griga fought back and Doorbal killed him."

"Was Lugo surprised?" Levine wanted to know.

"Yes. He was mad and surprised that Doorbal killed him."

As Lugo was explaining what had happened, Delgado saw Doorbal come downstairs with the girl over his shoulder.

"What happened next?" Levine asked.

"She started to wake up," Delgado replied. "She started to ask where Frank was. She started to scream, 'Where's Frank? Take me to Frank. I want to see Frank.' And then Lugo told her 'Don't worry, we'll take you to see Frank, everything will be okay.' Then he told Doorbal to get a syringe, the horse tranquilizer from the refrigerator, and shoot her up with the needle to calm her down."

"What did he do after he retrieved it from the refrigerator?"

"He put it into a syringe and pushed it into the girl's ankle."

"Into her ankle?"

"Yeah."

"What did the girl do when he injected her in the ankle?"

"She moved around and she started to scream, and after he injected her he muffled her mouth." Krisztina, he said, stopped screaming. Later, while Doorbal held her up by her shoulders, Lugo tried to get Krisztina to reveal the keypad code for the Golden Beach house but she would become confused and stop, then start again.

"During the time that these questions were being asked of her, was she asking any questions?" Levine wanted to know.

Delgado said, "All she was asking was if they were taking her to see Frank, and Lugo kept telling her she'll be taken to see him soon enough, after she answered all the questions." But instead of calming down, Krisztina became more agitated and started shaking and screaming, so Doorbal injected her again, this time in her thigh.

"After the injection, she calmed down a little bit," Delgado recalled. "She screamed as soon as she got the injection and then she started to calm down, and Doorbal laid her back down flat on the floor and held her mouth so she can calm down, and she started to move around, but she finally calmed down and fell back to sleep."

"George, did you do anything to help her?" Levine wanted to know.

"No."

Levine was incredulous. "You didn't feel the need to call the police?" she asked.

"No."

"You knew you were in it, right?"

"Yes."

"You did nothing to save her?"

"No."

Not only did Delgado admit that he did nothing to save Krisztina, he testified that he helped his muscle-bound pals remove the bodies from the townhouse to the warehouse, and he stood by while they carved up their bodies.

They drove there in a rented U-Haul cargo van, with Lugo behind the wheel, Delgado in the passenger seat, and Doorbal in the back with the wardrobe box into which the muscleman had stuffed Krisztina's body and Marc Schiller's black leather couch, which held Frank Griga's body.

Levine had Delgado identify the tools the musclemen used to dismember the couple: The hatchet, chain saw, and pliers, as well as the barrels and buckets they used to hold the body parts.

He described how Lugo and Doorbal prepared—how they laid out plastic bags on the warehouse floor, cleaned the bodies with Windex, and positioned the barrels and buckets. Delgado said he sat quietly looking out a window while the musclemen decapitated the couple, chopped off their hands and feet, and removed their teeth. While court-room spectators gasped and the couples' relatives, who were seated in the first two rows, cried, Delgado emotion-lessly related the grisly details, and he described what he saw when his pals were finished: Legs sticking out of bar-rels and heads, hands, and feet stuffed into buckets.

Before Levine was finished with direct examination, Jorge Delgado testified that he helped the musclemen in their attempts to cover up the murders—he pitched in to clean Doorbal's apartment and he assisted Lugo in remov-ing potentially incriminating items to the love nest he shared with Sabina. Three defense attorneys took turns trying to impeach Delgado's testimony. At times, their questioning was grueling, but Delgado held his own, and in the days ahead, forensic evidence would corroborate his testimony. Anita Matthews, DNA expert from LabCorp, a clinical testing laboratory in Raleigh, North Carolina, tes-tified that she had matched the couples' DNA to the swabs Sergeant Jimenez brought back from Hungary. A blood expert testified that bloodstains from Doorbal's townhouse and from the warehouse matched Frank Griga's. And a fin-gerprint expert testified that the latent prints MDPD Police Officer Agnes Sarisky Duncan lifted from the glasses on the coffee table in Griga's house were Doorbal's.

On April 21, nearly two months after the trial began, Dr. Roger Mittleman, the associate medical examiner, took the stand to testify about the autopsies he conducted on Frank Griga and Krisztina Furton two-and-a-half years before. He testified that he took photographs during the postmor-tem procedures, and he brought with him color slides for the jurors to see. Gail Levine had the photos entered into evidence and then asked the bailiff to dim the lights in the courtroom. Jurors and courtroom spectators were about to see things that no one should ever see: Photos of decom-posed skulls and severed hands and feet, as well as arms without hands and legs without feet. The first two pho-tos were heart wrenching and sickening. Dr. Mittleman narrated.

"What we are seeing here is a torso," he explained. "There is no head. The head had been removed at the upper neck area or upper cervical area, as we call it. And the hands had been removed." The next photo showed the point at which Krisztina's neck had been severed from the torso. Both heads had been removed with a hatchet. Furton and Griga's torsos showed no signs of trauma other than the dismemberment.

Dr. Mittleman recalled receiving the buckets containing heads, hands, and feet in July 1994. The face and jaw had been removed from Furton's skull, which had been in a corrosive agent. Only fragments of teeth remained and the brain was decomposed. The face had also been removed from Griga's skull, and there was evidence of blunt force trauma to the top of the skull. The trauma could have been fatal and would have caused bleeding. The fingertips had been removed from the hands. Furton's right hand had been removed with a chain saw and her right foot had been removed with a hatchet. Griga's hands and feet had also been removed with a hatchet.

The medical examiner testified that he was able to match the heads to the torsos despite the decomposed state of the body parts. He also testified that toxicology reports revealed significant amounts of the horse tranquilizer Rompun in both bodies. Krisztina, he said, probably died from it. A veterinary pathologist who read the toxicology report estimated that at the time of her death, Furton's liver contained more Rompun than would be needed to kill several fully grown horses.

The medical examiner ruled both deaths homicides, but he said he was unable to definitively determine the cause of death for either victim. However, Furton probably died from asphyxia either from an overdose of horse tranquilizer or strangulation, and Griga probably died from blunt force trauma to his head, bleeding from the wound to his head, or a combination of these factors.

"Is it possible that the animal tranquilizer caused his death?" Gail Levine asked.

"Yes."

"And it's possible that he was strangled or suffocated?"

"Correct."

"And is it possible that all three of these things happened to him?"

"Of course."

"So it's possible that any of these things could have killed him?"

"Yes."

"As well as the possibility of all three?"

"Yes, or any combination thereof."

A few minutes later, Gail Levine announced, "Nothing further, your honor."

Only Ron Guralnick rose to cross-examine Dr. Mittleman: "Your examination cannot tell who it was that stuck or shot up these people with this drug, can it?"

"No, of course not," the medical examiner replied.

CHAPTER TWENTY-THREE

Who so sheddeth man's blood,
by man shall his blood be shed.

—GENESIS 9:6

Dr. Mittleman's testimony marked the beginning of the end
of the Sun Gym trial. Over the next few days, neighbors
of Adrian Doorbal testified that they heard thuds coming
from his apartment the night of May 24, 1995, at around
eleven in the evening. There was also testimony from
forensic accountant Christopher McFarland who testified
that he reviewed Doorbal's brokerage accounts, Sun Fitness Consultants' records, Mese's escrow account records,
and banking statements, including Schiller's accounts. He
opined that John Mese had indeed laundered Marc Schiller's money.

On Wednesday, April 22, Gail Levine announced that
the State of Florida rested. Lugo's and Doorbal's attorneys
chose not to put on a case, but Bruce Fleischer, John Mese's
court appointed attorney, did. He called one witness, a
forensic accountant who said that Mese did not commit
money laundering. Then Fleischer filed a motion for a
directed judgment of acquittal for his client on the RICO
counts and the counts charging him with the Griga-Furton

murders and kidnappings and the conspiracy to kidnap Winston Lee. Prosecutors argued that the evidence against Mese was sufficient for the jury to consider because it established that the Sun Gym owner was involved in the Schiller crimes, and his role was to launder all monies secured by his codefendants from all their crimes. Judge Ferrer reserved ruling and allowed the case to go to the jury, but before that could happen there would be closing arguments and a charge from the judge to the juries. Neither Lugo, nor Doorbal, nor Mese took the stand in their own behalf.

On Tuesday, April 28, Gail Levine was ready to deliver her closing argument. Before she began, Judge Ferrer addressed the jurors.

"The State and the defendant have now rested their case. The attorneys will now present their final arguments. Please remember that what the attorneys say is not evidence. However, do listen closely to their arguments. They're intended to aid you in understanding the case. Each side will have equal time, but the State is entitled to divide this time between an opening argument and rebuttal argument after the opponent has spoken. With that, Ms. Levine, you may start your closing argument."

Gail Levine rose and, as she had done in her opening argument on February 24, she addressed the court, the defense attorney, and the jurors, then she launched into one of the most eloquent and passionate summations ever heard in the Richard E. Gerstein Justice Building.

"Torturous, violent, just horrible, horrible crimes for simple greed. Each man motivated by greed. Each man with a planned, premeditated mind to gain wealth for himself. You know, when you reflect on this case, look back on it, you might think to yourself, it's really a work of fiction, a bad TV movie, all the blunders, all the gratuitous violence. How could it be real? How could something like this occur in our society? How could there be evil people like these men? Individuals so motivated by their own gain that would go to any length, place no value on human life, and only think about themselves and the wealth that they could acquire. Unfortunately, nothing, not one thing presented in this case, is fiction. Every single bit of it is real. It's all supported by the facts and the evidence."

Then she reviewed the evidence and the facts, twelve hundred exhibits and ninety-eight witnesses, all but one a prosecution witness.

"Frank Griga was a successful man," she said. "He started out with nothing and he became the American dream. You heard that from his own accountant. You heard that his net worth at the time of his death was an abundant ten million dollars. You heard that Krisztina Furton was his constant companion, the love of his life. They shared a home. They had cars. They had friends. And they had each other. And that is why they both were murdered."

Then she pointed first to Lugo, then to Doorbal, saying, "Unfortunately, this man and this man wanted what they had. Now, they didn't want similar things, like they wanted a nice house or they wanted a nice car. They actually wanted Frank and Krisztina's things. They wanted to live their life, basically assume their identity. And to do this, Frank Griga would have to die. And because Krisztina Furton would be with him or would be looking for him, she would have to die, too. Murdered horribly, despicably. They had to lose their lives for these men. You see, they had done this before, and they had been pretty successful at it."

As for Mese, "he is down on his luck and needs money badly for that pretty wife, to keep her in the style that he wants her to be accustomed to. He doesn't want to work at an accounting firm anymore. He wants somebody else's money."

These three men, Levine said, are "in it for a penny, they're in it for a pound. They're principals to every single crime, and they created their own organization."

She spoke for more than two hours during which she recounted Marc Schiller's monthlong ordeal, and Jorge Delgado's role in it. "Let's face it," she conceded, "Delgado is the stoolie, a murderer but a stoolie." They never expected him to talk, she said, but he did. And by the way, "don't let anybody stand up here and say it starts with Delgado and it ends with Delgado. It's not about Delgado."

He got a deal, "the deal of a lifetime," she admitted, but "that's not your concern, whether you like the deal or not." And she asked the jurors not to think of Adrian Doorbal as a victim or a dupe of Danny Lugo. Instead, they should think of him as the hands-on killer of Frank Griga and Krisztina Furton, and the abductor of Marc Schiller. Doorbal, she said was the gang's muscle. Lugo was its brains, and Mese was its chief financial officer.

She reminded the jurors of the grisly autopsy photos they had seen. "Those pictures are engraved in your mind. I wanted you to see them so you could have a full picture of what they did to Frank and Krisztina, to make sure there was nothing left of them so they could not be identified." She apologized for the length of the trial, saying that she wanted to leave "no stone unturned." When she finished it was Tony Natale's turn.

Doorbal's lawyer began his summation claiming that prosecutors had failed to prove their case beyond a reasonable doubt. "In a criminal case," he said, "the allegations that are made by the prosecution are a promissory note. They promised to bring evidence, truthful competent evidence to prove beyond a reasonable doubt what they said."

They failed, he said, calling the State's case "a house of cards." He attacked the witnesses, especially Delgado, because they made deals with prosecutors. Referring to Delgado's plea deal, Natale said, "Fifteen years for attempted murder. Fifteen years for kidnapping. Fifteen years for extortion. That's forty-five years. Not. They all run concurrent. They all run at the same time. He gets credit for time he's already been in jail. The devil makes a deal. He knows what he's doing."

Natale reminded the jury that Marc Schiller never named Doorbal as one of his kidnappers, and that the only testimony connecting Adrian Doorbal to the death of Frank

Griga and Krisztina Furton came from the mouth of Jorge Delgado, who wasn't even there. Instead, he was relating what Danny Lugo, "a man of many faces," told him.

"I come to you with Adrian's life in my hand," he said. "Verdict, Adrian not guilty."

Bruce Fleischer, John Mese's attorney, said his client "was not involved" in what happened to the Hungarian couple, or to Marc Schiller. The prosecutor had lots of evidence, he conceded. "They have quantity, but they don't have quality." No evidence that Mese knew Frank Griga or Krisztina Furton ever existed, and no evidence that, after the Schiller kidnapping, John Mese's lifestyle changed.

"Who used Marc Schiller's credit cards?" Fleischer asked. "Lugo and Delgado. Who had all of Schiller's property? Not John Mese. Who used false names and aliases? Danny Lugo and Adrian Doorbal. Who had false passports? Lugo. John Mese didn't have any false passports. John Mese didn't have any aliases. Whose fingerprints were all over the evidence? Mr. Lugo, Mr. Delgado, and Mr. Doorbal."

One could say "that John Mese is guilty of being stupid, and maybe he did notarize those documents, but you can't make that leap of faith to think that he was involved in the abduction and kidnapping and torture of Mr. Schiller, nor can you think he was involved in those murders."

He reminded the jury about reasonable doubt. "The court doesn't instruct you that you need X number of reasonable doubts to equal not guilty. You only need one reasonable doubt . . . to find John Mese not guilty."

Gail Levine had the last say, a chance to rebut the closing arguments of the defense attorneys. She began by telling the jurors that when she was just starting out in her career, she learned a valuable lesson that has stayed with her: "When a defense attorney has the facts on his side or her side, they bang on the law. When the law's on their side and the facts aren't, they bang on the facts, and when they've got nothing, they bang on the prosecutor." She reviewed the evidence and the testimony once again, and she asked the jurors to find the defendants guilty on all counts, which is what they did.

After deliberating on Monday, May 4, the two juries announced they had reached verdicts, but the decisions were sealed until the following day, when they were read to a standing-room-only courtroom. Danny Lugo's verdicts were read first. His jury of three men and nine women found him guilty on all counts: guilty of conspiracy to commit racketeering; guilty of racketeering; guilty of the first-degree murders of Frank Griga and Krisztina Furton; guilty of kidnapping them; guilty of kidnapping Marc Schiller; guilty of first-degree attempted murder, of robbery, extortion, and arson.

Adrian Doorbal was next. The seven men and five women on his jury found him guilty on all counts, too. Guilty of conspiracy to commit racketeering and racketeering; guilty of two murders, three kidnappings, attempted murder, extortion, forgery, robbery, burglary, grand theft, burglary, and arson.

John Mese squirmed in his chair, then he, too, heard the word guilty again and again. Guilty of thirty-nine counts including two counts of first-degree murder; guilty of conspiracy to commit racketeering; guilty of racketeering; guilty of kidnapping, forgery, and multiple counts of money laundering.

Listening to the verdict in the courtroom were Kristzina's mother and father. They wore headphones through which they listened as a translator repeated the verdicts in Hungarian. Zsuzsanna Griga, Frank's sister, sat nearby. A high school English teacher in her homeland, she didn't need a translator. She did, however, need tissues. Outside the courtroom, defense attorneys spoke briefly to reporters.

"Blood was all over the courtroom, the body parts were all over the courtroom, we could not overcome that," said Bruce Fleischer, Mese's attorney. He vowed to appeal and he said he hoped to try the case again. Tony Natale, Doorbal's attorney, said he faced a daunting challenge: Saving his client's life.

The verdicts were in, but the case was not over. Ferrer set John Mese's sentencing date for June 30, while the penalty phase for Doorbal was set for June 1, the first day of hurricane season. The six years since Hurricane Andrew, a category five, roared across Miami had been relatively mild, but forecasters at the National Hurricane Center were predicting a more turbulent season ahead, but that's not what was on the minds of the seven men and five women who returned to Judge Ferrer's courtroom that rainy Monday morning for the penalty phase in the trial of Adrian Doorbal; they were there to decide whether he would live or die.

First, jurors heard powerful testimony from the families of the murdered couple. Through an interpreter, Krisztina's father spoke lovingly of his youngest daughter, an avid swimmer who never had a bad word to say about anyone. His wife suffered a nervous breakdown over the murder of their daughter and of Frank Griga. "To this day we cannot accept that they are dead. I often feel that they are just around the corner in the house. We know it's not true, but we have this hope."

Zsuzsanna Griga said her brother was her best friend, godfather to her two children, and very close to her husband. She spoke to Frank on the phone nearly every day. Her mother, she said, "is not the same anymore." Their lives had been shattered, she said tearfully. Her mother "cannot speak of him in the past tense. I cannot speak of him in the past tense either."

The first to take the stand to plead for Doorbal's life was Sachi Lievano. She had been a receptionist and secretary at Penny Burke's law office when she developed a romantic relationship with Noel Adrian Doorbal while he was awaiting trial. Burke asked her to explain how their relationship began. Sachi said that she initiated it.

"We were speaking and I felt just so comfortable during

one of our conversations, I felt so comfortable with him, and whenever he talked to me I felt happy, and I said I wanted to put a face to the voice."

She asked if she could visit him, and the muscleman said she could, whenever she wanted to. Since then, he has been her alarm clock. She explained:

"I work two jobs. I wake up with a ring and I get it and when I do it's Noel and, you know, when someone calls from jail it's a machine, and it asks if you'll accept a collect from an inmate, and they are supposed to say their name, and I would accept and he would tell me, 'Good morning beautiful. Have a wonderful day.' And then he hangs up. Then he will call me again and tell me that God loves us, and he'll call me again and tell me, 'Don't forget to eat breakfast,' and then he will call again and say, 'Be careful driving' and 'Tell the girls I love them.' "

Lievano described herself as Doorbal's fiancée. She described Doorbal as a gentle person and testified that he had helped her to be a better person and a better Christian. Lievano's mother testified, too. She reiterated her daughter's testimony and testified that since Sachi had become involved with the muscleman she had become a better mother.

Coworkers from his days as a worker at Fiesta Taco appeared. Kathleen Pelish testified that she worked with Doorbal from 1990 to 1992. He was a hard worker and a good friend. He never raised his voice, was very appreciative, and claimed that his parents were dead and rarely spoke of his family. She also admitted that the defendant was capable of making his own decisions and running a restaurant. Andrea Franklin testified that she dated Doorbal for six months in 1993. He was very interested in bodybuilding and used steroids, but they had no effect on his personality, that he was very inquisitive about business because he wanted to better himself, that he was a spiritual person and that Lugo was a smart, commanding person with a magnetic personality.

Another Fiesta Taco worker, Steven Bernstein, testified

that he met the muscleman at the restaurant in 1990 and they became friends. Doorbal did not have a temper, he said, and he was a very nice person. Danny Lugo gave him money to buy a car, and he offered to give him a place to live and to set him up in business because Lugo could not have a business in his own name. Despite the fact that Bernstein advised against it, Doorbal decided to take Lugo up on his offer. After that, the defendant seemed to change. He became more interested in having money, Bernstein said. He described the relationship between Doorbal and Lugo as one of brothers and stated that as far as he could see, Doorbal was not afraid of Danny Lugo.

Patsy Hernandez, Doorbal's half-sister, testified that Doorbal was the product of a liaison between her father and a thirteen-year-old who "hated the very sight of him" and physically abused him. But he was loved by his father and his grandmother, and he was always considerate and obedient.

Petra LaRoche, Doorbal's elderly grandmother, testified that her daughter Winifred became pregnant with Doorbal at the age of thirteen. According to LaRoche, Winifred had mental problems, refused to care for her son, and was jealous of him. LaRoche claimed that Winifred once banged Doorbal's head into a wall, broke his hand, and hit him with sticks. LaRoche said that because of this mistreatment, she sent him to live with relatives. Adrian, she said, told her that Lugo was like a brother to him.

It took the nine women and three men of Doorbal's jury about twenty minutes to make their recommendation. They voted eight to four for the death penalty.

One week later, it was Danny Lugo's turn to fight for his life. Once again, Furton's father and Griga's sister spoke movingly. Ron Guralnick presented two witnesses on Lugo's behalf—his mother, Carmen, and Santiago Gervacio, a longtime friend. Lugo's mother testified about two isolated incidents in which her son had been mistreated by his father when he was a child. One incident involved corporal punishment with a clothes hanger. The other occurred when Lugo's father poured a bowl of spaghetti over young Danny's head when he refused to eat. Lugo's mother testified that on the whole, however, Lugo was raised in a loving home, that both she and his father loved him, and that he was loving toward them both.

"I love him with all my heart," Carmen said. After all, he had been an altar boy and he was awarded a scholarship to Fordham University. "How could I not love such a good son?" she asked.

Santiago Gervacio testified that Lugo was a passive person. He had never seen him commit a violent act. He also stated that Lugo showed great love toward his deceased sister's four children, and had even adopted them. Gervacio added that Lugo showed love toward his parents.

The nine women and three men on Lugo's jury needed just ten minutes to make their recommendation. They voted eleven to one for the death penalty.

But the final decision was Judge Ferrer's. He held a death penalty hearing on July 8. Gail Levine invited Marc Schiller to return Miami. "She said it was imperative that I be there," Schiller recalled, so he flew in from Colombia one more time to confront his kidnappers, who sat shackled and handcuffed in prison-issued jumpsuits in the courtroom.

He spoke to them and to Judge Ferrer. He was still suffering, he said, as was his wife, Diana, whose lupus was made more severe because of the kidnapping. He recounted the details of his ordeal and stated that he could not understand how human beings could commit such heinous crimes. Neither Lugo nor Doorbal deserved to live in society, Schiller said.

His statement finished, Schiller bade the prosecutors good-bye and walked from the courtroom. The elevator took him to the main floor where he exited the building. He had just stepped onto the courthouse steps and was thinking about his return flight to Bogota when he heard the shouts: "Marcelo Schiller, you are under arrest." Before he could turn around, Schiller was surrounded by FBI agents who hustled him to a waiting car and drove away. He had been indicted for Medicare fraud and money laundering based on information Jorge Delgado had given the U.S. attorney. The twenty-three count indictment was unsealed that very day. It charged Schiller with masterminding a $14 million Medicare fraud scheme. The feds had been patiently waiting for the Sun Gym trial to end before arresting Marc Schiller.

"We knew since 1995 that one of the kidnapper-killers went to the government with this Medicare fraud story," Schiller's attorney Jeffrey Tew told the *Miami Herald*. "We were advised by the state attorney's office, but Mr. Schiller kept returning to Florida to do his duty and be a witness."

According to the indictment, Schiller set up several corporations and recruited associates to operate them while he billed Medicare. The associates recruited physicians who, for one hundred dollars per prescription, prescribed nutritional supplements and feeding tube kits for real Medicare patients who did not need them. One of the companies was Dadima Corporation, which Schiller sold to Delgado.

Considered a flight risk, Schiller was cooling his heels in the Federal Detention Center on Friday, July 17, 1998, when Judge Ferrer took the bench to sentence Lugo and Doorbal. He had written an eighteen-page sentencing order for each muscleman, and he set about reading them into the record. Danny Lugo was first.

> On May 4, 1998, three and a half months after trial began, the defendant, Daniel Lugo, was convicted by a jury for the crimes of first-degree murder, two counts; conspiracy to commit racketeering; racketeering; kidnapping, two counts; armed kidnapping; attempted extortion; grand theft, three counts; attempted first-degree murder; armed robbery; burglary of a dwelling; first-degree arson; armed extortion; money laundering, nine counts; forgery, six counts; uttering a forged instrument, six counts; possession of a removed identification

plate; and conspiracy to commit a first-degree felony. On June 11, 1998 the jury recommended, by a vote of eleven to one, that the court sentence Lugo to death.

Section 921.141 of the Florida Statutes requires that this court consider all aggravating and mitigating circumstances set forth by statute. Lugo is entitled to an individual consideration of those aggravating and mitigating circumstances.

Judge Ferrer explained the aggravating factors:

- Lugo was previously convicted of another capital felony or of a felony involving a threat of violence to another person.
- The murders were committed while he was engaged in and/or an accomplice in the commission of or an attempt to commit the crime of kidnapping.
- The murders were committed for the purpose of avoiding or preventing a lawful arrest.
- The murders were committed for financial gain.
- The murders were committed in a cold, calculated, and premeditated manner without any pretense of moral or legal justification.
- The murders were especially heinous, atrocious, or cruel.

Judge Ferrer said he gave "great weight" to the aggravators, and had this to say about the last one:

The State has proven this aggravator beyond and to the exclusion of every reasonable doubt. It has been held that fear, emotional strain, and terror of the victim during events leading up to the murder may allow an otherwise quick death to become heinous, atrocious, and cruel. The murder of Ms. Furton had all of those components and much more. She did not die quickly by any stretch of the imagination. After seeing her fiancé being strangled by Doorbal, she screamed in fear and was immediately tackled by Lugo who proceeded to gag her, handcuff her hands, and secure her ankles with duct tape. She was then injected with Xylazine in order to reduce her resistance.

The evidence showed that Xylazine works on the nervous system and is used as a horse tranquilizer. An injection of Xylazine would be painful, provide a burning feeling, would cause agitation, salivation, and extreme thirst. The person's respiration would lower, which, when combined with being bound and gagged, would likely cause a feeling of suffocation. She was kept with a hood over her head to limit her vision.

On the day following Griga's murder, during Delgado's conversation with Lugo in Doorbal's apartment, Doorbal brought Ms. Furton downstairs and laid her on the steps. He was carrying her over his shoulder and she was bound hand and foot.

She woke up and begged to see Griga, her fiancé, whom she had last seen being strangled by Doorbal. At Lugo's direction, Doorbal injected her again in the ankle and Ms. Furton screamed. Doorbal covered her mouth to muffle her scream. Doorbal held her upright by the shoulders while Lugo questioned her as to the location of the safe and the house codes. She continued begging to see Frank Griga. When Lugo told her she would be taken to see Frank if she answered all of their questions she became nervous again, started shaking, and began screaming. Doorbal gave her another injection in the thigh and she screamed out in pain again. It had been less than an hour since the last injection of Xylazine. When she passed out again, they left her lying on the stairs while they continued discussing the crime.

He found no statutory mitigators, and gave little or no weight to non-statutory mitigators that had been presented by the defense during the penalty phase: Lugo was not a totally immoral person and had exhibited great acts of kindness in the past—little weight; Lugo's execution would have a negative impact on his elderly mother—little weight; Lugo exhibited appropriate courtroom behavior—little weight; Lugo assisted police after the murders had been committed in finding the torsos of Griga and Furton—very little weight; life terms for Lugo for each of the murders would permanently remove him as a menace to society—little weight; if incarcerated, Lugo would be able to assist other prisoners in learning computer skills—no weight; Lugo should not be sentenced to death because he was not the "hands-on" killer—no weight.

Judge Ferrer declared that the evidence proved that "Lugo was the leader of the organization." The others "were certainly independent players and able to make decisions on their own," but they "followed his lead." Danny Lugo was "the brains," and he "is legally and morally responsible for every single thing that was done to Frank and Krisztina in this case. He was the director and the driving force."

With that said, Ferrer pronounced sentence: Thirty years for conspiracy to commit racketeering; thirty years for racketeering; death for the murder of Frank Griga; death for the murder of Krisztina Furton; life for the kidnapping of Marcello Schiller; life for the kidnapping of Frank Griga; life for the kidnapping of Krisztina Furton; five years for extortion; five years for grand theft of a motor vehicle; fifteen years for grand theft from Schiller's bank and brokerage accounts; life for the attempted murder of Marcelo Schiller; thirty years for extortion with a firearm; thirty years for arson; five years for each of three counts of forgery; fifteen years for conspiracy to commit a first-degree felony. Each death sentence would run consecutively as would every other sentence.

"It is hereby ordered that you, Daniel Lugo, be taken by the proper authority to the Florida State Prison, and there be kept under close confinement until the date of your execution is set. It is further ordered that on such scheduled date, you, Daniel Lugo, shall be put to death. You are hereby notified that this sentence is subject to automatic review by the Florida Supreme Court. May God have mercy on your soul."

Lugo showed no emotion as he was led from the courtroom. In the afternoon it was Doorbal's turn. Judge Ferrer read a lengthy sentencing order. He said he gave great weight to five aggravators applicable to the Griga-Furton murders: Prior violent felonies including the kidnapping of Marc Schiller and the "contemporaneous murder" of the other victim; the murders were committed while Doorbal was engaged in the commission of a kidnapping; the murders were committed to avoid arrest; the murders were committed for financial gain; the murder of Krisztina Furton was heinous, atrocious, and cruel.

As with Danny Lugo, Judge Ferrer said he found no statutory mitigators for Doorbal, and he gave little weight to non-statutory mitigators: Difficult childhood; hardworking and loyal employee; loyal friend and positive influence on others; religious devotion and ability to help others with their religious beliefs; life in prison without parole would permanently remove him from society.

Judge Ferrer said that he agreed with the jury's recommendation, and imposed two death sentences. He also sentenced Doorbal to thirty years for conspiracy to commit racketeering and racketeering; thirty years for extortion; thirty years for arson; life in prison for armed robbery and armed kidnapping; fifteen years for burglary, grand theft, and conspiracy to commit a felony, and five years for attempted extortion and grand theft auto. All the sentences, Judge Ferrer said, would be served consecutively.

Before the proceeding ended, Ferrer said: "It is hereby ordered that you, Noel Adrian Doorbal, be taken by the proper authority to the Florida State Prison, and there be kept under close confinement until the date of your execution is set. It is further ordered that on such scheduled date, you, Noel Adrian Doorbal, shall be put to death. You are hereby notified that this sentence is subject to automatic review by the Florida Supreme Court. May God have mercy on your soul."

On Monday, July 20, it was John Mese's turn to appear
in Judge Ferrer's courtroom for sentencing. His attorney
had filed a motion to set aside the jury verdict as to all of
the RICO counts, the Griga-Furton counts, and the Winston Lee count. Ferrer granted the motion, which meant
the former Sun Gym owner, bodybuilding impresario, and
pillar of the community stood convicted for the Schiller
kidnapping, money laundering, and forgery only. Ironi-
cally, long before the Sun Gym case went to trial, Mese
was offered a plea deal: Nine years in prison in exchange
for his cooperation. But he turned it down, electing to
take his chances with a judge and a jury. Judge Ferrer pronounced sentence—fifty-six years in state prison. The Sun
Gym case was closed.

AFTERWORD

It was the longest and most expensive trial in Miami-Dade County history. It began on February 24, 1998 and it didn't end until July 20, when John Mese, the last of the Sun Gym ringleaders, was sentenced to state prison. More than fifty MDPD detectives took part in the investigation. Thirty-four men and women put their lives on hold to serve as jurors. They heard testimony from ninety-eight witnesses, and they viewed twelve hundred pieces of evidence, including what courthouse regulars said were the most gruesome photos ever seen in a Miami-Dade County courtroom.

Danny Lugo and Adrian Doorbal are among more than three hundred prisoners on Florida's Death Row. They are incarcerated at the Union Correctional Institution in Raiford. When the musclemen arrived there in 1998, the method of execution was the electric chair, which Floridians nicknamed "Old Sparky." It was built out of oak by prison inmates in 1923, and it lived up to its name in 1997, when an electrode in the headpiece malfunctioned, sending sparks shooting from the head of convicted murderer Pedro Medina. After a three-year moratorium on executions,

Florida pulled the plug on Old Sparky, opting for lethal injection instead, but inmates can still choose the electric chair.

Florida's Death Row inmates live in tiny cells, six by nine by nine-and-a-half. Cells are not air-conditioned and temperatures in them can exceed one hundred degrees. Inmates shower every other day, are counted once an hour, wear handcuffs whenever they are outside their cells, and are not allowed to mingle with each other.

Lugo and Doorbal have been appealing their convictions since 1998. When all their appeals have been exhausted, Florida's governor will sign a death warrant, and they will be moved into a Death Watch cell adjacent to the windowless execution chamber. At the appointed hour, they will be escorted into the chamber and strapped to a gurney. Curtains will be pulled back and witnesses will be able to watch as two executioners attach intravenous tubes to each arm. One of them will administer the first drug, two syringes of Sodium Pentothal, which should cause unconsciousness. Two syringes of pancuronium bromide, a muscle relaxant that paralyzes the muscles needed for breathing, will then be injected into the other IV, followed by a dose of potassium chloride, which will cause cardiac arrest and then death within fifteen minutes.

In the years since the musclemen were convicted and sentenced to death, their Sun Gym pals, with the exception of John Mese, have served their time and been released. Carl Weekes was a free man again in May 2002, Stevenson Pierre in May 2001. Jorge Delgado left prison in November 2002. Jail guard John Raimondo served three years for kidnapping, and Mario Sanchez served two. Mario Gray, charged as an accessory after the fact, and Dan Pace, charged with replacing a motor vehicle VIN number, were placed on probation. John Carl Mese was never a free man again. He died in a prison hospital on October 8, 2004, after suffering a stroke at age sixty-six.

As for the others who were affected by the depravity of the Sun Gym thugs, Marc Schiller pleaded guilty to one count of Medicare fraud and served twenty-seven months in a federal correctional facility in Florida. Sabina Petrescu gave up nude dancing and became a restaurant hostess. The state attorney decided not to prosecute her for possession of an automobile with an altered VIN number. Doorbal's ex-wife, Cindy Eldridge, resumed her nursing career. She lives in northern Broward Country. Judge Alex Ferrer, whose patience and case management skills were remarkable, left the bench in 2005 to star in "The Judge Alex Show," a syndicated television courtroom drama featuring real people seeking solutions to everyday disputes. After settling her brother's estate, Frank Griga's sister, Zsuzsanna, returned to Budapest. Today she is an astrologer specializing in karmic astrology. She also teaches astrology and past life regression.

As for Chopin the dog, he found a new home with friends of Frank and Krisztina, but every now and then, especially on balmy nights when the wind blew in from the ocean, he would stand by the front door scratching and whimpering, just as he had done on the night of May 24, 1995, when Frank and Krisztina followed Danny Lugo and Adrian Doorbal, never to be seen again.